Adobe

Photoshop Elements

2024

The Ultimate Mastery Guide to Effortlessly
Learn the Latest Tools, Techniques and Tricks
in Adobe Photoshop Elements 2024

Disclaimer and Terms of Use

The author and publisher of this book and the accompanying materials have used their best efforts in preparing this book. The author and publisher make no representation or warranties with respect to the accuracy, applicability, fitness, or completeness of the contents of this book. The information contained in this book is strictly for informational purposes. Therefore, if you wish to apply the ideas contained in this book, you are taking full responsibility for your actions.

Printed in the United States of America

Table of Contents

TABLE OF CONTENTS...III

INTRODUCTION 18

MAKE ADJUSTMENTS THAT ARE IMPACTFUL IN A SWIFT MANNER 18
   Learn as you are working 18
   Make amazing designs and share them with ease 18
   Remain organized 19
WHAT'S NEW IN ADOBE PHOTOSHOP ELEMENTS 2024 19
   New light and dark modes 19
   Color Match 19
   Photo Reel 20
   Add Text Guided Edit 20
QUICK ACTIONS 21
   Free Adobe Stock Photos 21
   New Artistic Effect 21
   One-click selection 22
PHOTOSHOP ELEMENTS MOBILE AND WEB COMPANION APPS (ENGLISH-ONLY BETA) 22
   Mobile 22
   Web 23
OVERVIEW OF THIS BOOK 23
   Chapter 1: Things You Need to Know 24
   Chapter 2: Get to Know Photoshop Elements 2024 24
   Chapter 3: Quick Fixes and Effects 24
   Chapter 4: Guided Edits 24
   Chapter 5: Get to Know the Photoshop Elements Toolbox 25
   Chapter 6: Select and Isolate Areas in Your Photos 25
   Chapter 7: Resize Your Images 25
   Chapter 8: Fix and Enhance Your Picture 25
   Chapter 9: Work with Photoshop Elements Layers 25
   Chapter 10: Create and Edit Text 25
   Chapter 11: Add Photo Effects and Filters 26
   Chapter 12: Photoshop Element Tricks 26
   Chapter 13: Advanced Photo Editing Tools 26
   Chapter 14: Learn about Your Photoshop Elements File 26
   Chapter 15: Manage Your Files with the Organizer 26
   Chapter 16: Create Fun Pieces 26
   Chapter 17: Share Your Photos and Videos 26

CHAPTER 1 27

BASIC THINGS YOU OUGHT TO KNOW **27**

PIXELS 27

    Megapixel 28

    PPI and DPI 28

    Resolution 29

RASTER VS. VECTOR GRAPHICS 29

    Raster 29

    Vector 30

IMAGE SIZE VS. CANVAS SIZE 31

    Selections 31

    Layers 32

ALPHA CHANNELS 33

COLOR 34

    About color 34

    HSB model 34

    RGB model 35

    Color wheel 35

    The Photo Bin 35

WHAT IS A NATIVE PSD FILE? 36

    Uses 37

ACTIVITY 38

CHAPTER 2 .... **39**

GET TO KNOW PHOTOSHOP ELEMENTS 2024 .... **39**

THE ELEMENT HUB 39

THE EDITOR WORKSPACE 39

CREATE A NEW BLANK FILE 39

    Open a file 40

OPEN A PDF FILE 42

    Place a PDF file in a new layer 43

PROCESS MULTIPLE FILES 44

    Close a file 46

GUIDES AND RULERS 47

    Change the rulers' zero origin and settings 47

    Change the guide and grid settings 48

THE TOOLBOX 49

    Toolbox in the Quick Mode 49

    Toolbox in the advanced mode 49

    Tools in the View group of the advanced mode toolbox 49

    Tools in the Select group of the Advanced mode toolbox 49

Tools in the Enhance group of the Advanced mode toolbox.. 50

Use a tool 51

Choose a tool 51

Select options from the Tool Options bar.. 52

Edit tool preferences 52

THE PANEL BIN 53

WORK WITH PANELS 54

Panels in the advanced mode 54

The Photo Bin 55

Save files 57

Save changes... 57

Save changes with a different file format, name, or location... 58

Save a file in GIF format 58

Save a file in JPEG format 60

Save a file in Photoshop PDF format 60

Save a file in PNG format 61

Save a file in TIFF format 61

SET PREFERENCES FOR SAVING FILES 62

FREE ADOBE STOCK PHOTOS AND IMAGERY 64

In Guided Mode... 65

In Advanced Mode 67

QUOTE GRAPHIC 68

ACCESS LICENSED IMAGES FROM THE ADOBE STOCK WEBSITE... 68

ACTIVITY.. 68

CHAPTER 3 69

QUICK FIXES AND EFFECTS 69

THE QUICK FIX TOOLBAR 69

EFFECTS, ADJUSTMENTS, TEXTURES AND FRAMES... 69

Effects 69

Artistic Effects 70

Class Effects 70

COLOR MATCH EFFECTS.. 72

Textures... 74

Frames 74

ADD QUICK EFFECTS (FX) 74

Quick Actions 75

Apply Quick Textures... 75

Add Quick Frames 75

ACTIVITY.. 76

CHAPTER 4 .... **77**

GUIDED EDITS **77**

BASICS: GUIDED EDITS 77

ADD TEXT GUIDED EDIT 77

USING THE TEXT ON SELECTION TOOL 80

    Using the Text on Shape Tool 80

    Use the Text on Path tool 81

THE MOVE & SCALE OBJECT GUIDED EDIT 82

OBJECT REMOVAL GUIDED EDIT 82

CORRECT SKIN TONE GUIDED EDIT 84

    Crop Photo Guided Edit 84

    Lighten and Darken Guided Edit 84

    Resize Guided Edit 84

VIGNETTE EFFECT GUIDED EDIT 87

COLOR GUIDED EDITS 88

    Adjust saturation and hue 89

    Change color saturation or hue 89

    Modify the range of Hue / Saturation sliders 90

    Change the color of an object 91

BLACK & WHITE EDITS 91

B&W COLOR POP GUIDED EDIT 93

    B&W Selection guided edit 94

    High Key guided edit 95

    Low Key guided edit 95

    Fun Edits 95

    The Meme Maker Guided Edit 96

    The Multi-Photo Text Guided Edit 97

    The Double Exposure Guided Edit 100

    The Painterly Guided Edit effect 101

    The "Out of Bounds" Guided Edit effect 102

    Save As / Save: Save 103

    Proceed with Editing: In Swift / In Skill 103

    Share on Twitter or Flickr 103

    Create a Picture Stack 104

    Create a Puzzle Effect 105

SPECIAL EDITS 106

    The Depth of Field Guided Edit 106

    Simple Method 106

CUSTOM METHOD 108

    The Text and Border Overlay Guided Edit 109

Get Faces Clean Up with the Perfect Portrait Guided Edit 110

Photomerge Guided Edits 111

    Paste between photos with Photomerge Compose 111

    Combine the best-lit elements from two photos with Photomerge Exposure 112

Automatic Photomerge Exposure 113

    Manual Photomerge Exposure 114

Combine photos with Photomerge Panorama 115

Activity 117

CHAPTER 5 118

GET TO KNOW THE PHOTOSHOP ELEMENTS TOOLBOX 118

The Tool Options 118

The Color Picker 118

    Color 120

    HSB model 120

    RGB model 121

    Color wheel 121

The Eyedropper/Sampler Tool 121

    Choose a color from the toolbox 123

The Color Swatch panel 123

    Make a color choice with the use of the Color Swatches panel 123

    Add a color to the Color Swatches panel 124

    Save and make use of custom swatch libraries 125

    Delete a color from the Color Swatches panel 126

    Additional Foreground /Background color options 126

About Blending Modes 126

The Zoom Tool 128

    Zoom in or out 128

    Display a picture at 100% 129

    Fit a picture to the screen 129

Modify the size of the window while zooming 130

    Navigator panel 130

The Hand Tool 130

The Move Tool 131

    Move a selection 131

    Move tool options 132

Copy selections or layers 133

    Copy selections with the Move tool 133

    Copy a selection with the use of commands 134

    Add to and subtract from a selection 134

The Marquee Selection Tools 134

Lasso Selection Tools 135

Quick Selection Tools 136

The Refine Selection Brush and Push Tool 138

Eye Tools: The Red Eye Removal Tool 138

Open Closed Eyes 139

The Spot Healing Brush Tool 140

What is Anti-Aliasing? 141

    Content-Aware *142*

The Healing Brush Tools 142

The Smart Brush Tools 143

Modify Smart Brush tool correction settings 145

The Clone Stamp Tool 146

    The Pattern Stamp Tool *148*

    Make use of the Pattern Stamp tool *148*

Blur, Smudge, and Sharpen 149

    The Blur Tool *149*

Blur filters 150

    Gaussian Blur *150*

    Lens Blur *150*

    Radial Blur *150*

    Smart Blur *151*

    Surface Blur *151*

    The Smudge Tool *151*

    The Sharpen Tool *152*

Precisely sharpen a picture 152

Unsharp Mask Filter 153

The Sponge, Dodge, and Burn Tools 154

    The Sponge Tool *154*

    The Dodge Tool *154*

    The Brush Tools *155*

The impressionist Brush 155

Brush Settings and options 156

Adding a new brush to the brush library 157

    Delete a brush *157*

Create a custom brush shape from a picture 158

Tablet Settings 158

The Eraser tool 158

The Background Eraser Tool 159

The Magic Eraser tool 160

The Paint Bucket (Fill) Tool 161

FILL A LAYER WITH A COLOR OR PATTERN 162

THE GRADIENT TOOL 163

APPLY A GRADIENT 163

APPLY A GRADIENT FILL TO THE TEXT 164

DEFINE A GRADIENT 164

SPECIFY GRADIENT TRANSPARENCY 165

THE SHAPE SELECTION TOOLS 166

TRANSFORM A SHAPE 166

THE RECTANGLE TOOL, ELLIPSE TOOL, AND ROUNDED RECTANGLE TOOL 167

Drawing a rectangle, square, or rounded rectangle 167

ELLIPSE TOOL 167

THE POLYGON TOOL 168

THE LINE TOOL 168

TYPING TOOLS 169

ADD TEXT 169

TYPE TOOL OPTIONS 171

USING THE TEXT ON THE SHAPE TOOL 171

USING THE TEXT ON SELECTION TOOL 172

USING TEXT ON CUSTOM PATH TOOL 172

THE PENCIL TOOL 173

THE CROP TOOL 173

CROP TO A SELECTION BOUNDARY 175

AUTOMATIC CROPPING SUGGESTIONS 175

PERSPECTIVE CROP TOOL 176

THE COOKIE CUTTER TOOL 177

THE PERSPECTIVE TOOL 177

THE RECOMPOSE TOOL 178

RECOMPOSE A PHOTO IN GUIDED MODE 178

RECOMPOSE A PICTURE IN ADVANCED MODE 179

RECOMPOSE OPTIONS 180

THE STRAIGHTEN TOOL 181

MANUALLY STRAIGHTEN A PICTURE IN ADVANCED MODE 181

FILL EMPTY EDGES INSTANTLY 182

MANUALLY STRAIGHTEN A PICTURE IN QUICK MODE 183

ACTIVITY 183

CHAPTER 6 184

SELECT AND ISOLATE AREAS IN YOUR PHOTOS 184

WHY SELECT AND ISOLATE? 184

Feathering 184

Blur the edges of a selection by feathering 185

Define a feathered edge for a selection tool 185

Define a feathered edge for an existing selection.. 186

Select Subject, Background, or Sky 186

Refine the edge of your selection 187

Edit and Refine Selections... 189

Defringe a selection.. 190

Cut and paste a selection into another photo 191

Copy a selection using commands 191

Paste one selection into another 191

Fill or stroke a selection... 192

Fill a layer with a color or pattern 192

Stroke objects on a layer 193

Activity.. 194

CHAPTER 7 195

RESIZE YOUR IMAGES 195

Image Resizing 195

About monitor resolution... 196

Display the image size of an open file 196

View the print size on the screen 196

Change print dimensions and resolution without resampling.. 197

Resample an image 198

Maximum image size limits in Photoshop Elements 200

Maximum image size limit in the Editor... 200

Maximum image size limit in the Organizer 200

Canvas Resizing 201

Activity.. 202

CHAPTER 8 203

FIX AND ENHANCE YOUR PHOTOS 203

Auto Fixes.. 203

Auto Smart Tone 203

Apply Auto Smart Tone to a picture 203

Auto Smart Tone Learning 204

Adjust Color.. 205

Correct color in Quick Mode... 205

Fix Photos with touch-up buttons 207

Correcting color in advanced mode... 208

About Histograms 209

PREVIEW CHANGES 210
    Adjust Hue/Saturation 210
    Change color saturation or hue 210
    Modify the range of Hue/Saturation sliders 212
    Replace Color 212
    Adjust Color Curves 214
    Adjust Color for Skin Tone 215
    Adjust Lighting 216
    Brightness/ Contrast 216
    Shadows/Highlights 217
LEVELS 218
CONVERT TO BLACK AND WHITE 219
    Precisely convert to black and white 219
AUTOMATICALLY CONVERT TO BLACK AND WHITE 220
    Add custom presets for black-and-white conversion 221
ADD COLOR TO A GRAYSCALE IMAGE 221
COLORIZE PHOTO 221
CHANGE COLORS IN CERTAIN REGIONS OF A PICTURE 222
HAZE REMOVAL 223
    Auto Haze Removal 223
    ; 223
UNSHARP MASK 223
SMOOTH SKIN 224
ADJUST FACIAL FEATURES 225
SHAKE REDUCTION 226
    Automatic Shake Reduction 227
    Manual Shake Reduction 227
WORK WITH ADJUSTMENT AND FILL LAYERS 228
    Creating adjustment layers 228
    Create fill layers 229
    Edit an adjustment or fill layer 230
    Merging adjustment layers 230
    Edit the layer masks 230
ACTIVITY 231

CHAPTER 9 .... **232**

WORK WITH PHOTOSHOP ELEMENTS LAYERS **232**

HOW LAYERS WORK 232
    Select a layer to edit 233
    Show or hide a layer 233

Lock or unlock a layer 234

Delete a layer 234

The Layers panel 234

Adding layers 235

CREATE AND NAME A NEW BLANK LAYER 235

CREATE A NEW LAYER FROM PART OF ANOTHER LAYER 236

CONVERT THE BACKGROUND LAYER INTO A REGULAR LAYER 236

MAKE A LAYER THE BACKGROUND LAYER 237

SIMPLIFY OR FLATTEN A LAYER 237

COPY LAYERS FROM ONE IMAGE FILE TO ANOTHER 237

MOVE THE CONTENT IN A LAYER 238

CHANGE THE STACKING ORDER OF LAYERS 238

LINK AND UNLINK LAYERS 239

Merge layers 239

MERGE LAYERS INTO ANOTHER LAYER 240

FLATTEN AN IMAGE 241

TRANSFORM AND WARP A LAYER 241

ACTIVITY 242

CHAPTER 10 .... **243**

CREATE AND EDIT TEXT **243**

TEXT IN AN IMAGE 243

Choose characters 243

CHOOSE A FONT FAMILY AND STYLE 244

Choose a font size 244

Change text color 245

Apply style to text 245

OTHER TRANSFORM OPTIONS 246

ACTIVITY 246

CHAPTER 11 .... **247**

ADD PHOTO EFFECTS AND FILTERS **247**

THE FILTER / ADJUSTMENT MENU 247

TIPS FOR CREATING VISUAL EFFECTS WITH FILTERS 248

Apply a filter 248

THE FILTER GALLERY 251

Improve performance with filters and effects 251

THE EFFECT PANEL 252

Classic Effects 252

Artistic Effects 253

Photo Effects 254
COLOR MATCH 255
Applying Color match effect in Quick mode; 255
RENDER FILTERS 256
Cloud 256
Difference Clouds 256
Fibers 257
Lens Flare 257
Texture Fill 257
ADJUSTMENT FILTERS 257
Equalize filter 257
Gradient Map filter 258
APPLY THE INVERT FILTER 259
APPLY THE POSTERIZE FILTER 259
APPLY THE PHOTO FILTER 260
THE STYLES PANEL 262
WORK WITH LAYER STYLES 263
Apply a layer style 263
Hide or show all layers styles in an image 263
Edit a layer's style settings 264
Copy style settings between layers 264
Remove a layer style 264
GRAPHICS PANEL 264
Add stylized shapes or graphics to a picture 265
Add an artistic background to a picture 265
Add a frame or theme to a picture 266
ACTIVITY 266

CHAPTER 12 267

PHOTOSHOP ELEMENTS TRICKS 267

SWAP OUT A FACE 267
SWAP OUT A BACKGROUND 267
REMOVE WARTS AND BLEMISHES 268
REMOVE BIG THINGS FROM YOUR PHOTOS 268
ACTIVITY 269

CHAPTER 13 270

ADVANCED PHOTO EDITING TOOLS 270

SCAN YOUR PHOTOS 270
GET PHOTOS FROM SCANNERS 270

Scan photos using a TWAIN driver 271
Download photos from your digital camera 271
Camera RAW installation 272
    Edit in Camera RAW 272
    Opening and processing camera raw files 273
    Adjust sharpness in camera raw files 275
    Reducing noise in camera raw images 275
    Save changes to camera raw images 276
    Supplementary choices 276
    Open a camera raw image in the Edit workspace 276
    Important controls for Camera Raw 276
Custom camera settings 277
Photoshop Elements Preferences and Presets 278
    Preferences 278
    Switching to Light and Dark mode 278
    Restore default preferences 278
Redisplay disabled warning messages 279
    About Presets 279
    Use preset tool options 279
Change the display of items in a pop-up panel menu 281
Use the Preset Manager 281
    Load a library 281
    Save a subset of a library 282
    Rename a preset 282
Activity 282

CHAPTER 14 283

LEARN ABOUT YOUR PHOTOSHOP ELEMENTS FILE 283

The Info panel 283
Set color modes and units of measurement in the info panel 284
Display file information in the info panel or status bar 284
Save or delete metadata templates 286
File Info 286
    View or add file information 286
Activity 287

CHAPTER 15 288

MANAGE YOUR FILES WITH THE ORGANIZER 288

Auto Curate 288
    Instantly edit photos 288

CREATE OR ADD PHOTOS TO AN ALBUM 289

THE MEDIA BROWSER AREA 289

CONFIGURE VIEWING PREFERENCES FOR THE MEDIA VIEW 290

SORT FILES IN MEDIA VIEW 291

HIDE AND SHOW MEDIA FILES IN THE MEDIA VIEW 291

    Hide media files by marking them 291

    Remove the Hidden icon from the media files 292

    View and manage files by folders 292

    Select files in the Media view 294

THE ORGANIZER CATALOG 294

CREATING A CATALOG 295

OPEN A CATALOG 297

MOVING OR MODIFYING MEDIA FILES 297

    Moving files 297

    Renaming files 298

    Deleting 298

    Editing files 299

    Delete a catalog 299

SWITCH BETWEEN ALBUM AND FOLDER VIEWS 300

SYNC YOUR MEDIA TO THE CLOUD 300

    Auto Sync Preferences 300

    Auto Sync details 301

    Sync selective media 301

AUTO ANALYZE YOUR MEDIA 301

MANAGE YOUR FILES WITH KEYWORD TAGS 302

USING THE KEYWORD TAGS PANEL 302

    Create a keyword tag 303

    Attach keyword tags to media files 303

    Find media files by their keyword tags 304

CREATE AND APPLY TAGS QUICKLY 304

    Create tags quickly 305

    Apply tags quickly 305

    Create new keyboard tag category or subcategory 305

    Write keyword Tag Information into your files 305

IMPORT AND EXPORT KEYWORD TAGS 306

IMPORT KEYWORD TAGS FROM THE FILE 306

FIND PEOPLE IN YOUR FILES 307

    Add People to Groups 307

MANAGE YOUR PHOTOS BY PLACE 307

PINNED AND UNPINNED TABS 308

VIEWING MEDIA FILES BEFORE ADDING LOCATION INFORMATION 308

ADDING LOCATION INFORMATION TO YOUR MEDIA FILES 308

MANAGE YOUR MEDIA FILES BY DATE OR EVENT.. 310

VIEW AND FIND MEDIA FILES USING THE TIMELINE 311

INSTANT FIX A PHOTO 311

    Editing photos using Instant Fix 312

APPLYING EDITS AND EFFECTS 312

APPLYING OR UNDOING CHANGES.. 313

BACK UP YOUR ORGANIZER CATALOG 313

    Auto Backup and Restore Catalog Structure.. 313

    Manually Backup and Restore 313

    Manually backing up a catalog 314

    Manually restoring a catalog 314

RESTORE A CATALOG FROM ONE COMPUTER TO ANOTHER 315

ACTIVITY... 315

CHAPTER 16 316

CREATE FUN PIECES 316

CREATE AN ORGANIZER SLIDESHOW.. 316

    Quickly create a slideshow 316

CUSTOMIZE THE SLIDESHOW 317

ADD MEDIA FROM THE CATALOG TO THE SLIDESHOW 317

ADD MEDIA FROM A FOLDER TO THE SLIDESHOW 319

    Add captions to the slideshow 319

    Add text slides to the slideshow 319

    Add music to a slideshow 320

    Save changes to the slideshow 320

CREATE A PHOTO COLLAGE 320

CREATE A COLLAGE 321

RESIZE, REPOSITION, AND ROTATE THE IMAGES OR LAYERS IN THE COLLAGE 322

CREATE A PHOTO REEL 323

CREATE A QUOTE GRAPHIC 324

    Enter the workspace 324

CHANGE BACKGROUND 325

    Add text.. 326

    Customize the Quote Graphic 326

SAVE AND PRINT 327

    Save... 327

    Print.. 327

CREATE PHOTO PRINTS 327

PRINT PHOTOS AT HOME.. 328

Select multiple media files *330*

PRINTING CHOICES 331

Custom print size *331*

CREATE A PHOTO BOOK 332

CREATE A GREETING CARD 333

CREATE A PHOTO CALENDAR 335

CREATE PRINTS AND GIFTS 336

CREATE A VIDEO STORY 336

Create a video story *337*

ADD CAPTIONS AND NARRATION TO THE WORKFLOW 340

CREATE A HIGHLIGHT REEL 340

ACTIVITY 341

CHAPTER 17 .... **342**

SHARE YOUR PHOTOS AND VIDEOS **342**

DEVICE 342

Social Media *343*

Audio *344*

Image *344*

SHARE YOUR PHOTOS VIA EMAIL 344

SETTING UP THE PROFILE FOR A PRESET SERVICE PROVIDER 345

SET UP THE PROFILE FOR OTHER SERVICE PROVIDERS 346

SHARE FILES BY EMAIL 347

SHARE A PDF SLIDESHOW BY EMAIL 348

SHARE YOUR PHOTOS ON FLICKR 349

SHARE YOUR VIDEO ON VIMEO 350

SHARE YOUR VIDEO ON YOUTUBE 351

CREATE AN ELEMENTS ORGANIZER CONTACT BOOK 351

Add an entry to the contact book *351*

Import addresses into the contact book (Windows only) *351*

Delete or modify an entry in the contact book *352*

Edit an entry in the contact book *352*

Create a group in the contact book *352*

EXPORT CONTACT INFORMATION TO VCARD FILES (WINDOWS ONLY) 353

ACTIVITY 353

CONCLUSION 354

INDEX **355**

INTRODUCTION

Adobe Photoshop (Elements) is a graphics editor designed for photographers, image editors, and enthusiasts. It has the majority of the functionality included in the professional edition, but with lesser and simpler alternatives. Users can use the program to generate, edit, organize, and share photographs. It is the replacement for Adobe Photoshop (Limited Edition). Automatic modifications can be used to improve images, or you can use guided edits to acquire knowledge as you go. With these tools, you will be amazed at how simple it is to wow clients, relatives, and friends or gain more social media attention. Photoshop Elements contains all the capabilities you require if you're new to photo editing or you simply want to make fast modifications or enhancements. Start by looking at the auto-generated content on your home screen, such as photo and video highlights and slideshows, collages, and slideshows of great occasions. Additionally, you can get courses, innovative concepts, and new tools.

You can get to do the following with your pictures when making use of Photo Elements;

Make adjustments that are impactful in a swift manner

With the use of Photoshop Elements, it is now very possible to perform fast alterations that once required hours of pixel-by-pixel retouching, such as opening closed eyes or making frowns into grins. You now can also get to colorize black-and-white photographs, create 3D effects, and more with Adobe Sensei's advanced capabilities.

Learn as you are working

You don't have to acquire all the needed knowledge before you commence with the use of Photoshop Element. You can now get detailed instructions for almost any edit you wish to make. You can follow 58 guided modifications and have more fun with your images than ever, from simple adjustments like correction of colors and getting the horizon straightened to more difficult ones like double exposures or color pops.

Make amazing designs and share them with ease

It's simple to include quotes or any special notes to your images with Photoshop Elements. Create quote graphics by customizing templates with your own text or by creating your own graphics right from the beginning. Increase attention by adding so many catchy animations. You can also share your images as prints or on items like clothes, mugs, artwork, and gadget cases if you live in the US. Use the built-in FUJIFILM Prints and Gifts service in Photoshop Elements to order prints.

Remain organized

The whole of your photo catalog will be more organized with the use of tags for people, places, events, and others. Videos are instantly tagged with Smart Tags which are dependent on topics like sunsets, birthdays, dogs, kittens, and more. Your photo and video library's entire contents are now regularly backed up for quick recovery.

What's New in Adobe Photoshop Elements 2024

Fast photo correction, whole alterations, and Photo editing are made simple with AI, automation, and a modernized user interface. Match the color and tone of any image automatically, or choose a background or sky with a single click. Create customized text and play around with different backgrounds and Artistic Effect settings to achieve distinctive styles. Post images in quick-moving photo reels. With a revamped design, all of your Quick Actions in one location, and instant access to many free Adobe Stock images, get ready for a whole new experience. Try the one-click repairs in the English-only beta Elements Mobile companion app and the creative overlays in the Elements Web companion app when you're on the go. Your films and photographs will automatically sync, making them accessible anywhere.

New light and dark modes

Experience editing in a modern, fresh way with eye-pleasing fonts, buttons, symbols, and colors. You can also select between light and dark mode settings. Modernized workspaces (Advanced, Guided, and Quick), dialog boxes, buttons, panels, toolbars, action bars, and more are all visible. The application's UI color mode can be adjusted to either light or dark from the options.

Color Match

After just a single click, you can adjust hue, saturation, and brightness by selecting from pre-made presets or by using your own photo. Examine the new Quick and Advanced Color Match features.

- After selecting one of the pre-built presets in the Quick mode, **adjust the brightness, saturation, and hue.**
- In addition to the pre-made presets in the Advanced mode, you may also use a picture of your own as a customized preset and adjust the output's parameters.

Photo Reel

Favorite shots are sped through in reels, each with unique text, effects, and graphics. For simple sharing, save them as GIFs or MP4s.

Add Text Guided Edit

Adobe has combined all the text options into a simple guided edit for this edition. Text can be aligned on a path, a form, or horizontally or vertically. Use gradients and patterns to customize and warp it.

To utilize this guided edit tool, take these actions:

- Navigate to **Guided mode** when you have opened your preferred picture.

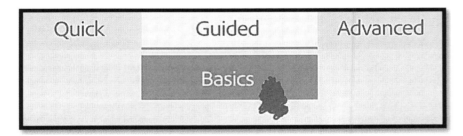

- Choose the **Add Text guided edit** card that can be found in the **Basics category** in order to have an initiation of the workflow.

- Follow the guided edit steps.

Quick Actions

In this section are 25 of the most widely used one-click modifications that you can access instantly. With just one handy panel, you can instantly blur or eliminate a background, smooth skin, dehaze or colorize a photo and much more. When in Quick mode, the Quick Actions panel is adjacent to Effects.

Some of the most well-liked one-click modifications in Quick Actions are listed below:

- JPEG Artifacts Removal
- Auto Smart Fix
- Remove Background
- Select Subject
- Smooth Skin

Free Adobe Stock Photos

Get free images from Adobe Stock to increase your creative potential. Use Photoshop Elements to create an inspirational Quote Graphic, experiment with different backgrounds, or collages with thousands of gorgeous stock photographs.

Using Adobe Stock, get free photos and backgrounds for these four Photoshop workflows:

- **File menu > Search on Adobe Stock**
- **Advanced mode > Graphics > Background**
- **Guided > Replace Background**
- **Create > Quote Graphic**

New Artistic Effect

The new Artistic Effect options let you turn images into works of art. To add effects influenced by well-known pieces of art or common art genres, simply click. Powered by Sensei* from Adobe.

One-click selection

For simpler editing, choose a background or sky with a single click. Selecting an automatic option makes it easy to improve or replace a single area. Powered by Sensei* from Adobe.

There are two ways that you can use these one-click select options:

- Make your preferred choice between **Subject, Background, or Sky from the list in the Select menu.**
- Open the **Tools panel and select any of the Selection Tools.** Then, use any of the action bar's Subject, Sky, and Background options.

Photoshop Elements Mobile and Web Companion Apps (English-only beta)

Mobile

- To upload mobile images and videos to Elements on the desktop and web, try the redesigned companion app. From there, you may edit more creatively and in a more advanced manner on the desktop, and then access, watch, and share the edited content back on your mobile device.
- With only one click on **Quick Actions,** you can automatically adjust tone, eliminate backgrounds, adjust white balance, and much more. You may now see creations

from Elements Web and import images from a larger variety of files and directories on your phone.

- With 2GB of free storage in the cloud, get started right away.

Web

- Discover how to access and watch your modified Elements images and movies from any browser by exploring the redesigned web companion app. You can also make collages and slideshows and share them as you like.
- Enhance your photographs with colorful patterns, then use the desktop application to edit them in greater detail.
- To give the impression of depth and to frame your topic, use peek-through overlays.
- Use the right layouts to ensure that your work is print- or social media-ready.
- To make more extensive edits, launch your web creation on the desktop app.
- Start using 2GB of free cloud storage right away.

Overview of This Book

You can basically do anything you would like to with digital photographs when making use of Photoshop Elements. You can add color to black-and-white pictures, remove evil red-eyed expressions, or alter the looks of persons who have harmed you. The drawback is that, especially if you're new to the application, all those options might make it challenging to navigate Elements. There are several Photoshop Elements books available, but the majority of them are usually of the opinion that you are familiar with the fundamentals of digital image and/or photography. Getting to locate decent books for intermediate readers on Elements is much simpler than finding books to get you started with the program. By eliminating jargon that is technically related as much as possible and describing why and when you should use (or avoid) specific software features, it aims to make learning Elements easier. People who are experienced photographers as well as those who are just starting out with their first digital cameras can both benefit from this book.

Both users of Windows and Mac computers can immensely benefit from the use of this book's chapter on utilizing Elements. On a Mac, pop-out menus, for instance, are more likely to have a white background rather than a black one.) Regardless of the type of computer you're using, Elements' Editor (the section where you edit images) operates exactly the same way. However, the Organizer and the projects you can choose from might be slightly different, and those variances are usually shown where there is a need for them. There are seventeen (17) chapters in this book and each of the chapters is well illustrated with screenshots to ensure that you have a perfect understanding of the instructions and steps to get things done with ease. Below is a sneak peek into what each of the chapters in this book contains. Note however that there are activities at the end of each of the chapters that you should take in order to get your knowledge tested as regards what you must have read and practiced in that chapter!

Chapter 1: Things You Need to Know

In this chapter, you will learn about the basic things you need to know in order to get perfectly started with the use of Photoshop Elements especially if you are new to this software. Here you will learn about Pixels, resolution, the difference between raster and vector graphics as well as the difference between image size and canvas size, selections, layers, alpha the tool options bin, etc. Pay close attention to the details in this chapter as it will help you with other things you will be learning in the other chapters of this book.

Chapter 2: Get to Know Photoshop Elements 2024

In this chapter, you will learn about the new features embedded in this new edition of Photoshop Elements; the editor workspace, light or dark interface, toolbox, photo bin, saving files to the cloud, and the section that deals specifically with all of the new features you will be introduced to.

Chapter 3: Quick Fixes and Effects

In this chapter, you will learn how to swiftly make certain fixes and apply some effects without taking so much time. You will learn about the quick fix toolbar where you will be able to add quick effects, quick textures, quick frames, etc.

Chapter 4: Guided Edits

In this section, you will learn about search-guided edits, the move and scale object-guided edit, color-guided edits, black and white edits, fun edits, special edits, photo merge-guided edits, and the use of the action panel.

Chapter 5: Get to Know the Photoshop Elements Toolbox

In this section, you will learn about so many tools that you are expected to make use of in Photoshop Elements. Some of these tools include the color picker tool, the zoom tool, the hand tool, the move tool, the lasso selection tool, the quick selection tool, the refine selection tool, the spot healing brush tool, the smart brush tool, the clone stamp tool, the pattern stamp tool, the blur tool, etc. This chapter is quite comprehensive and filled with so many instructions to help you get through the practicable steps with ease.

Chapter 6: Select and Isolate Areas in Your Photos

Here you will learn about all that has to do with making selections in your picture. You will also learn about edge detection, refining edge adjustment, the background or sky selection, cutting and pasting a selection into another picture, and filling or stroking a selection.

Chapter 7: Resize Your Images

In this chapter, you will learn about the image size and canvas size, you will also learn about how to resize an image and also how to resize a canvas.

Chapter 8: Fix and Enhance Your Picture

Enhancing your picture is absolutely important so you get the best of pictures. In this chapter, you will learn about auto-fixes, adjusting color, removing color, adjusting color curves, adjusting color for skin tone, adjusting lighting, quick fixes and guided fixes, converting to black and white, colorizing photo haze removal, adjusting sharpness, unsharp mask, smooth skin adjust facial features.

Chapter 9: Work with Photoshop Elements Layers

In this chapter, you will learn about how layers work, the use of the layers panel, simplifying or flattening a layer, and transforming and warping a layer.

Chapter 10: Create and Edit Text

In this chapter, you will learn how to create and edit text with the use of the type tool; you will also learn to shape and resize your text.

Chapter 11: Add Photo Effects and Filters

In this chapter, you will learn about the filter gallery, the effects panel, the filters panel, the styles panel, and also the use of graphics.

Chapter 12: Photoshop Element Tricks

Here you will learn some tricks like swapping out a face, swapping out a background, and removing warts and big things from your picture to ensure that they are clear and distinct.

Chapter 13: Advanced Photo Editing Tools

Here you will learn to scan your picture, screen captures, and download pictures from your camera.

Chapter 14: Learn about Your Photoshop Elements File

In this chapter, you will learn about the info panel, and also file information.

Chapter 15: Manage Your Files with the Organizer

Going a little in-depth, in this chapter, you will learn about auto-curate, the organizer catalog, what metadata is all about, managing your files with keyword tags, adding people to groups, instant-fixing a picture, and lots more.

Chapter 16: Create Fun Pieces

In this chapter, you will get to create loads of fun stuff which include; creating a photo collage, photo reel, photo prints, photo book, photo calendar, video story, and lots more.

Chapter 17: Share Your Photos and Videos

In this chapter, you will learn how to share your photos through email, share your pictures on Flickr, and share your pictures on all other social media platforms like Facebook, and YouTube. You will also learn how to create an element organizer contact book.

CHAPTER 1
BASIC THINGS YOU OUGHT TO KNOW

In the first chapter of this book, you are welcomed into the world of digital photography. It is assumed that you have no prior knowledge of how to make simple edits and also that you have never been involved in the editing of any book hence, you will get to learn about various terminologies that are often used in Elements and also in the world of digital photography.

Pixels

The fundamental color-programming unit on a computer screen or in a digital image is often regarded as the pixel; it is a word that was created from the phrase "picture element." Take it more as a logical as a physical unit. In a digital display, pixels are the smallest unit. On a device's screen, an image or video may have millions of pixels or much more than that. Red, green, and blue (RGB) colors, which are shown at various intensities, are emitted by a subpixel within each pixel. The range of various colors that appear on a display or computer monitor is made up of the RGB color components which you will get to learn more about as you read on. The resolution of a computer monitor or the screen of a television is oftentimes determined by the number of pixels, and generally speaking, the more pixels you have, the sharper and clearer the image tends to be. The 8K full ultra-high definition TVs on the market has a resolution of 7680 × 4320, or roughly 33 million pixels. When you multiply the horizontal and vertical pixel measurements, you will get the total number of pixels. For instance, HD has 2,073,600 total pixels, 1,920 horizontal and 1,080 vertical. Typically, it is displayed in 1080p or 1920 x 1080 resolutions. Progressive scan is shown by the pixel also. For instance, an 8K video resolution has 16 times as many pixels as a 1080p video while a 4K video resolution has four times as many pixels as full high definition (HD).

Other very common display resolutions include;

- 480p, which is the default definition, is 640 x 480 and is most times used for smaller mobile devices;
- 720p, which is High Definition (HD), is 1280 x 720;
- 1440p, which is 2550 x 1440 and often referred to as quarter HD (QHD), is most times used for PC gaming monitors; and

- 4K video resolution, which is known as ultra HD, is 3840 x 2160 pixels.

A pixel's description of a specific color is most times a combination of RGB, the color spectrum's three primary colors. A pixel's color can be indicated with the use of up to three bytes of data, one byte for each significant color component. All three bytes are employed in a true color or 24-bit color system. The display can only show 256 different colors because many color display systems only use one byte. The resolution that has been chosen for the display screen determines the main size of a pixel. The physical size of a pixel will match the dot pitch, or dot size, of the display if it is configured to its highest resolution. A pixel, nevertheless, will be larger than the ideal size of the screen's dot if the resolution is configured to a value that is lower than the maximum resolution. Literally, this means that a pixel will consume more than one dot.

Megapixel

A million pixels make up one megapixel (MP). The term "megapixel" is often used in relation to photography, although it can also be used to describe screen resolutions. As an illustration, 4K is roughly 12 MP, and 1080p is 2.1 MP. Megapixels are a common term used in photography to describe both the resolution of an image and the quantity of image sensor components in digital cameras. For instance, the Sony A7 III camera can capture images at a resolution of 24,200,000 pixels, or 24.2 MP. Smartphone cameras normally have a resolution of 12 MP, whereas interchangeable-lens cameras often have a resolution of 20 to 60 MP. Smaller action cameras like GoPros and Insta360 can have 12-48 MP resolutions.

PPI and DPI

Pixels per inch (PPI) are a unit of measurement used in the description of screen image sharpness. PPI and dots per inch (DPI) are two closely related and often mixed-up ideas. PPI is regarded as the measure of how many pixels make up an inch of a digital image. DPI, on the other hand, helps with the measurement of the quantity of printed dots within an inch of an image. PPI has to do with the quality of a digital image shown on-screen, whereas DPI refers to the quality of a physical, printed photo. This is the main distinction between the two concepts. The number of printed ink dots is indicated by the dots in DPI.

Resolution

The number of pixels—picture components or individual color points—that may fit onto a display screen or on a camera sensor is known as resolution. Resolution, in real-world terms, refers to how clear or sharp an image is. It is defined in terms of how many pixels can be shown in both a vertical and horizontal manner. For a proper evaluation of the visual quality of digital photographs, photos, and videos, the resolution is a very important aspect. An image with a greater resolution will have more pixels; this simply means it can display more visual data. A high-resolution image is consequently crisper and more distinct than a low-resolution one.

Raster vs. vector graphics

Raster

Raster files, also referred to as bitmaps, perform best when it has to do with storing and displaying high-quality pictures. If they are digital or print, the majority of images are in the raster file format. You can alter individual pixels within a raster file to alter the look of a photograph with the use of tools like Adobe Photoshop Element. The size and resolution of each raster picture are, however, constrained by the unique dimensions and pixel count that it has. An image that does not have sufficient pixels can become pixelated if its size is increased, which is often not desirable. For this reason, logos or graphics that need to be utilized in a range of sizes frequently arrive in vector format. If you have the thought of making use of a raster file when creating your next project, ensure you are well aware of its ups and downs before you commence your project;

Below are some of the very important of the raster graphics;

- **Attention to detail**: when shown in the perfect dimensions, raster files are capable of displaying all of the details and colors that seem intricate in resolutions that are quite high. When a pixel has more pixels, the image quality tends to be stronger/
- **Precise editing**: You are capable of altering each pixel when you are modifying a raster graphic or picture. With this, you can enhance and also get the image tailored to meet your specific needs.
- **Widely compatible**: A wide range of applications and browsers can be launched with the use of the raster files, ensuring it becomes much easier to see, alter, and distribute as your pictures.

The very few disadvantages with the use of raster graphics include;

- **Limited resolution**: Raster files do not keep their resolution when enlarged when compared to vector images. The number of uses for these photographs is usually reduced since when they are expanded, their colors and details may get distorted.
- **Larger file sizes**: Millions of pixels can be found in a raster file. While doing so produces a well-detailed image, it might also affect the file size and times it loads.

Vector

When you require high-quality visuals that can be swiftly scaled to multiple sizes, the vector format can be a very nice option. No matter how big or small you make them, vector files won't get fuzzy or deformed due to the fact they were produced with the use of mathematical methods. So what purposes does vector generally serve? If the design has to be scaled up or down for a diverse range of advertising mediums, digital graphics, and company logos usually employ the use of this form. A logo saved in vector format will not lose resolution when used on anything from T-shirts and posters to bite-sized business cards. The most popular vector file types are SVG (Scalable Vector Graphics), EPS (Encapsulated PostScript), PDF (Portable Document Format), and AI (Adobe Illustrator).

Some very important benefits of making use of vector files include;

- **Infinite resolution**: Almost no size is possible for a vector image without having to let go of resolution. Raster files, on the other hand, only maintain their resolution when sized to a specific area. The quality may suffer more the further you stretch them.
- **Lighter file sizes**: Vector files typically weigh less than raster images like photos since they do not have blocks of pixels, which might contain loads of camera data.

There are also certain disadvantages to making use of vector images;

- **Less useful for complex pictures**: Raster formats are usually ideal for highly detailed digital images since they allow for the editing of individual pixels. Photographs typically don't work as well with vector files as they do with graphics.
- **Conversion difficulties**: Given that it takes more processing power, converting a raster image to a vector file is usually far more difficult.

The resolution of raster and vector files is one of their primary differences. The resolution of a raster file is often expressed in terms of DPI (dots per inch) or PPI (pixels per inch). Raster images enable you to zoom in or increase their size so that you will be able to see the individual pixels. Raster files display a much wider variety of colors than vector files, allow for more color tweaking, and show a finer light and shade, but they lose image quality when they are scaled. Increasing an image's size is a simple approach to determine if it is a raster or vector graphic. The image is most likely a raster file if it blurs or becomes pixelated.

Image Size vs. Canvas Size

While the size of an image and the size of a canvas may have similar sound, they each affect an image in different ways. When you change the canvas size of an image, you either make the canvas's surface area larger or less. This means that expanding the canvas size will give rise to more space surrounding the image. Contrary to that, shrinking the canvas size will lead to the image being cropped, which means that based on where you crop it, you may lose some of the images. On the other hand, when you adjust the image size of an image, you affect how big or tiny the image becomes. If you expand an image too much, it may look as though it is blurry and appear larger. Similar to this, if you reduce the size of the photograph, some detail will be lost in the process. Hence, all you have to do to crop an image or add additional space to it is just to modify the canvas size. If on the other hand, you would like to decrease, increase, or change the resolution of the image, alter the image size.

Selections

The editable pixels of a photo are usually determined by selections. For example, you can make use of them in the darkening of a specific part of a picture without having a major influence on others. A selection tool or a selection command can be used to make selections. The selection is often surrounded by a selection outline that you can hide. The pixels inside a selection border can be edited, but until the selection is deselected, you cannot gain access to the pixels outside the selection perimeter. For various selections, Photoshop Elements provides selection tools. For example, the Magic Wand tool may quickly choose an area of like colors, the Rectangular Marquee tool chooses square and rectangular areas, and one of the Lasso tools enables freeform choices. Furthermore, you can employ the use of feathering and anti-aliasing to soften a selection's edges. Various selection tools perform diverse functions in Photoshop Element; the rectangular marquee tool draws square or rectangular selections, the elliptical marquee helps with the drawing of round or elliptical selections, the lasso tool draws freehand selections, the polygonal lasso tool draws various multiple straight-edged portions of a selection. Furthermore, you have the magnetic lasso tool that draws a selection that instantly snaps to make a contrast of the edges you move over in the picture. The quick selection tool instantly creates a selection that is dependent on color and texture when you choose or click-move an area. The selection brush tool instantly chooses or deselects the portions you paint, based on if you are in Selection or Mask mode.

Layers

When you work on individual picture layers in Photoshop Elements it enables you to make modifications without permanently making changes to the source image. You can add new layers, give them names, and also rearrange, organize, or even merge particular layers. When you want to make so many adjustments to photographs, layers are very important. You can add adjustment layers that affect brightness, color, saturation, and other characteristics against changing the pixels in the image itself. When you separate the edit from the image on layers, you may experiment with various configurations without having to constantly undo your changes. There is just one default layer when you first import or scan an image into Photoshop Elements. Layers make the process quite simple once you start using some of the more involved and complex picture modification and retouching tools. Layers act like transparent, clear sheets layered on top of one another, but when you check the last image, they blend together to form just one, cohesive image. You might notice that when you copy and paste selections, your image automatically adds new layers. Given that you can edit just one layer at a time, you can select and change particular portions of your shot without having a direct impact on the data on other layers. This then is the actual beauty of layers; the ability to work on and also experiment with one aspect of your picture while leaving the remaining of it totally untouched. Adjustment layers are quite more flexible, giving you room to make corrections to tone and color to individual or various layers without a need to alter the main pixels.

When it comes to transparency, layers look like clear acetate sheets, enabling you to see through to the levels below. In your image, layers are displayed in the same order as they are in the Layers panel. The background layer can be found at the bottom of the list of layers on the Layers panel, while the top layer of your image is displayed first. The Layers panel immediately shows in the Panel Bin in the lower-right corner of your screen when Photoshop Elements is launched first. The Layers panel can be dragged out into the work area and it can also be used from the Panel Bin. The active layer can be changed, layers can be shown or hidden, and layers can be locked in order to prevent unauthorized modifications. Also, you have control over layer names, opacity (transparency), and blending modes.

Alpha Channels

In order to alter certain components of an image without changing the rest of the image, an additional channel which is known as an alpha channel is usually added to the image. It lets you save a selection for later use and makes it simple to create transparent sections. An alpha channel basically is a kind of mask that simplifies image editing. You must first be familiar with ordinary channels and how they operate on an image in order to understand how an alpha channel operates. In Photoshop, there are three channels by default for any image you edit. The channels are Red, Green, and Blue, which together make up RGB. You will be able to see how much of each color is present in the image when choosing these channels. You can also add an additional channel, known as an alpha channel, which enables more creative image editing.

Using an alpha channel, you can accomplish the following:

- Change the opacity of some elements of your picture.
- Isolate elements of the picture to create a background that is transparent.
- Save selections that are quite difficult so you can use them much later.

The creation of transparent areas that transfer to other programs that accept alpha channels is the main advantage of making use of an alpha channel. This is useful if you want to isolate a specific element from an image so you can use it in other applications, like video editing software. After you have made your choice, you can save it as an alpha channel. The alpha channel will be chosen by the new program when you import the image, allowing you to continue to work with the selection.

Color

There are two color models in Adobe Photoshop Elements that are used to modify color. The human eye perceives color in terms of hue, saturation, and brightness (HSB), while computer monitors display color as a combination of red, green, and blue (RGB) values. Another tool that can be used for understanding the connections between colors is the color wheel. There are basically four image modes in Photoshop Elements that control the amount of colors that are visible in an image: RGB, bitmap, grayscale, and indexed color.

About color

The human eye sees color in terms of three characteristics; hue, saturation, and brightness (HSB) while computer monitors show colors by producing diverse amounts of red, green, and blue (RGB) light. In Elements, you make use of the HSB and RGB color models to choose and tweak color. The color wheel can help you have a perfect understanding of the relationships between colors.

HSB model

Depending on the perception of human color, the HSB model describes three basic features of color;

- **Hue**: this is the color that is emitted or transmitted by an object. On the standard color wheel, it is measured as a position, which is then stated as a degree between 0 and 360. Basically, the name of the color, like red, orange, or green, serves as the hue's identifier.
- **Saturation**: this is basically the strength or the purity of the color. Saturation, which oftentimes is referred to as chroma, shows the amount of gray in proportion to the hue, measured in the form of a percentage from 0 (gray) to 100 (fully saturated). On the standard color wheel, saturation becomes increased directly from the middle to the edge.
- **Brightness**: this is simply the relative lightness or darkness of the color which is often measured as a percentage from 0(black) to 100 (white). Even though you can always make use of the HSB model in Photoshop Elements for the definition of a color in the dialog box of the Color Picker, you are unable to make use of the HSB mode for the creation or the modification of the images.

34

RGB model

A considerable section of the visible spectrum can be shown by varying the quantities and intensities of red, green, and blue (RGB) light. The additive primaries are these three colors. When red, green, and blue light are added together, they form white light. Cyan, magenta, and yellow are formed when two hues overlap. Lighting, video, and monitors all use additive primary colors. For example, color is created by producing light through red, green, and blue phosphors in your display.

Color wheel

The color wheel is a useful tool for understanding and remembering the relationship between colors. The additive primaries are red, green, and blue. Subtractive primaries are cyan, magenta, and yellow. Each additive primary's complement is directly across from it: red-cyan, green-magenta, and blue-yellow. Each subtractive primary has about two additive primaries but not their complement. With this, increasing the amount of a primary color in your image will lead to a reduction of the amount of its complement. Yellow, for example, is made up of green and red light but contains no blue light. When you modify the color values in the blue color channel in Photoshop Elements, you change the color values in the yellow color channel. You eliminate yellow from your image by adding blue to it.

The Photo Bin

The Photo Bin, which can be found close to the bottom of the Photoshop Elements window, above the taskbar, shows thumbnails of open photos. It comes in handy when you are flipping between numerous pictures that are opened in your workstation. The Photo Bin has controls for opening and closing photographs, hiding images, navigating between open images, making a specific image the frontmost image, duplicating an image, rotating an image, and seeing file information. Open photos can be simply brought into Quick mode for editing. In the Create panel, multipage projects created with the Create tab are open.

Do any of the following when you happen to be in the Photo Bin;

- (Windows alone) To launch a picture, move a file from just about any location on your computer which also includes the Photo Browser and you can also choose to move from any storage device that is linked to your computer into the Photo Bin.

- To bring to the front a picture that is opened, choose **a thumbnail.**
- Move the thumbnails that are in the Photo Bin to reorganize pictures. The order here has no impact on the order of the photos in the organizer of the Elements.
- Right-click **on a thumbnail in the Photo Bin and select Close to have an image closed.**
- If there is an image in the floating and you would like to have it concealed, right-click **on the thumbnail and select Minimize from the context menu**.
- To access the file details for a photo, right-click **a thumbnail and select File Info within the context menu.**
- Duplicate an image by right-clicking it, selecting **Duplicate from the context menu, and naming the file.**
- Right-click **a thumbnail and select Rotate 90° Left or Rotate 90° Right from the context menu to rotate it.**
- Right-click **in the Photo Bin and select Show Filenames from the context menu to display Filenames.**
- Click the **Photo Bin taskbar icon to manually show or hide the bin.**
- **The flyout of the Photo Bin has more choices to work with the pictures that can be found in the Photo Bin;**
    - **Print Bin Files**: this helps with the opening of the dialog box of the Photoshop Elements Print, with choices available to print the pictures selected at the moment in the Photo Bin.
    - **Save Bin as an Album**: this choice allows you to give a name to an album and also save the album that has the pictures in the Photo Bin. The new album can be found in Organizer.
    - **Show Grid**: this choice shows a grind around pictures in the Photo Bin.

What is a native PSD file?

PSD files are Adobe Photoshop's native file type. You've probably come across files with the.psd suffix, especially if you've used Adobe Photoshop. Photoshop Documents, which are most typically used by designers and artists, are sophisticated tools for picture data storage and creation.

- A PSD can help with the storage of multiple lares, pictures, and objects, most times in high resolution, ensuring that it becomes the standard of the industry for creative.
- A PSD can provide support for about 30, 000 pixels in height and breadth, providing these files with an amazing range for both the image depth as well as the color spread.

The PSD debuted alongside Adobe Photoshop and is now regarded as the industry standard file type for digital image processing and editing. PSD files, as the software's native files type, enabled Photoshop creations to be saved as high-quality, editable documents. Adobe, then known as Adobe Systems Incorporated, created Photoshop in 1988 and made it available to the public in 1990. The software, as well as its PSD file format, has progressed substantially over time, establishing the firm as the global leader in image editing.

Uses

PSDs can hold a huge amount of picture data, including multiple layers of various images or graphical elements. They can create significantly huge, editable files with PSD sizes of up to two gigabytes.

- **Digital design**: with Photoshop being the Swiss army knife in toolkits for designers, it is no surprise that PSDs are files that are commonly used in digital design work. The ability to get the job done across various layers, and import, and alter various graphics and high-quality images make PSDs a must-have for various digital projects.
- **Photography manipulation**: Photographers who employ Photoshop and other Adobe Creative Cloud products for post-production work, such as picture editing, retouching, and compositing, will be quite familiar with PSD files. A photographer may do practically anything inside a PSD, from adjusting an underexposed photo to creating high-gloss editorial graphics.

The advantages of making use of the PSD files include;

- PSDs have the ability to keep about 30, 000 pixels in both height and breadth; this means they have the ability to save a huge amount of color and picture quality information for their size.

- They are one of the very few image files that can be edited across various layers; this means that various images can be overlaid and manipulated individually.
- PSDs can be transported with ease into other Adobe products like Illustrator and Premiere Pro.

Activity

1. What are pixels?
2. Differentiate between raster and vector graphics.
3. Differentiate between image size and canvas size.
4. What are layers?
5. What is a native PSD file?

CHAPTER 2
GET TO KNOW PHOTOSHOP ELEMENTS 2024

The Element Hub

In this section, you will get to learn about the various important sections that make up the element hub and how best to make use of this aspect when you have to edit your pictures.

The Editor workspace

Working in Photoshop Elements' Edit workspace gives you options for working with your files. You can choose to configure settings for opening, saving, and exporting files based on file type, file size, and resolution. Camera raw files can also be processed and saved. These tools make it simple to integrate and optimize files of various sorts in Adobe Photoshop Elements. You may open a recently used file, create a blank file, define which file formats to open in Photoshop Elements, and more in the Edit workspace. The Guided Edit function is another alternative for operating in the Edit workspace. When you're unsure about a workflow or how to complete a task, Guided Edits can aid. They enable users to perform complex altering workflows in a few simple steps.

Create a new blank file

You might have a need to design a web graphic, the logo of a company, or letterhead. Or banner; whichever the case is, you will have to commence with the use of a new blank file.

- Select **File > New Blank File.**

- **Insert the various options for the new picture and then select the OK button.**

  o **Name**: give the new picture a name. Ensure it is a name that tallies what you are about to design so that you will be able to remember much later.

  o **Preset**: this choice helps with the provision of configuring the breadth, height, and resolution of the picture you would like to print or to see on-screen. Choose Clipboard to employ the size as well as the resolution of the data that you have copied to the clipboard. You are also able to base a fresh picture on the size and the resolution of any image that is opened by selecting its name from the lower part of the menu of the preset.

  o **Size**: you can make your choice from a list of standard sizes that can be chosen for the current preset.

  o **Width, Height, and Resolution:** this choice configures these options individually. The default values are dependent on the last picture that you have just created unless you have gotten the data copied to the clipboard.

  o **Color Mode**: this helps with the configuration of an image to RGB color, grayscale, or bitmap.

  o **Background Contents**: this option colorizes the image Background layer. White is the standard color. To utilize the current background color (as shown in the toolbox), select Background Color. Choose translucent to make the default layer translucent and remove all color values—the fresh image will have Layer 1 instead of a Background layer.

Open a file

You can launch and import pictures in diverse file formats. The available formats will be displayed in the dialog box of Open, the dialog box for Open As, and also the submenu for Import. To launch a file from Elements Organizer

- Choose the **file, and select Editor in the taskbar.**
- **Do any of the following;**
  - Select **File and then click on Open**. Navigate and choose the specific file you would like to have opened. If the file is not displayed, select **All Formats from the Files of Type menu. Select Open.**
  - Choose t**he Open drop-down (at the top of the toolbox)**. The Open drop-down is a rundown of files that have just been opened.

- Move an image from a folder on your storage or your computer then proceed to drop it in the Editor.
- In the dialog box that is displayed, configure format-specific choices, and proceed to launching the file. Sometimes, there are always instances where Photoshop Elements is unable to determine the right format for a certain file. For instance, sending a file between Mac OS and Windows can make the format become mislabeled. When this happens, you must then indicate the right format in which you would like to have the file opened.

To open a file that you have just edited;

- Click on **File > Open Recently Edited File**,

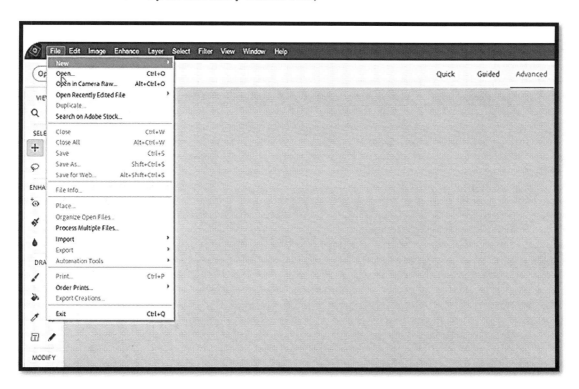

And then choose a file from the submenu that is shown. It is worth noting that if you would like to indicate the number of files that can be found in the Open Recently Edited File submenu, click on **Edit > Preferences > Saving Files**, and then insert a number in the text box of the Recent File List Contains.

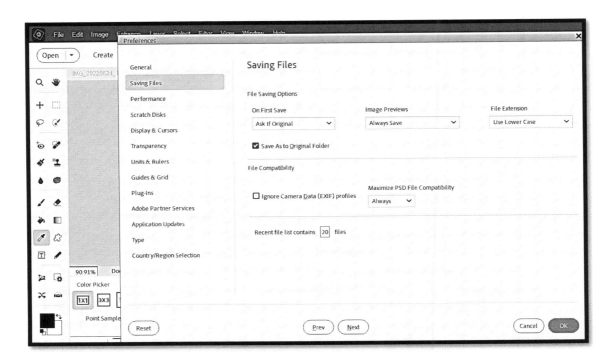

If there is a need for you to indicate the file format in which you would like to have your file opened;

- Select **File > Open As**, and then choose the file you would like to have opened. Then make a choice of the preferred format from the Open As menu, and then select Open.

Open a PDF file

Portable Document Format (PDF) is a dynamic file format that can incorporate electronic document search and navigation features as well as vector and bitmap data representation. Adobe Acrobat's primary format is PDF. You can preview the pages and images in a multipage PDF file using the Import PDF dialog box before deciding whether to open them in the Photoshop Editor. You can either import whole pages (with text and graphics) or simply the photos from a PDF file. If you merely import the photographs, the quality, size, and color mode stay untouched. You can modify the resolution and color mode when you import pages.

- Select **File > Open.**

- Choose your preferred **PDF file**, and then select **Open.** You can choose to alter the types of files that are displayed by choosing an option from the **Files of Type menu.**
- If you would like to bring in just the pictures from a PDF file, select the **picture or pictures you would like to have opened**. If you would like to choose more than one image, press down Ctrl (Windows) or Command (MacOS) and then choose the images you would like to open. If there is no need for you to have pages imported, you can choose to skip the fourth step.
- **To import pages from PDF files, select the Pages choices from the Select area in the dialog box of the Import PDF, and then you can choose to do any one of the following;**
  - If the file has numerous pages, choose **one or the various ones** you want to open and click **OK**. (To select multiple pages, hold down Ctrl (Windows) or Command (Mac OS) and click each one individually.)
  - Accept **the existing name or input a new filename in the Name field under Page Options.**
  - Choose **Anti-aliased** to reduce jagged edges when the image is rasterized (bitmapped).
  - Enter the **width and heigh**t. Activate **Constrain Proportions** to prevent visual distortion caused by size changes.
  - Accept the default (300 ppi) or enter a different value for Resolution. The file size grows as the resolution increases.
  - Make a choice from the Mode menu (RGB in order to keep the pictures in color, Grayscale to instantly make them black and white). If per adventure the file has an ICC (International Color Consortium) profile embedded, you can decide to pick the profile from the menu.
- Choose **Suppress Warnings** to conceal any error message while the process of import is ongoing.
- Choose **OK** to have the file opened.

Place a PDF file in a new layer

You can place pages or images from PDF files into a new layer in an image, but you cannot modify text or vector data in placed artwork since it is rasterized (bitmapped).

The artwork is rasterized at the resolution of the file into which it is placed.

- In Elements, launch **the picture** into which you would like to have the artwork placed.
- Select **File > Place**, make a choice of the file you would like to place, and then choose Place.
- If you happen to be placing a **PDF file** that has various pages, choose the page you would like to place from the dialog box given and then choose **OK**. The artwork that has been placed will be displayed inside a bounding box in the middle of the image of the Photoshop Elements. The artwork will keep its initial aspect ratio; nevertheless, if the artwork happens to be larger than the image of the Photoshop Elements, the size will be altered so that it becomes a fit.
- Get the placed artwork repositioned by placing the pointer inside the bounding box of the placed artwork and move it.
- **Scale the artwork you have placed if need be by doing any of the following;**
    - Move one of the handles at the corners or the sides of the bounding box.
    - In the bar for the Tool Options, insert values for the width and height in order to make an indication of the height of the artwork. By default, these choices show scale in the form of a percentage. Nevertheless, you can insert a different unit of measurement in either (inches), cm (centimeters), or px(pixels). If there is a need for you to constrain the proportions of the artwork, choose the box for Constrain Proportions. This choice will be on when the icon has a white background.
- If there is a need for you to blend edge pixels while rasterization is ongoing, choose the Anti-alias choice. To generate a hard-edged transition between edge pixels while rasterization is ongoing, deselect the **Anti-alias choice.**
- To get the placed artwork committed to a new layer, choose **Commit.**

Process multiple files

The Process Multiple Files command applies settings to a group of files in a folder. You can also import and process several photographs if you have a digital camera or a scanner with a document feeder. (The software driver for your scanner or digital camera may require an acquisition plugin module that enables these actions.) When working with files, you have the option of leaving all of them open, closing and saving the changes to the original files, or saving modified versions of the files to a new location (leaving the originals unaltered).

If you're going to save the processed files somewhere else, you should make a new folder for them before starting the batch.

- Select **File > Process Multiple Files**.
- **Make a choice of the files from the pop-menu of Process Files From;**
  - **Folder**: this choice helps with the processing of files in a folder you indicate. Choose Browse to indicate and choose the folder.
  - **Import:** this choice goes ahead to process pictures from a digital camera or scanner.
  - **Opened Files**: this choice processes all open files.
- Choose **Include All Subfolders** if there is a need for you to process files in subdirectories of the folder that is indicated.
- For Destination, choose **Browse** and make your preferred choice of folder location for the processed files.
- **If you choose Folder as your preferred destination, indicate a file-naming convention and choose file compatibility choices for the files that are being processed;**
  - Select **components** from the popup menus or type text into the areas for Rename Files to be integrated into the default names for all files. The fields allow you to adjust the order and formatting of the filename components. To prevent files from overwriting each other, you must include at least one field that is unique for each file (for example, file name, serial number, or serial letter). Starting Serial Number defines the number that should be used as the first digit in any serial number field. When you choose Serial Letter from the drop-down menu, serial letter fields always begin with the letter "A" for the first file.
  - For the sake of compatibility, select **Windows, Mac OS, and UNIX in order to make filenames compatible with the Windows, Mac OS, and UNIX operating systems.**
- Beneath Image Size, choose **Resize Images** if there is a need for each of the sizes of the processed file to be altered to a uniform size. Then input a width and height for the pictures, and then make a choice of an option from the menu for Resolution. Choose **Constrain Proportions** to maintain the width and height proportional.

- To add an instant adjustment to the pictures, choose your **preferred choice from the Quick Fix pane.**
- If you would like to include a label to the pictures, make a choice from an option from the menu containing Labels, then personalize the text, position of the text, font, size, opacity, and color. To alter the text color, choose **the color swatch and make a choice of a new color from the Color Picker.**

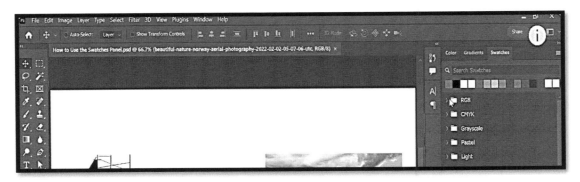

- To record each error in a file without halting the operation, select **Log Errors That Result from Processing Files.** After processing, if errors are logged to a file, a message appears. After the Batch command has been completed, open the error file in a text editor to review it.
- Select **OK** to have the files processed and stored.

Close a file

- **Do one of the following in Elements;**
  - Select **File > Close.**
  - Select **File > Close All.**
- **Make a choice of whether you are saving the file or not;**
  - Select **Yes** to have the file saved.
  - Choose **No** to close the file without getting it saved.

Choose the **Apply to All** choice to apply the present action to all files being closed. For example, if you select **Apply to All** and hit Yes to store the first file, all other open files are retained and then closed.

Guides and Rulers

In Advanced mode, rulers, grids, and guides can assist you in accurately positioning elements (such as selections, layers, and shapes) across an image's width or length. Only grids are available in Quick mode. When rulers are enabled, they show along the top and left sides of the active window. When you move the pointer, the ruler's markers reflect its position. You can also measure from a specific place on the image by changing the ruler origin (the 0, 0 mark on the top and left rulers). The point of origin of the grid is also determined by the ruler's origin. Employ the use of the View menu option to display or conceal the rulers (Advanced mode alone), the grid, or the guide. The View menu option also helps the enablement or disables the snapping of items to either the grid or the guide.

Change the rulers' zero origin and settings

- **In Advanced mode, get any of the following done;**
- To modify the zero origin of the rulers, put the pointer at the top of the intersection of the rulers in the upper-left corner of the window and drag in a diagonal manner down onto the image. The rulers' new origin will then be marked by a set of cross hairs. The new zero origin will be established when you let go of the mouse button.
- To alter the settings of the ruler, click twice on a ruler, or select **Edit > Preferences > Units & Rulers. For Rulers**, select a unit of measurement. Choose **OK.**

It is worth taking into consideration that if there is a need for you to reset the origin of the ruler to its default value, clicks **twice on the upper-left corner of the ruler.** Also, modifying the units on the info panel instantly alters the units that are on the ruler.

Change the guide and grid settings

- Select **Edit > Preferences > Guides & Grid**.

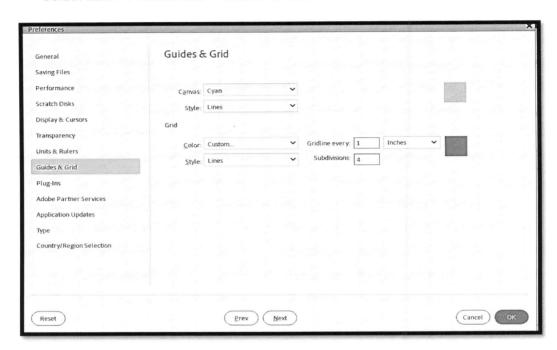

- Beneath the **Guides or Grids area**;
  - Make a choice of a preset color, or select the color swatch to make a choice of a custom color.
  - Select **the line style for the grid.** Make a choice of lines for solid lines, or select **dashed lines or Dots for the broken lines**.
- For Gridline every, insert a number value, and then select the unit of measurement to make a definition of the spacing of major grid lines.
- For the case of subdivisions, insert a number value to specify the frequency of minor grid lines, and then choose **OK**.

The Toolbox

Photoshop Elements includes a toolkit in Quick and Advanced modes to assist you in working with your photos. The toolbox contains tools for selecting, enhancing, drawing, and viewing images.

Toolbox in the Quick Mode

In Quick Mode, the toolbox contains a minimal set of simple tools. Zoom, Hand, Quick Selection, Eye, Whiten Teeth, Straighten, Type, Spot Healing Brush, Crop, and Move are the tools available in this mode.

Toolbox in the advanced mode

In the Advanced mode, the toolbox is quite richer than the one in the Quick mode. The tools are arranged in the following logical groups;

- View
- Select
- Enhance
- Draw
- Modify

Tools in the View group of the advanced mode toolbox

- **Zoom tool (Z)** This tool helps with zooming in or out of your picture. The tools that are related to this tool displayed in the Tool Options bar are Zoom In and Zoom Out.
- **Hand tool (H)** This tool drags your picture into the Photoshop Elements workspace. You can move your image with the use of this tool.

Tools in the Select group of the Advanced mode toolbox

- **Move tool (V)** used in dragging selections or layers.
- **Rectangular Marquee tool (M)** chooses a portion in your image in a rectangular box. Press and hold the Shift key in order to select a square.
- **The Elliptical Marquee tool (M)** chooses a portion in your picture in an elliptical shape. Press and hold the Shift key to ensure that the selection is a circle.

- **The Lasso tool (L)** chooses a part in your picture in a free-form shape.
- **Magnetic Lasso tool (L)** chooses an area of your picture by making a choice of the high-contrast edges that are around a shape.
- **The Polygonal Lasso tool (L)** creates straight-edge segments of a selection border.
- **Quick Selection tool (A)** creates a selection depending on the color and texture similarity when you choose or click-drag the part you would like to choose.
- **Selection Brush tool (A)** makes a choice of the part where you will paint with the use of the brush.
- **Refine Selection Brush tool (A)** helps to add or take off parts to and from a selection by instantly detecting the edges.
- **Auto Selection tool (A)** instantly creates a selection when you create a shape around the object you would like to choose.

Tools in the Enhance group of the Advanced mode toolbox

- **Eye tool (Y)** takes off the red-eye effect and pet eye effect and helps with the correction of closed eyes in your pictures.
- **Spot Healing Brush tool (J)** takes away spots from your pictures.
- **Healing Brush tool (J)** takes away spots from your picture by choosing an aspect of your picture as the point of reference.
- **Smart Brush tool (F)** adds tonal and color modifications to certain parts of a picture.
- **Clone Stamp tool (S)** Paints with an image sample that you can use to reproduce things, repair picture flaws, or paint over objects in your photograph. You can also clone a portion of one image to another.
- **Pattern Stamp tool (S)** This tool colors with the use of a pattern that has been defined from your picture, another picture, or even from a preset pattern.
- **Blur tool (R)** This tool helps with the softening of hard edges or parts in a picture by reducing the details.
- **Sharpen tool (R)** This tool helps with the sharpening of a picture by placing focus on soft edges in the picture to make an increase in clarity or focus.
- **Smudge tool (R)** the actions of dragging a finger across wet paint are simulated. Color is picked up where the stroke begins and pushed in the direction you drag.

The tool groups are those of the draw and modify group of the advanced mode toolbox. You will learn more about these tools much later in the fifth chapter of this book.

Use a tool

To make use of a tool in the Quick or Advanced mode, you will have to first choose the tool from the toolbox. Once that has been done, make use of the various options in the Tool Options bar to get your task done.

Choose a tool

Do any of the following;

- Choose **a tool in the toolbox.**

- Enter the tool's keyboard shortcut. To pick the Brush tool, for example, press **B**. A tool's keyboard shortcut is indicated in the tooltip. A collection of useful keyboard shortcuts can also be found in Keys for selecting tools.

You cannot deselect a tool; once selected, it remains selected until you select another tool. If you've used the Lasso tool and wish to select your image without choosing anything, choose the Hand tool.

Select options from the Tool Options bar

In the Photoshop Elements window, the Tool Options bar is located at the bottom. It provides the options for the currently selected tool. For example, if you select the Crop tool from the toolbox, the Tool possibilities bar displays related tools (Cookie Cutter tool and Perspective Crop tool) as well as other possibilities. If you cannot see the Tool Options bar, choose **the tool icon in the toolbox or select Tool Options in the Taskbar**.

Edit tool preferences

The default preferences for tools can be changed. You can, for example, hide tooltips or alter the appearance of a tool pointer.

- **Do any of the following;**
    - ○ In Windows, select **Edit > Preferences > General**.
    - ○ In Mac, select **Photoshop Elements > Preferences > General.**
- **Choose one or more of the options below;**
    - ○ Choose **Show Tooltips to display tooltips.**

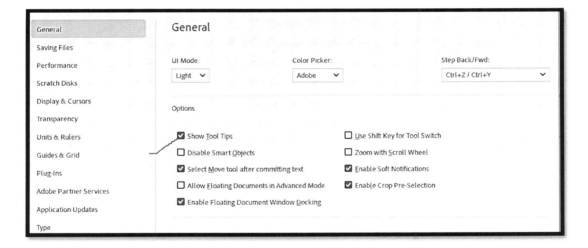

- ○ Choose **Use Shift key for Tool Switch** to move through a set of concealed tools by **holding down the Shift key**. When you have deselected this option, you can then move through a set of tool options by tapping the keyboard shortcut. For instance, tapping **B on your keyboard** continuously moves through all the options of Tool.

- ○ Choose **Select Move tool After Committing Text** to choose the Move tool after you made use of the Type tool to include text to your picture.
- Choose **OK.**

The Panel Bin

Panels can be found in both Photoshop Elements and Elements Organizer, but their behavior is not the same. Panels assist you in managing, monitoring, and modifying photos. Menus on several panels provide extra commands and settings. In Advanced mode, you can arrange panels in the basic and custom workspaces. Panels can be stored in the Panel Bin to keep them out of the way but easily accessible.

- **Panel menus**: some commands are shown in both the panel menu and the menu bar. While some other commands are just for the panel menus. Select **the panel menu** to see the various commands in each panel.
- **Pop-up sliders within panels**: Some panels and dialog boxes have pop-up slider settings (for example, the Opacity option in the Layers panel).

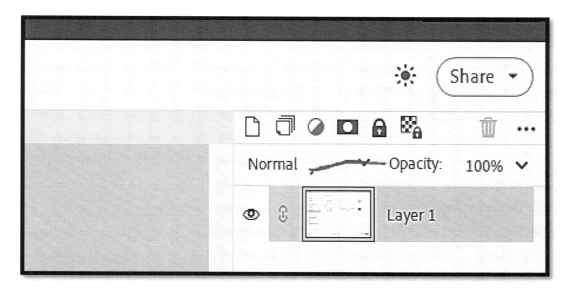

You can activate the popup slider by clicking the triangle that appears next to the text box. Place the pointer over the triangle adjacent to the setting, then move the slider or angle radius to the appropriate value while holding down the mouse button. To close the slider box, click **outside it** or press **Enter. Press Esc** to cancel changes.

Work with panels

Panels gather together features, information, or functionality for quick and easy access. Photoshop Elements' Panel Bin is located on the right side. Depending on the mode you're in or the type of items you wish to work with, it shows tabs and panels.

The Panel Bin shows:

- **Quick mode**: this helps to list the quick-mode effects that can be added to a picture.
- **Guided mode**: this helps to make a list of all the guided-mode edits that can be added to a photo.
- **Advanced mode**: this helps to list the choices for a chosen panel (Layers, Effects, Graphics, or Favorites).

Panels in the advanced mode

In the Advanced mode, panels can be shown in two basic ways; Basic Workspace, and Custom Workspace.

Basic Workspace: The Basic Workspace is the default workspace that is shown. The taskbar has buttons for the most frequently used panels in this view. Layers, Effects, Graphics, and Favorites are the buttons in this workspace. For example, choosing the Layers button exposes all options related to layers. Click **More** to see all of the other available tabs or to close any open tabs.

Custom Workspace: To display panels in the Panel Bin in a tabbed arrangement, click the **arrow** next to More and then Custom Workspace. Click **More** to see a list of all possible tabs, then choose one from the drop-down menu. The selected tab is shown. In the personalized workspace, you can keep commonly used panels open. Dock one panel at the bottom of another or group panels together. You can drag and drop the tab's title bar into the tabbed layout, or drag and drop the tab dialog into the tabbed layout.

- To display or conceal the Panel Bin, select **Window > Panel Bin.**
- In the Panel Bin (Custom Workspace)
    - To take off a panel from the Panel Bin, move **the title bar of the panel out of the Panel Bin.**
    - To include a panel in the Panel Bin, move **the title bar of the panel into the Panel Bin.**

- Move **the title bar** of the panel to another location if you would like to organize panels in the Panel Bin.
- Click **twice on the name of the panel** if you would like to expand or collapse panels in the Panel Bin.
- To make use of panels that are outside the Panel Bin, navigate to the view of the Custom Workspace, and then do any of the following;
  - To open a panel, select it from the **Window menu,** or click **the arrow next to the More icon in the taskbar and choose a panel.**
  - To close a panel, select the panel's name from the Window menu. Alternatively, hit the **Close button** in the panel's title bar.
  - To modify the size of a panel, drag **any of its corners.**
  - Drag a panel onto the body of the target panel to group panels (one panel with many tabs). When the pointer is over the appropriate area for grouping, a thick line appears around the body of the target panel. Drag the panel's tab to another group if you wish to move it. Drag **the panel tab outside the group to separate it from the group.**
  - Dragging the title bar will allow you to shift a panel group.
  - Double-click **the panel or panel group's tab or title bar to expand or collapse it**.
  - Drag a panel's tab or title bar to the bottom of another panel to dock them together (stacked panels). When the cursor is over the appropriate location, a double line appears at the bottom of the target panel.
  - Choose **Window > Reset Panels** to return all panels to their default placements.

The Photo Bin

The Photo Bin located near the bottom of the Photoshop Elements window, above the taskbar, displays thumbnails of open photos. It comes in handy while flipping between numerous open photographs in your workstation. The Photo Bin has controls for opening and closing photographs, hiding images, navigating between open images, making a specific image the frontmost image, duplicating an image, rotating an image, and seeing file information. Open photos can be simply brought into Quick mode for editing. In the Create panel, multipage projects created with the Create tab are open.

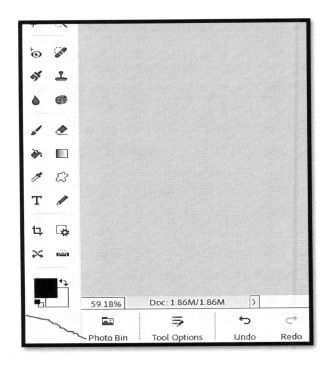

- **Do one of the following;**

  o (Windows alone) To have an image opened, move a file from any location of your choice on your computer which also includes the Photo Browser, or from just about any storage device that is linked to your computer into the Photo Bin.

  o To bring an opened image to the front as the frontmost picture, choose a **thumbnail of your choice**.

  o To reorganize pictures, move **thumbnails in the Photo Bin**. Note that the order does not impact the order of the photo in the Elements Organizer.

  o To close a picture, **right-click a thumbnail** in the Photo Bin and pick **Close**.

  o To conceal a picture that is a floating window, right-click the thumbnail and pick Minimize from the context menu displayed.

  o To have a view of the information of the file of a picture, **right-click on a thumbnail and pick File Info from the context menu.**

  o For the duplication of an image, **right-click a thumbnail, pick Duplicate from the context menu, and give the file a name.**

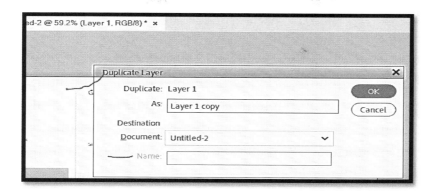

- To have the image rotated, **right-click a thumbnail and pick 90 degrees Left or Rotate 90 degrees right from the context menu.**
- To display the names of the files, right-click in the **Photo Bin** and select **Show Filenames from the context menu**.
- To manually display, show, or hide the bin, select the **taskbar icon of the Photo Bin.**
- **The flyout menu of the Photo Bin has more choices that can be used to work with the images that can be found in the Photo Bin;**
  - **Print Bin Files:** this choice opens the Photoshop Elements Print dialog box, with the choice to print the picture presently chosen in the Photo Bin.
  - **Save Bin as an Album**: this choice allows you to give a name to an album and also save the album that has images in the Photo Bin. The new album can then be found in the Organizer.
  - **Show Grid:** this choice shows a grid around pictures in the Photo Bin.

Save files

Save changes to the current file with the Save command, or Save As to save changes with an alternative format, name, or location.

Save changes

Do any of the following;

- Choose **File > Save**.
- Tap **Ctrl + S (Windows) or Command + S (Mac OS).**

Save changes with a different file format, name, or location

You can configure parameters for saving picture files, such as the format and whether to include the saved file in the Elements Organizer catalog or to preserve layers in an image, by using the Save as option in the File menu. Other options may be available to you depending on the format you choose.

- **Do any of the following;**
    - ○ Choose **File > Save As.**
    - ○ Tap **Ctrl + Shift + S (Windows) or Command + Shift + S (Mac OS).**
- Configure the following file saving choices, and then choose Save;
  File Name: indicate the name of the file for the image saved.
  File format: indicates the file format for the image saved.

Include in the Elements Organizer: this choice Includes the saved file in your catalog so that it can be seen in the Photo Browser. Some file formats that work in the Edit workspace do not work in the Elements Organizer. This option is not available if you save a file in one of these formats, such as EPS. Save In Version Set with Original Saves the file and then includes it to a copy configured in the Photo Browser to manage the various versions of the image.

Unless Include in the Organizer is selected, this option is not available. Layers All layers in the image are preserved. There are no layers in the image if this option is disabled or unavailable. A caution icon next to the Layers checkbox warns that your image's layers will be flattened or combined for the format you've chosen. All layers are combined in some formats. Choose another format if you want to keep the layers.

Save a file in GIF format

- **Do any of the following;**
    - ○ Choose **File > Save As.**

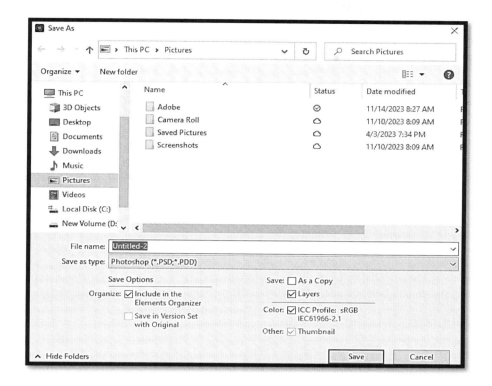

- Tap **Ctrl + Shift + S (Windows) or Command + Shift + S (Mac OS).**

- Indicate the name of a file and its location, and pick **CompuServe GIF format from the list of formats. Your picture will then be stored in the indicated directory.**

- Choose **Save.** If your initial image is RGB, the dialog box of Indexed Color will be displayed.

- If need be, indicate indexed color choices in the dialog box of Indexed Color and select **OK.**

- In the dialog box for GIF, choose a row order for the GIF file and choose **OK;**

Normal shows the picture in a browser alone when the picture has been completely downloaded. Interlaced shows a series of low-resolution copies of the pictures while the complete image file is being downloaded to the browser. Interlacing can make the time for downloading seem as though it is shorter and bring an assurance to viewers that the download is still ongoing. Nevertheless, interlacing also contributes to an increase in the size of the file.

Save a file in JPEG format

- **Do any of the following;**
  - ○ Choose **File > Save As.**
  - ○ Tap **Ctrl + Shift + S (Windows) or Command + Shift + S (Mac OS)**
- Select **JPEG from the list of formats.**
- Indicate a name for a file and location, choose options for file-saving, and then choose Save. The dialog box for JPEG options will then open.
- If the picture has transparency, choose a Matte color to simulate the look of background transparency.
- Indicate picture compression and quality by selecting a choice from the Quality menu, moving the Quality slider, and inserting a value between 1 and 12.
- Choose your preferred format choice;

Baseline (Standard) makes use of a format that can be recognized by most browsers. Baseline Optimized this helps with the optimization of the quality of the color of the picture and produces a slightly smaller file size. All web browsers do not offer support for this choice. Progressive designs a picture that is gradually shown as it is downloaded to a web browser. Progressive JPEG files are usually a bit larger in size, have a need for more RAM for viewing, and are not supported by all applications and web browsers.

- Select **OK.**

Save a file in Photoshop PDF format

- **Do any of the following;**
  - ○ Choose **File > Save As.**
  - ○ Tap **Ctrl + Shift +S (Windows) or Command + Shift + S (Mac OS)**
- Make a choice of Photoshop PDF from the list of formats.
- Indicate the name of the file and the location; choose file-saving choices, and then select **Save.**
- Navigate to the dialog box of **Save Adobe PDF,** and choose **a compression method.**
- Select **a choice from the menu of the Image Quality.**
- To have a view of the PDF file, choose **View PDF after Saving to open Adobe Acrobat or Adobe Reader (based on the application that you have installed on your computer).**

- Choose **Save PDF.**

Verify the Saving File Preferences dialog box if you've made modifications to an Acrobat Touchup file but the changes aren't reflected when you open the file. Select **Edit > Preferences > Saving Files**, and then from the On First Save menu, select **Save Over Current File.**

Save a file in PNG format

- **Do any of the following;**
  - Choose **File > Save As.**
  - Tap **Ctrl + Shift + S (Windows) or Command + Shift + S (Mac OS).**
- Make a choice of PNG from the list of formats.
- Indicate the name of a file as well as its location, choose file-saving choices, and then choose Save.
- In the dialog box for PNG Options, choose an Interlace choice and select **OK.**

None shows the picture in a web browser only after it has fully downloaded. Interlaced shows low-resolution copies of the picture while the complete image is being downloaded in the browser. Interlacing can ensure that the time for downloading is quite shorter and it can also assure that download is ongoing. Nevertheless, interlacing also helps to increase the size of the file.

Save a file in TIFF format

- **Do any of the following;**
  - Choose **File > Save As**
  - Choose **Ctrl + Shift + S (Windows) or Command + Shift +S (Mac OS).**
- Pick **TIFF from the list of formats.**
- Indicate a name for the file and the location; choose file-saving options, and then select **Save.**
- In the dialog box for TIFF Options, choose **choices;**

Image Compression indicates a method for the compression of the composite image data.

Pixel Order picks interleaved to be able to include the picture in the Elements Organizer.

Byte Order The majority of modern apps can read files in either Mac or Windows byte order. If you don't know what program the file will be opened in, choose the platform on which it will be read.

Save Transparency Saves information in many resolutions. Photoshop Elements does not support opening multi-resolution files; the image opens at the highest quality available inside the file. Adobe InDesign and some image servers, on the other hand, support opening multiresolution formats.

Layer Compression Describes a method for compressing data for pixels in layers (rather than composite data). Many apps are unable to read layer data and therefore skip it when opening a TIFF file. Layer data in TIFF files can be read by Photoshop Elements. Although files with layer data are larger than those without, saving layer data saves the need to save and manage a separate PSD file with the layer data.

- Select **OK.**

Set preferences for saving files

- **Do any of the following;**

    o (Windows) Choose **Edit > Preference > Saving files**.

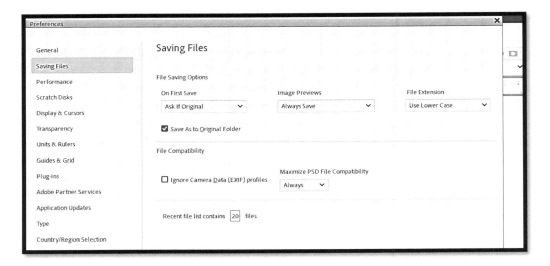

    o (Mac OS) choose **Adobe Photoshop Elements Editor > Preference > Saving Files.**

- **Configure the following preferences;**

    o On First Save provides the ability to manage how files are being saved.

Ask If Original (default) in this option, the first time you change and save the original file, it displays the Save As dialog box. The preceding version is overwritten by all subsequent saves. When you open the changed copy in the Edit workspace (via Elements Organizer), the initial save and all future saves overwrite the previous version.

Always Ask this choice launches the dialog box of Save As the first time you modify the initial file. All the saves done subsequently will overwrite the former copy. If you launch the edited copy on the Edit workspace, the initial save will launch the Save As dialog box. **Save Over Current File** this choice in no way launches the dialog box for Save As. The initial save overwrites the original save.

Image previews in this choice, a preview image is saved along with the file. Choose **Never Save** if you want to save files without previews, Always Save if you want to save files with specified previews, or Ask When Saving if you want to assign previews on a file-by-file basis.

File Extension Specifies a value for the three-character file extensions that specify the format of a file: Choose Use Upper Case if you want to append file extensions with uppercase characters, or Use Lower Case if you want to append file extensions with lowercase characters. In general, it's best to leave this option configured to Use Lowercase.

Save As Original Folder Specifies the default folder location in the Save As window. When this option is deselected, the Save As box always opens in the folder where you last saved a file. When this option is chosen, the **Save As** dialog typically opens the folder from where you last opened a file. **Preferences > Saving Files** is where you'll find it.

Ignore Camera Data (EXIF) profiles Select this option to have any color profiles used by your digital camera instantly discarded. The color profile created in Photoshop Elements is kept alongside the image. Maximize PSD File Compatibility This choice saves a composite picture in a layered Photoshop file so that you can import it or launch it by a much wider range of applications.

Do any of the following;

- Choose **Never** if you would like to have this step skipped.
- Choose **Always** to instantly save the composite.
- Choose **Ask** if you would like to be prompted anytime you store a file.

The recent file list containing this choice indicates the number of files that can be found in the **File > Open Recently Edited File submenu**. Insert a value from 0 to 100. The default value is usually 20.

- Select **OK.**

Free Adobe Stock photos and Imagery

With access to thousands of great stock photographs from within Photoshop Elements, you can experiment with a new background or create an intriguing Quote Graphic. Adobe Stock pictures can now be accessed from the File menu in both Quick and Advanced mode.

To use Adobe Stock photos in your projects, follow these steps:

- Choose **File menu > Search on Adobe Stock in Quick or Advanced mode**.

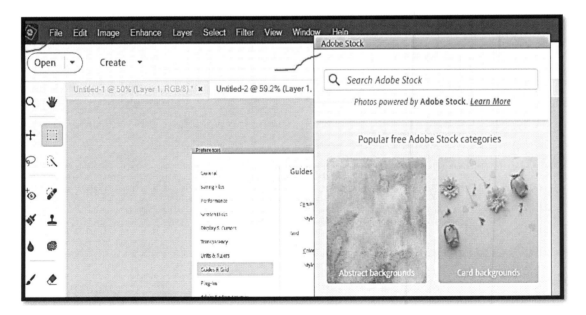

- Explore a variety of categories in the dialog box of Adobe Stock to locate the picture you are searching for. You are also able to make use of the search bar to locate certain pictures with the use of keywords.
- Choose the License for Free button to download the picture and get it licensed for free.

In Guided Mode

Follow the steps below to make use of Adobe Stock Picture in your projects;

- Choose **File > Open** to launch the preferred picture.

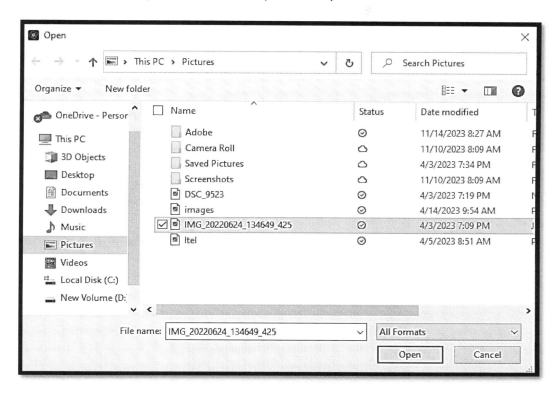

- Choose **Guided > Special Edits**

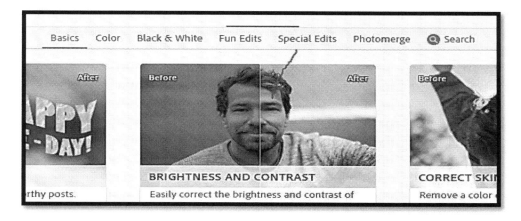

> Replace Background.

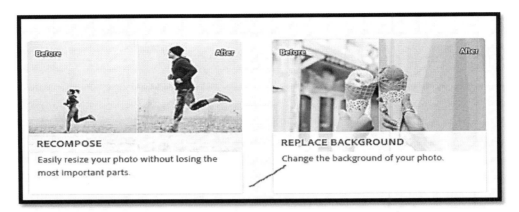

- Pick the primary subject by hitting the **Select Subject button.**

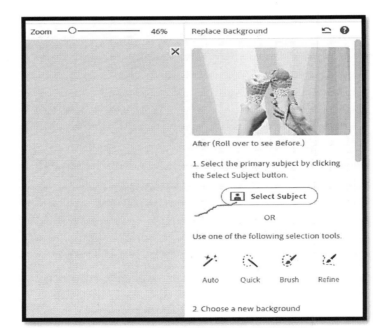

- Choose **St** to make use of pictures from Adobe Stock.
- Explore a variety of categories in the dialog box of Adobe Stock to locate the picture you are looking for. You can also make use of the search bar to locate certain pictures with the use of keywords.
- Choose the License for Free button to download the picture and get it licensed for free.

In Advanced Mode

Follow these steps to make use of the Adobe Stock pictures in your projects;

- Choose **File > Open** to launch the preferred picture. Choose **advanced mode**.
- Launch the **Graphics panel > Select Adobe Stock.**

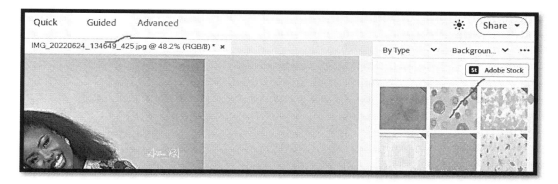

- Explore various categories in the Adobe Stock dialog box to locate the picture you are searching for. You can also make use of the search bar to look for certain pictures with the use of keywords.
- Configure **License for Free button to download pictures and get them licensed for free.**

- Choose **Layers to see the Adobe Stock picture** which is added as a background layer.

Quote Graphic

Follow the steps below to make use of Adobe Stock Picture in your projects;

- Choose **Create > Quote Graphic**.
- You can either select a picture of yours by choosing **Start** with a photo or make your preferred choice from the custom templates.
- Choose **Adobe Stock from the Backgrounds panel.**
- Explore a variety of categories in the dialog box of Adobe Stock to locate the picture you are looking for. You can also choose to make use of the search bar to look for certain pictures with the use of the keywords.
- Choose License for free button to download the picture and get it licensed for free.
- Your default background for the specific picture will be replaced by the Adobe Stock picture.

Access licensed images from the Adobe Stock website

Follow the steps to make use of licensed pictures from the Adobe Stock website;

- Sign in to the **Adobe Stock website**.
- Choose **User Profile icon > License History.**
- Once done, you will then be able to see and download all your licensed assets.

Activity

1. Edit pictures in the editor workspace.
2. With the use of guides and rulers modify your pictures.
3. Adjust panels in the panel bin.

CHAPTER 3

QUICK FIXES AND EFFECTS

The Quick Fix Toolbar

After you've imported and categorized your photographs, you're ready to perform some simple modifications. Photoshop Elements provides multiple degrees of editing, ranging from rapid, basic photo fixes with simple editing workflows to advanced color correction and composition in the Editor workspace.

- Select a photo to edit in the Organizer workspace, and then click the **Editor icon** in the taskbar. This will bring up the photo for modification in the Editor workspace.

Your photo is now accessible for modification in Photo Editor. You may utilize Photoshop Elements' basic photo-fixing tools to rapidly do some common editing jobs, such as adjusting the exposure or applying the pencil sketch effect to your photo. The Quick view allows you to do the most frequent editing operations fast. This view collects basic photo-editing tools in one location. Use this view to quickly correct an image's exposure, color, sharpness, and other elements. You may use the Effects, Textures, and Frames panel in this view to transform your photos into professional-looking images in addition to fixing them.

Effects, Adjustments, Textures and Frames

In order to quickly adjust exposure, color, how sharp the image is, and other elements of an image, the Quick mode gathers common photo-fixing features into one location. Aside from the Adjustments panel, you may also alter your images with the Effects, Quick Actions, Textures, and Frames panels.

Effects

One place wherein you can choose to apply photo effects is provided via the Effects panel. You can find it easily on the taskbar in both Quick and Advanced modes in the Effects panel. To edit or apply effects to a photo, it shows thumbnail representations of the artwork. The menu of category selections and related subcategories is available in most sections. Artistic, Classic, and Color Match are the three types of effects available.

Artistic Effects

You can easily add effects to your images that are modeled after well-known paintings or prominent art movements with the use of just one click. You can also choose to apply one of the incredible artistic effects to all or portions of your shot, and you can still quickly edit the results to get the precise appearance you so desire. These creative effects are available in both Quick and Advanced settings. It is worth taking into consideration that there are about five new artistic effects that have been added in the new version of Photoshop Elements.

Class Effects

There are about fifty-five classic effects, from cross-process presets to vintage looks to black and white. To see the presets available versions, select any **Classic effect. Auto-Smart Styles** This helps to evaluate the provided image and presents options with various effects added based on the image's content. Obtainable variants;

- Auto1
- Auto2
- Auto3
- Auto4
- Auto5

Please take note: A layer mask is used when you are applying effects as a new layer. In Advanced mode, you can choose to modify the layer mask to eliminate or lessen impacts in specific regions.

Tint: gives the picture a color tint (for example, green, sepia, or golden). Obtainable variants include;

- Copper
- Golden
- Sepia
- Green
- Blues

Seasons: this one I really do love because it adds a seasonal touch to the picture. Obtainable variants include;

- Spring

- Summer
- Autumn
- Winter
- Snow

Pencil Sketch: adds a technique to give the image the appearance of a pencil drawing. It is often used by so many artists. Obtainable variants include;

- Soft Lines
- Pencil Sketch
- Charcoal
- Stippling
- Colored Pencil

Toy Camera: This option helps to apply a technique that gives the impression that the image was captured with a toy camera. Obtainable variants include;

- Toy Camera
- Lomo Blue
- Lomo Contrast
- Lomo Green
- Holga

Black & White: It gives the image a Black & White look, as the name implies. Obtainable variants are;

- Simple B & W
- Silver
- Old School
- Platinum
- Tinted Black

Cross Process: interprets the results of processing photographic film in a solution of chemicals meant for another kind of film. Variations that is accessible:

- Deep Blue
- Orange Wash
- Blue Wash

- Green Wash
- Purple Wash

Split Tone: applies the effect of applying a different color to the shadows and a different color to the brightest areas in a black-and-white image. Obtainable variants are;

- Split Tone
- Blue Tone
- Red Tone
- Green Tone
- Grey Tone

Vintage: this option simply gives the picture a retro feel. Obtainable variants are;

- Vintage Leak
- Faded Vintage
- Vintage Color
- Sepia Glow
- Heavy Vintage

Light Leaks: applies light's impact to an image's negative that has seeped into a camera's light-tight chamber. Obtainable variants include;

- Diffused Colors
- Burnt Edges
- Soft Leak
- White Leak
- Yellow Streak

Color Match effects

In this effect, you are free to select from pre-made presets or upload your own image. Further adjustments can also be made to brightness, saturation, and color. Examine the Quick and Advanced versions of the Color Match effect.

To apply the color match effect in quick mode, follow the steps below;

- To open the photo you would like to apply the effect to, either pick **File > Open or click the Open button**.

- Select **from pre-made settings in the Color Match section of the Effects panel.**

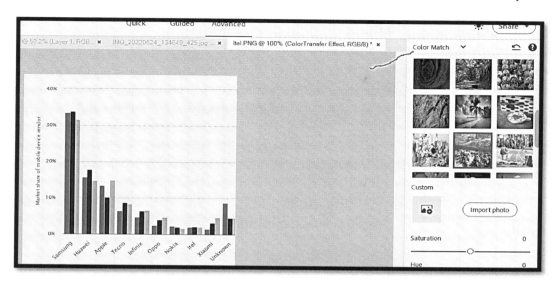

Please note: Since layers are not introduced, color-match effects are mutually exclusive. Any presets applied to the primary input photo will be substituted with the effect of another preset.

One of the following two methods can be employed to put one preset over another:

- When using the next preset, save the result of the previous one and use it as the input photo.
- Add the initial preset in Quick mode, and then go to **advanced mode**. In Advanced mode, use the Quick mode result as your input photo, and choose **the preset you want to apply.**
- The brightness of the picture, its hue as well, and its saturation can be fine-tuned more based on the requirements of the picture. It is worth noting that you can choose to make use of both the redo and the undo edit options by simply touching their icons whenever the need to make use of these options arises.
- You don't have to just keep your pictures to yourself; the globe can now be accessed right from the comfort of your home with the use of your devices. Choose **Share** to share the photo on all various social media platforms or you can click on **File > Save As to have the picture saved.**

Textures

You can add ten different textures to your photo anytime you make use of the Textures tab. Textures mimic different backdrops or surface that you can use to print the image. Consider the rough blue grid, cracked paint texture, aged paper appearance, and chrome feel. Using a layer mask, textures are added as new layers. In Advanced mode, you can adjust the layer mask to lessen or eliminate texture from specific areas (skin/face).

Frames

To select and apply one of the various frames for your photo, use the Frames panel. The optimal fitting of the frame is done automatically. The image and frame can also be moved or altered. Double-clicking **the frame with the move tool will accomplish this**. In Advanced mode, you can alter the Color Fill layer to change the backdrop color from white to any other shade of color you like.

For a combined way to include either an effect, frame, or texture, follow the set of instructions below;

- In Photoshop Elements Editor, open a picture of your choice and choose **Quick mode.**
- Apart from the Adjustments panel, there are three other panels available: Effects, Textures, and Frames. To gain access to any of the panels, select **their respective icon.**
- The open images live preview thumbnails are shown in the Panel bar. To add an effect, texture, or frame, click **on a thumbnail.**
- Make changes to the effect, texture, or frame you applied to the picture by switching to the advanced mode. The alteration that was made in Quick mode is accessible in a different layer. (note that this is optional)

Add Quick Effects (FX)

You apply picture effects from a single spot in the Effects panel. In both Quick and Advanced modes, the Effects panel can be seen on the taskbar. It shows a preview of the artwork or effects that you can apply or add to a picture. A menu of available categories and their respective subcategories is provided in the majority of sections. You can select effects from three categories: Color Match, Classic, and Artistic.

Quick Actions

The Textures option allows you to apply ten different textures to your picture. Textures simulate various surfaces or backdrops that the image might be printed on. Think about the old paper look, the cracked paint texture, the rough blue grid, and the chrome feel.

Auto: in the auto option you can make the following; smart fix, color correction, dehaze, red eye fix.

AI Edits: you can do the following quick actions in AI edits; JPEG Artifacts removal, adding blue sky, smoothening skin, and coloring a black-and-white picture.

Background: here you are able to choose a background, remove the background, change the color background to black and white, blur the background, and change a photo background to a white background.

Subject: here you can choose Subject, choose Sky, convert the subject in your picture to black-and-white, pop subjects, or transform the subject in your photo to a sticker.

Creative: in this section, you can do the following; add lens flare, make photo borders by getting the corners darkened, create the appearance of a stained glass window in your picture, and add a duotone effect to your picture for a much more beautiful two-color creation.

Effect: here you can convert your picture to black and white, add the woodblock effect to your picture, and improve your picture with the captivating oceanic sunset filter effect.

Apply Quick Textures

You can swiftly add ten different textures to your photo using the Textures tab. Textures mimic different backdrops or surfaces that could be used to print the image. Consider the rough blue grid, cracked paint texture, aged paper appearance, and chrome feel.

Add Quick Frames

Utilizing the Frames window, you can quickly select and apply any available frames for your picture. The optimal fit for the frame is automatically determined. Additionally, you can resize and modify the picture and frame. You can accomplish this by double-clicking the frame while using the move tool. By adjusting the Color Fill layer in Advanced mode, you can switch the backdrop color from white to any other color you like.

Activity

1. Add effects, textures, and frames to your pictures.
2. Add quick frames to your picture.
3. Add quick textures to your photo.

CHAPTER 4
GUIDED EDITS

Basics: Guided Edits

With the help of the wizard-like interface that can be found in the Guided mode, you may make guided modifications to achieve specific predetermined effects. There is always an image for every guided edit. The area to the left of the slider shows how the image is, prior to when the effect is applied when you drag the mouse horizontally over it. After the effect is applied, the image is shown in the area to the right of the slider. This makes it very easy for you to be able to compare both images.

Add Text guided Edit

You can make use of the ADD TEXT guided edit to create engaging text for posts that deserve to be shared. Text can be aligned on a path, a form, or horizontally or vertically. Use gradients and patterns to customize and warp it.

In order to utilize this guided edit, follow these steps:

- **Take one of the subsequent actions:**
    - Launch **Photoshop Elements and open a picture.**
    - Choose **a picture to take out of the Photo Bin.**
- Go to **Basics > Add Text under Guided mode.**

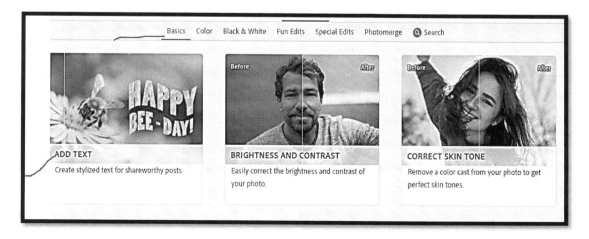

- **Once you have been able to complete the above, you can then proceed to choose any of the following from the panel on the right side;**

  o **Horizontal Type Tool**: You can enter text horizontally with the help of the horizontal type tool.
  o **Vertical Type Tool**: You can enter text vertically with the help of the Vertical Type Tool.
  o **Text on Selection Tool**: Enables you to enter text around the quick selection's boundaries by doing a rapid selection.
  o **Text on Shape Tool**: This tool lets you add text to the edges of the customized shape that's drawn over an image.
  o **Text on Path Tool**: This tool lets you type text to go around the edge of a personalized path that is drawn over the picture.

Please take into consideration that the Tool settings panel offers you the ability to experiment with different formatting settings, including fonts, font techniques, sizes, colors, leading, tracking, and text alignment.

- **Text can be customized the most by choosing the appropriate Style, Bend, Horizontal Distortion, and Vertical Distortion from the Warp Text window after choosing the Create warped text icon from the action bar.**

- Include the style of a text that has shadow, stroke, and bevel. It is worth noting that you can also choose to further customize the text style in the panel that contains the style configurations depending on your own preferred requirements by choosing the **advanced button.**

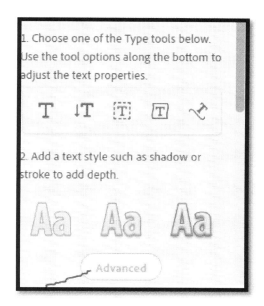

- You can ensure that the text looks rather more appealing when you add gradients or patterns to the text.

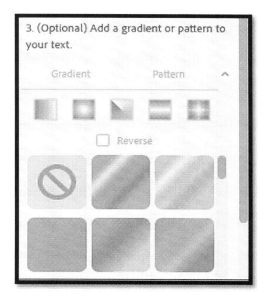

- **Once you are sure you have gotten the results you like, choose Next to make a choice of how you would like to move on;**
  - o **Save-Save/Save As** Save the newly edited image with stylized text using any of the formats that are available.
  - o **Proceed with editing in Quick/Advanced mode**. In either Quick or Advanced mode, choose where you want to keep editing the picture with stylized text.
  - o **Flickr**: Share Using one of the social media or sharing options offered by Photoshop Elements, choose to share your photo online with customized text.

Using the Text on Selection Tool

When you use the text-on-selection tool, it enables you to enter text around the fast selection's boundaries by doing a rapid selection.

To employ the Text on Selection tool, take the following actions:

- To use the Text on Selection type tool, **choose it.**
- If you would like to choose the region of the picture where you want to add text, **drag the pointer over it.** The square brackets can then be used to increase and decrease the size of the selection tool.
- To confirm the choices, click the **Commit current action button.**
- To obtain the reference text over the chosen area, move the cursor over the boundary of the area that has been selected until the Text on Selection type tool icon changes to the Type tool icon. Then, click **over the border**. To add your preferred text, start typing. The reference text can be further altered based on your needs.
- To save the text, choose the **Commit current action button**; to reverse the changes, select the **Cancel current action button.**

Using the Text on Shape Tool

Making use of the text-on-shape tool enables you to draw a custom shape over the image and enter the required text around its perimeter.

To utilize the Text on Shape tool, ensure that you take the following actions:

- Choose the **Text on Shape tool; ensure you choose the preferred custom shape.**

- Choose from the Tool Options to utilize for the addition of the text. To build the shape, drag **the pointer over the image.**
- To have a perfect view of the original text over the selected shape, move the mouse pointer over its boundary until the Text on Shape type tool icon changes to the Type tool icon. Then, click **over the chosen shape's boundary**. To add your preferred text all you have to do is start typing. The reference text can be further altered based on your needs.
- To save the text, select the **Commit current action button;** to reverse the changes, select the **Cancel current action button**.

Use the Text on Path tool

Writing around a path can be quite amazing and that is just what this unique tool allows you to do. It enables you to write text around the edges of a custom route that has been drawn over the picture.

To adequately employ the Text on Path tool, take the following actions:

- Choose the **Text on Path tool.**

- On the picture that you want to add text over, draw the route.
- For a precise verification of the path, use the **Commit current action button.**

- When the Text on Path type tool icon changes to the Type tool icon, move the mouse **pointer over the drawn path.** Then, click **over the path's boundary** to see the reference text over the area that you have chosen. Input the desired text by beginning to type. Depending on your needs, you can further alter the reference text.
- To save the text and reverse the changes, choose the **Commit current action button** and the **Cancel current action button,** respectively.

The Move & Scale Object Guided Edit

With the help of the guided edit feature MOVE & SCALE OBJECT, you can always choose an object and alter its size, location, and other attributes to personalize the appearance of your project making it feel more like yours.

Object Removal Guided Edit

With the help of the guided edit called OBJECT REMOVAL, you can get rid of stuff from your images.

- **Take one of these actions:**
  - Launch **Photoshop Elements** and **open a photo**.
  - Choose **any picture of your choice from the Picture Bin.**
  - Choose **Basics > Object Removal underneath Guided mode**.

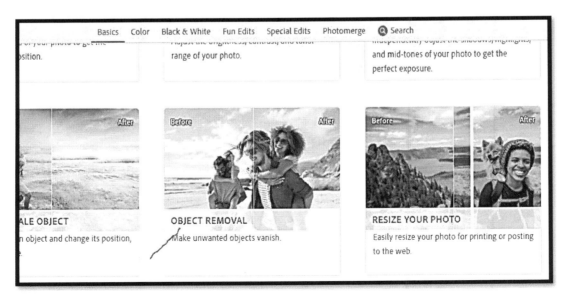

- **Choose any of the following selection tools from the panel on the right side;**

  o **Brush:** To erase an object, paint over it with the Selection Brush tool. The Brush Size adjuster allows you to change the brush's size.

  o **Lasso:** Whenever you have a need to make a free-form selection around the object you wish to eliminate, use the Lasso tool.

  o **Auto**: When you create a shape around an object you wish to delete, employ the **Auto Selection tool** to have the selection made for you automatically.

  o **Quick:** When you choose or select-drag the object you wish to delete, use the **Quick Selection tool** to create a selection based on edges. The Brush Size slider allows you to change the Quick Selection tool's dimensions.

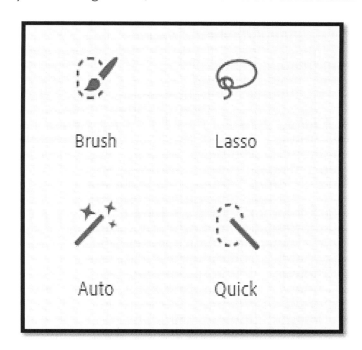

- If there is a need for you to remove the chosen object which is your picture, click on **Remove Object.**
- **Make a choice of any of the following choices if you have a need to get your results further enhanced;**
  o **Spot Healing Brush**: you can choose to make use of this feature to make small-scale edits. If there is a need to delete areas, simply **pick or drag this tool across the desired areas**. The Brush Size adjuster allows you to adjust the brush's size. Employ a brush of the smallest size to get the greatest effects.

- o **Clone Stamp Tool**: To alter a sizable region, use this feature. After selecting this tool, move your cursor over the area of the image that you wish to cover the object with, then hit **Alt+click on Windows or Option+click on macOS**. Drag the tool across the object after selecting it. The Brush Size adjuster allows you to change the brush's size.

- **Once the desired outcome has been achieved, pick Next and decide how you want to continue:**

  - o Save or Save As to keep the newly taken picture in any of the supported file formats.
  - o Edit in either Advanced or Quick mode going forward.
  - o Share **on Twitter or Flickr.**

Correct Skin Tone Guided Edit

Tan, blush, and light skin tones can all be corrected in an image by using the CORRECT SKIN TONE guided edit. You have the option to see the before and after photographs together, vertically or horizontally, or just the after image.

Crop Photo Guided Edit

To crop an image, employ the CROP PHOTO guided edit. You have the option to see the before and after photographs together, vertically or horizontally, or just the after image.

Lighten and Darken Guided Edit

To lighten or darken an image, use the guided edit LIGHTEN AND DARKEN. You have the option to see the before and after photographs together, vertically or horizontally, or just the after image.

Resize Guided Edit

To quickly generate a version of your photo that satisfies certain size requirements (in pixels, inches, or bytes), employ the **Resize Your Photo guided edit.**

- Choose a picture from the Photo Bin, then choose the guided edit option under **Guided > Basics > Resize Your Photo.**

- Determine why the photo was resized. Decide if you want to make a printed copy or use it online.

Web output: From the drop-down menu, choose a size option.

- **Long Edge**: Indicate the image's width. The aspect ratio is preserved by automatically adjusting the height.
- **Short Edge**: Give the image a height. The aspect ratio is preserved by automatically adjusting the width.
- **Give specific dimensions for the width and height**. A crop window highlights a section of the picture. To choose which area of the picture will be saved, move the crop window around with the mouse.
- **File Size**: Enter the largest possible size in kilobytes. The file size of the result that was produced was less than the amount you had given.

Print output: from the drop-down menu, choose your preferred dimension from the choice;

- **Long Edge**: Indicate the image's width. The aspect ratio is preserved by automatically adjusting the height.
- **Short Edge**: Give the image a height. The aspect ratio is preserved by automatically adjusting the width.
- **Width and Height**: Choose **Preview/Apply** after entering a custom width and height. A crop window highlights a section of the picture. To choose which area of the picture will be saved, move the crop window around with the mouse. The whole picture is compressed to fit one of the two measurements if the Shrink to

85

fit checkbox is selected; this could leave the photo with white edges at the top, bottom, or left and right.

- **Preset dimensions (such as 4 x 6):** Pick a size from the list and click **Preview/Apply.** A crop window highlights a section of the picture. To choose which area of the picture will be saved, move the crop window around with the mouse. The whole photograph is compressed to fit one of the two measurements if the Shrink to Fit checkbox is selected; this could leave the photo with white edges at the top, bottom, or left and right.

- To make a choice of what to get to do with the output, choose Next. In the former step, you will be presented with the subsequent choices if you prefer to make use of Web output;

  o **Save/Save As** Save the newly scaled picture in one of the supported file types.
  o **Proceed with editing in Quick/Advanced mode.** Choose **between Quick mode and advanced mode** depending on where you want to continue working on the enlarged image.
  o **Share on Twitter and Flickr**: Choose to share or post your resized photo on the internet using one of Photoshop Elements' social media or sharing options.

Options for print and web output are usually not the same hence, if you have chosen the print output choice in the previous step, you will be presented with the subsequent choices;

- **Save/Save As**: Store the resized image in one of the supported formats.
- **Proceed with editing in Quick/Advanced mode**. Choose whether you want to work in Quick mode or advanced mode on the image.
- **Print - Order Prints/Local Printer**: Choose to print the picture outline to a locally installed printer on this computer. Or use Adobe Photoshop Services to order prints.
- When you are done with the above configurations, choose **Done.**

Vignette Effect Guided Edit

Employ the vignette effect in your picture to draw attention to the significance of the subject, which could be a person, a group, or an object. Access the desired picture. Go to **Basics > Guided mode > Vignette Effect.**

- To make a choice of the color of the vignette you would like to add, select **either Black or White.**

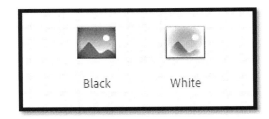

Black   White

- For a modification of the vignette's intensity (light or dark), use the Intensity slider.
- To adjust the vignette's size (Roundness) and edge (Feather slider), select **Refine Shape.** A smaller pixel value on the Feather slider denotes a harder, sharper edge, but a greater number denotes a softer, thicker edge.

  Positive values for the Roundness adjuster result in a less noticeable vignette, while negative values accentuate the effect.
- **Once the desired outcome has been achieved, pick Next to decide how to move forward:**
  - **Save - Save/Save As** Save the recently generated image in one of the supported file formats.
  - **Proceed with editing in Quick/Advanced mode.** Choose between the Quick and Advanced modes to continue working on the image.
  - **Twitter / Flickr Share**: Using one of Photoshop Elements' social media or sharing options, choose to post your photo online.

Color Guided Edits

In order to improve an image's color, saturation, and brightness, employ the **Enhance Colors Guided Edit.**

88

You have the option to see both the prior and subsequent photographs together, either horizontally or vertically, or just the after image.

Adjust saturation and hue

The Hue/Saturation command modifies an image's overall hue, specific color components, and saturation (purity) as well as lightness. Utilize the Hue slider to alter the color spectrum of a section of an image, add special effects, or color a black-and-white image (such as a sepia effect). To make colors more vibrant or subdued, adjust the saturation slider. For instance, by saturating the colors in a landscape, you may give it a color pop. Alternately, reduce the intensity of a striking hue, such as a bright red jumper in a photograph. To make a section of an image lighter or darker, use the Lightness slider in conjunction with the other modifications. Use caution when applying this modification to a whole image as it will decrease the tonal range.

Change color saturation or hue

- **Take any of the subsequent choices;**
  - Opt for **Enhance > Adjust Color > Hue/Saturation Adjustment**.
  - To modify Hue/Saturation, select **Layer > New Adjustment Layer > Hue/Saturation,** or open an already-existing adjustment layer.
  - The dialog box's two color bars show the colors in the color wheel's order. The lower bar displays how the adjustment impacts all hues at full saturation, while the upper bar displays the color as it was before the adjustment.
- **Make a choice of the colors you would like to modify in the edit drop-down menu;**
  - To instantly change all of the hues, select **Master.**
  - Select **the desired color adjustment** from among the available preset color ranges. You can modify any range of colors by dragging the adjustment slider that shows between the color bars.
- To adjust **Hue**, either input a value or move the slider until the desired colors are displayed. The text box's values indicate how many degrees the pixel has rotated from its original color around the color wheel. Clockwise rotation is indicated by a

positive value and counterclockwise rotation by a negative value. The possible values are −180 to +180.

- Enter a number for saturation, or drag the slider to the right to raise it or to the left to lower it. The range of values is −100 to +100.
- To adjust the lightness, either input a value or move the adjuster to the right or left to adjust the lightness. The values are between −100 and +100. Use caution while applying this slider to the full image. The image's overall tone range will be lowered.
- Select **OK.** Alternatively, press and hold **Alt (or Option in Mac OS) and select Reset to undo all of your changes.**

Modify the range of Hue / Saturation sliders

- **Get any of the subsequent choices done;**
    - Opt for **Enhance > Adjust Color > Hue/Saturation Adjustment.**
    - To modify **Hue/Saturation**, select **Layer > New Adjustment Layer > Hue/Saturation**, or open an already-existing adjustment layer.
- Directly from the edit menu, make a choice of a single color;
- **Consider any of the following for the adjustment slider;**
    - To change the degree of color fall-off without changing the range, drag one of the triangles.
    - To change the range without changing the amount of color fall-off, drag one of the gray bars.
    - To choose a new color area, drag the gray center portion of the adjustment slider to change the entire slider.
    - To change the color component's range, drag any of the vertically placed white bars close to the dark gray center portion. The color fall-off is reduced when the range is increased, and vice versa.
    - Ctrl-drag (Command-drag in Mac OS) the color bar to move it together with the adjustment slider bars.
- Select **the color picker and click the image** to modify the range by selecting colors from the image. To increase the range, use **the color picker + tool; to decrease it, make use of the color picker - tool.**

You may also use Shift to increase the range or Alt (Option in Mac OS) to decrease it when the color picker tool is selected.

Change the color of an object

An image's exact color can be changed with the Replace Color command. It is also possible to adjust the substitute color's hue, saturation, and lightness.

- Select **Improve > Modify Color > Switch Out Color**.
- Underneath the image thumbnail, choose **a display option**:
  - **Selection**: with the use of this option, you can show the mask in the preview box, it will resemble a black-and-white copy of the image.
  - **Image**: opens the preview box with the image displayed. When you have a small screen or are working with a magnified image, this option comes in handy.
- To alter the color of the image or the preview box, choose the color picker icon and then select **the desired color**. To prevent colors from changing, use the color picker – tool to delete colors or the color picker + tool to add colors.
- To adjust the degree to which associated colors are incorporated in the selection, drag **the Fuzziness slider.**
- To specify a new color, do one of the following:
  - You can input values in the text boxes or drag the Hue, Saturation, and Lightness sliders.
  - Select **an entirely novel color in the Color Picker** by clicking the Results box, then click **OK**.
- Press down **Alt (Option in Mac OS)** to start all over again after you have canceled your changes.

Black & White Edits

You can get guided edits done in the Guided mode, which offers a wizard-like interface for achieving specific preset effects. Every guided edit has a corresponding image. The area to the left of the switch helps to display the image without the effect when you move the mouse over it horizontally. The image with the effect applied is shown in the area to the right of the slider. For the conversion of colored photos into black and white, employ the Black and White Guided Edit on your pictures. A diffuse light effect can be added to the images to produce a surreal, dreamy look, or you can choose from a variety of black-and-white settings to make a clean, black-and-white picture.

- Choose **Black and White in the Guided mode** when a picture is opened.

- When you are on the chosen picture, make a choice of a preset you would like to work with.

Select a different setup if you're not happy with the way one is set up. Photoshop Elements does not place one preset on top of the other in this stage. Every time you choose a preset, the preset gets assigned to a new photo, and the chosen photo is returned to its initial form.

- You can utilize a diffused glow to draw attention to a particular area of your picture or if you have a prominent subject. To add a little glow to the picture, select the Diffuse Glow option. To alter them dispersed glow effect on particular areas of the image:
  - o To apply diffused glow, click **Add**; to remove the effect, click **Remove**.
  - o Select the brush size that will be utilized to apply the action.
  - o To adjust the glow's intensity, slide the **Opacity control.**
  - o Over some areas of the picture, **apply paint.**
- Select the **Increase Contrast icon** to get the contrast between the highlighted areas and other aspects of the picture increased.
- To make a choice of how you would like to proceed, click on **Next.** This must be after you have gotten the preferred result.
  - o **Save - Save / Save As** Use one of the available choices to save the newly created image.
  - o **Proceed with editing - In Fast / In Proficient**: Select whether you want to work in Advanced or Quick mode to continue editing the image.

- ○ **Share via Twitter / Flickr**: Select one of the social media or sharing options that Photoshop Elements offers to post your photo online.

B&W Color Pop guided edit

To bring attention to a particular color in an image while de-saturating the others, employ the B&W Color Pop Guided Edit. Red, Yellow, Blue, or Green is the default colors. You can adjust the effect by using the available choices.

- Ensure that the picture is opened, and then get to the Guided mode, and **choose B&W Color Pop.**

- Select a color that you want to maintain in the image. Choose **Select Custom Color** and select a sample in the picture using the color picker if you see more than one tone of the same color in this picture.

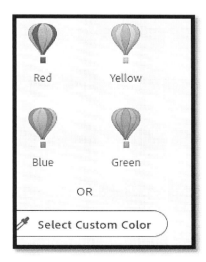

- Sections of the image that are the same hue as the one you choose will look saturated once you finish this step. The remaining portion of the picture begins to seem like a black-and-white image.
- Move the adjustment for Fuzziness to either the left or the right to add less or more tones of the chosen color.
- After selecting **Refine Effect,** adjust the **B&W Color Pop impact** to specific areas of the image. The brush's size can be changed using the Size slider, and the intensity of the effect can be adjusted with the Opacity slider.
- To bring the selected color to life, click **Increase Saturation**. Because of this, the items in that hue pop out from the otherwise flat black-and-white image.
- **Once you have been able to get the preferred result, choose Next to make a choice of just how you would like to move forward;**
  - **Save - Save / Save As** Use one of the available types to save the newly created image.
  - **Proceed with editing** - In Fast / In Proficient: Select **whether you want to work in Advanced or Quick mode to continue editing the image.**
  - **Share via Twitter / Flickr:** Select **one of the social media or sharing options that Photoshop Elements offers to post your photo online.**

B&W Selection guided edit

To make selected areas of a photograph appear lighter in color, employ the Selective Black and White Guided Edit. The other regions of a picture automatically seem highlighted when you desaturate certain areas of it. You can refine your pick after you've made it.

- Navigate to th**e Guided mode** after you have opened a picture and then choose **B&W Selection.**
- Select the **B&W with just a Click**. Select **if you would like to Add or Subtract areas to turn them into black and white from the available options**. To adjust the amount of area that is influenced by strokes throughout the picture, use the Brush Size slider.
- Select the **Refine Edge button** to further refine your selection if you plan on using this effect over an object (like hair) that has several fine edges.
- Click **B&W Detail Brush**, choose an action and brush size, and then color on the effect to carefully add or remove the black and white impact to more areas of the picture.

94

- Click **Invert Effect** to create the exact opposite effect of what has been created thus far.
- Once you have gotten the preferred options you can either save, keep editing, or share.

High Key guided edit

Include an ethereal dreamy impact to your pictures to offer them an upbeat and positive feeling.

- In the Guided Edits room, choose the **Black and White tab** then choose **High Key**. Pictures that must have been taken in excess light, or must have been overexposed will look as though they are bleached out when the High Key effect is added. Images that are slightly darker will give off much better results.
- Choose **Color or B&W,** to pick if you would like to work with a color or black and white high key effect.
- To accentuate the high-key look, apply a glow to the image's brighter areas by using the Add Diffuse Glow option. Press this **button multiple times** to keep adding a soft light to the image.

Low Key guided edit

Use the low-key effect to bring out the details in your photos, draw attention to your shadows, and give them a dramatic finish.

- Open a picture, then select the **Low Key** option under the **Guided Edits room > Black and White menu.**
- To select between working with a low-key color effect or a color one, click **Color or B&W**. The subdued effect is included. Brighter things seem slightly overexposed, while darker colors get pushed farther into the darkness. High contrast exists.
- To precisely apply the desired effect to your photo, utilize the **Background Brush and Reduce Effect buttons.**

Fun Edits

You can do guided edits in the Guided mode, which offers a wizard-like interface for achieving specific preset effects. Every guided edit has a corresponding image. The area to the left of the switch shows the image without the effect when you move the mouse over it horizontally. The image with the effect applied is shown in the area to the right of the slider.

The Meme Maker Guided Edit

Use Photoshop Elements to instantly turn any image into a humorous meme. With the aid of the guided edit feature in Meme Maker, you can combine text and photos to create a meme.

- Launch a picture in Photoshop Elements.
- Choose **Guided > Fun Edits > Meme Maker.**

- For the default meme template to be applied, click **Create Meme Template**. The meme template has the image centered with example text at the top and bottom.

- To select the sample text for modification, either **double-clicks on it or use the Type Tool.**
- Put in the text you want for your meme here. The Guided Workspace's Tool Options bar allows you to alter the text's font, size, color, and style. Press the **green check box** to finalize your changes when you're done typing.
- **Alter the size of your picture by doing any of the following;**
  - To zoom in or out, move the **Zoom slider** to the left or right.
  - To flip your photo, click **either the vertical or horizontal flip button.**
  - To make the photo fill the entire canvas, use the Fit Photo to Canvas option. By choosing this option, the Zoom and border customization functions are deactivated.
  - To see the heads-up display (HUD), double-click the picture. You can alter the primary photo and rotate it left or right using the HUD's zoom and magnification features. To commit your changes after making the necessary adjustments, click the **green checkmark.**

It is worth noting that you are also able to alter the size of the frame of your picture by simply moving the bounding box around the frame of the picture. Move a corner handle to have the picture scaled proportionally.

- **Get any of the following done to alter the border;**
  - To access the Border Presets dialog, click **the Border Preset button.** There are twelve unconventional border options.
  - Select **a solid color by clicking the color picker.**

The meme template is adorned with the chosen border or color.

- You can apply five predefined effects to your photo by clicking the Effects icon. Select **an effect to add to your photo by clicking on it.**
- Clicking the **Reset option** will allow you to go back to your original photo.

The Multi-Photo Text Guided Edit

You can generate visual writing with an additional photo within each letter by using the Multi-Photo writing guided edit. To create a visually rich shot, use any photo as the background, add text, and add a photo within each word using the Multi-shot Text guided edit.

- **Do any of the following;**
  - ○ Launch **a photo in Photoshop Elements.**
  - ○ Choose **a picture from the Photo Bin.**
- Choose **Multi-Photo Text under Fun Edits > Guided.**

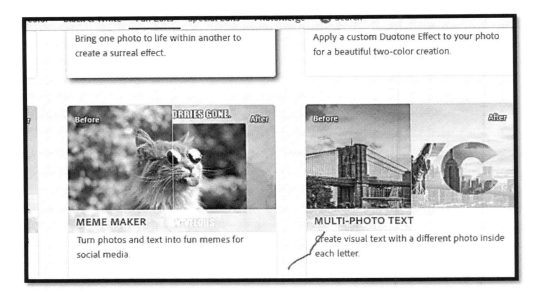

- Click **Type Tool,** and then click **any part of the image to start typing**.

- The Guided Workspace's Tool Options bar allows you to alter the text's font, size, and style. To commit your modifications after you've finished typing, select **the green checkmark ().**
- Decide if you would like to alter the size of the text on your picture with the use of the Fit of Fill choices;
  - **Fit**: stretches the text to fill the photo's width. The font maintains its aspect ratio.
  - **Fit:** Extends the text to fill the image's height and width.
- Choose **Create Frames** to transform each character that is in the text into a picture frame.
- **To include a photo in the text, do one of the following:**
  - To browse and choose a photo, click **on the instructions located within a character frame**. With this option, you can apply the selected photo to a character with more control.
  - Select one or more images from a single folder by clicking **Computer.**
  - To use any of the available photographs in the photo bin, click **Photo Bin.** You can pick images from an album or from a drop-down list in Elements Organizer in the Photo Bin.

Photos are arranged in an orderly fashion within each frame if you choose to select more images from the Computer or if the Photo Bin has more images than the number of character frames. Every extra picture is thrown away. You will, however, have some vacant character frames if you select fewer images.

- (Optional) Use the **Color Picker to select the desired color or make the background translucent, white, or black.**
- (Optional) Use any of the three presets to add effects to your text. Size options are Small, Medium, and Large. The buttons change the text's strokes, drop shadow, and bevel.
- **(Optional) To switch or modify a photo inside a text frame, do any of the following:**
  - To see the heads-up display (HUD), double-click **on a character frame**. You can change the photo and use the HUD to zoom in or out and rotate it left or right. To commit your changes after making the necessary adjustments, click the **green checkmark.**

- To swap out a photo, double-click **over a character frame and drag the picture onto the other frame**. Drop the image when the pointer changes to a double arrow. There is an image swap between the source and target frames.

The Double Exposure Guided Edit

By combining two photos, the Double Exposure guided edit allows you to produce an amazing double exposure effect. You can choose from one of the sample photographs that are given or import a picture from your PC.

- **Consider any of the following;**
  - Launch **a picture in Photoshop Elements.**
  - Choose **your preferred picture from the Photo Bin.**
- Select **Guided > Fun Edits > Double Exposure.**

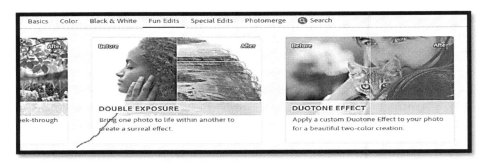

- (Optional) Use **the crop tool** to crop the image such that your topic remains in the middle of the frame.

- Employing the Auto or Quick selection tools, choose the focal point of your image.
- **Take one of these actions:**
  - To import a backdrop image from your computer, click **Import a photo.**
  - Choose **from the sample photos that are provided.**

The Intensity slider allows you to change the background's intensity.

- (Optional) To move the backdrop image or the subject, click the **Move Tool.**
- (Optional) Select **an impact from the list of possibilities**. The Intensity slider allows you to change the effect's intensity.
- Once you get your preferred results, choose **Next** to make a choice of how you would like to move forward;
  - **Save - Save / Save As** Use one of the available formats to save the newly created image.
  - **Proceed with editing - In Fast / In Proficient**: Select whether you want to work in Advanced or Quick mode to continue editing the image.
  - **Share via Twitter / Flickr:** With Photoshop Elements, you can use any of the social media or sharing sites to submit your photo online.

The Painterly Guided Edit effect

When you make use of Painterly, you will be able to produce artistic results by using a brush to paint your photo on various textured canvases and add various painting effects. This guided edit may be found under **Painterly > Guided > Fun Edits.**

- Launch **a picture in Photoshop Elements.**

- Choose **Guided > Fun Edits > Painterly.**

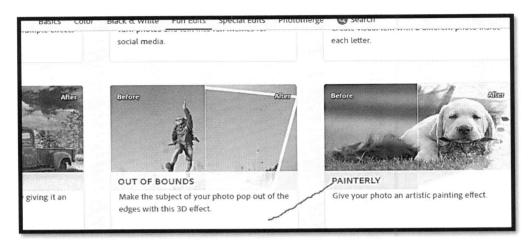

- Choose **Paint Brush.** You are then about to choose the portion of the picture that you will work on for the remaining part of this task.
  - o **Show / Hide**. To paint over sections you wish to reveal, use Show. To paint over sections you wish to remain hidden, use Hide.
  - o **Presets.** To get the desired impact for your painting, decide what sort of brush to use.
  - o **Size**. To adjust the brush stroke size on your photo, use the Size slider.
  - o **Opaque.** To find the intensity of the initial that is revealed when painting with the brush, use the opacity slider.
  - o **The angle of Brush**. To rotate the brush, use the Brush Angle parameter.
- Choose **a color for the remaining portion of the canvas**. There are two colors that you can select from: Black and White. To choose a different color, you can alternatively select **Select Custom Color** and press any place on the exposed portion of the image.
- Choose **a texture for the canvas (the background)**
- Choose **Effect and add an effect** in order to get the texture accentuated.

The "Out of Bounds" Guided Edit effect

With Guided Edit, you can add a frame to a picture and have a certain portion of the image appear beyond the frame by using the Out Of Bounds option.

- Choose **Out Of Bounds from the Guided Edits window.**

- To include a frame in the picture, click **Add Frame.**
- To have a portion of the primary subject remain outside the frame, drag the edges of the frame.
- To add a viewpoint, move the frame's handles while holding down the Command + Option + Shift keys. Press **Commit.**
- Drag the edges to change the frame border's width. Press **Commit.**
- Choose **the area of the picture** that should be outside the frame employing the **Quick Selection tool.**
- Select **Out of Bounds Effect.**
- To exit Out of Bounds Guided Edit, click **Cancel.** To proceed to the Sharing panel, click **Next.** Your picture appears with the Share panel to the right of it. This box allows you to save the image as a different image or at the same location. The image can be brought into the Advanced or Quick Edit rooms. The image can also be shared on Twitter or Flickr.

Save As / Save: Save

Save the altered photo to a computer folder. You are prompted to select a folder on your computer to store your photo if you haven't already saved the adjustments. To save the altered image to a different folder or with a different name, utilize the Save As option. You can choose from a number of sophisticated image formatting choices in the JPEG choices menu. To accept Photoshop Elements' applied settings, click **OK** if you don't wish to make any other adjustments.

Proceed with Editing: In Swift / In Skill

Bring your photo into the Advanced or Quick Edit rooms. This indicates that you have edited using the Guided Edit mode and are currently adjusting more in the Advanced or Quick modes.

Share on Twitter or Flickr

Use Twitter to post your altered photo to your loved ones. Alternatively, you can submit your images to Flickr and make shareable photo albums there.

- Select **Done.**

Create a Picture Stack

You can add frames to your photo with the Picture Stack Guided Edit, which gives it the appearance of an artistic collage.

- Launch **Photoshop Elements and open a picture.**
- Select **Picture Stack under Fun Edits > Guided.**

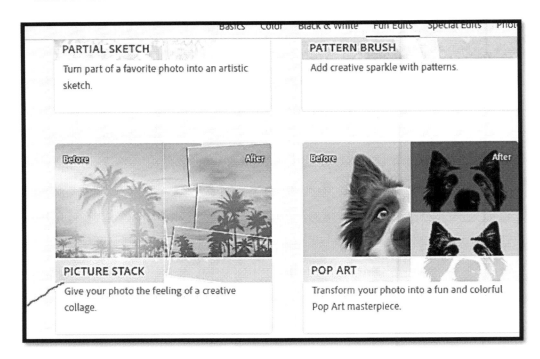

- From the list of options, choose how many photos you want in your photo collage.
- You can choose any of the three presets to give your photos a border. Size options are Small, Medium, and Large.
- **Choose one of the following buttons to later the background;**
  - Gradient
  - Solid Color

Indicate the color, blending mode, and opacity in the dialog box then choose **OK.**

- Once you have the desired outcome, select your preferred course of action by clicking **Next:**

- o **Save - Save / Save As** Use one of the available formats to save the newly created image.
- o **Proceed with editing - In Fast / In Proficient**: Select whether you want to work in Advanced or Quick mode to continue editing the image.
- o **Share - Flickr / Twitter:** Select one of the social media or sharing platforms that Photoshop Elements offers to post your photo online.

Create a Puzzle Effect

The Effect of The Puzzle The visual impression of assembling puzzle pieces into a photograph is produced by guided editing. You can take some of the puzzle pieces out of their places and rearrange them using the Guided Edit to create the impression that the puzzle is incomplete.

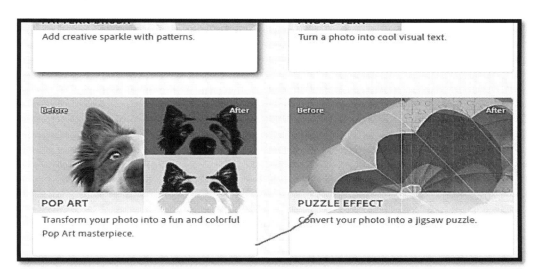

- To choose the size of the tiles into which your photo will be cut, click **Small, Medium, or Large.**

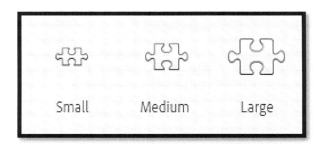

105

- You can choose which tiles are out of place in order to give the puzzle a more realistic appearance. To select a tile from the puzzle, click the **Select Puzzle Piece button. A tile has been chosen.**
- To move the chosen tile, click **Extract Piece**. It automatically selects the Move Tool.
- Use the controls to resize or rotate the selected tile, or drag it to any other spot on the canvas.
- To take off any artifacts that seem unnecessary or may have been introduced when you were adding this Guided Edit, choose **Eraser Tool.**
- To access the Share window, click **Next; to exit Pop Art Guided Edit, click Cancel**.

Your picture appears with the Share panel to the right of it. This box allows you to save the image as a different image or at the same location. The image can be brought into the Advanced or Quick Edit rooms. The image can also be shared on Twitter or Flickr.

Special Edits

You can do guided edits in the Guided mode, which offers a wizard-like interface for achieving specific preset effects. Every guided edit has a corresponding image. The area to the left of the scale shows the image without the effect when you move the mouse over it horizontally. The image with the effect applied is shown in the area to the right of the slider.

The Depth of Field Guided Edit

By opacifying the surrounding environment, the Depth of Field effect lets you concentrate on specific regions of the picture.

Simple Method

Using this technique, the backdrop layer is duplicated and given a uniform blur. Decide which areas you wish to concentrate on. The amount of blur used on the remaining portion of the image can be adjusted.

- Choose **Depth of Field from the Special Edits** part in the Guided mode.

- Choose **Simple.**

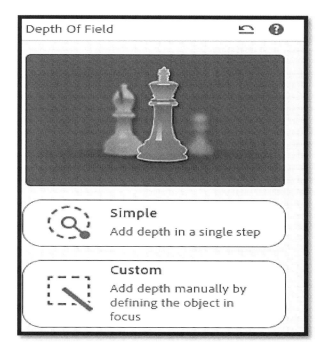

- Select **Add Blur.** A uniform blur will then be shown all over the picture.

- For a definition of area of focus, choose **Add Focus Area** and move the pointer over portions of the picture you would like to focus on.

- To personalize the blur for the remaining aspect of the image, move the Blur adjuster until you have been able to achieve the preferred blur impact.
- **Once you have been able to get the preferred effect, choose Next in order to make a choice of the manner in which you would like to move on;**
    - **Save - Save / Save As** Use one of the available types to save the newly created image.
    - **Proceed with editing - In Fast / In Proficient**: Select whether you want to work in Advanced or Quick mode to continue editing the image.
    - **Share via Twitter / Flickr:** Select one of the social media or sharing options that Photoshop Elements offers to post your photo online.

Custom Method

Employing the quick selection tool, you select the things you wish to focus on in this manner. Unselected portions of the image receive the blur. The amount of blur used on the remaining portion of the image can be adjusted.

- Choose **Depth of Field from the Special Edits part in Guided mode.**
- Choose **Custom.**
- Select the **Quick Selection tool and drag over aspects** of the picture you would like to focus specifically on.
- A uniform blur will be added to the remainder of the image when you choose Add Blur.
- Move the blur slider in order to personalize the blur for the remaining part of the image. Continue to move until you have gotten your preferred blur impact.

The Text and Border Overlay Guided Edit

Stylish border text that tells your story can be added to your images. Employ the Text and Border Overlay guided edit to add well-polished borders and text to your photo to give it a whole new look.

- **Do any of the following;**
  - ○ Launch **a picture in Photoshop Elements.**
  - ○ Choose **a picture from the Photo Bin.**
- Navigate to **Guided then choose Text and Border Overlay from Special Edits.**

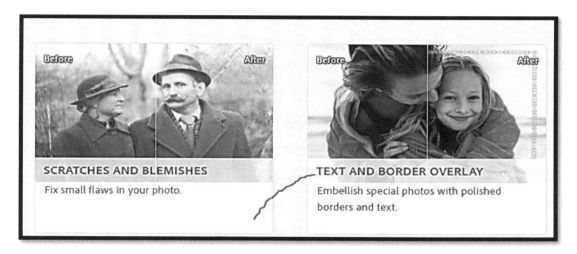

- Choose **Select a Border** and then make a choice of a border from the choices available.

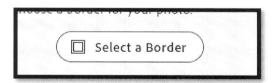

- To change the border's size, use the **Resize Border slider.**
- After selecting the color you wish to use for the border, press the **Color Picker option.**
- To add text overlay, click the **Add Text Overlay option**. Over the border, a text frame shows up and the Type Tool opens.

- Enter the new text by typing it in. The Guided Workspace's Tool Options bar allows you to modify the text's font, size, color, and style. Once you have finished typing, select **the green check box () to save your changes.**
- Click **a dot on the border to reposition the text.**
- You can apply predefined text styles to the text by clicking the **Text Style button.** To apply a text style, click **on it within the text**. By selecting the Reset () option, you can go back to your initial text style.

Get Faces Clean Up with the Perfect Portrait Guided Edit

With Guided Edit, you may use simple tools to enhance different aspects of the image and get rid of imperfections to produce the ideal portrait.

- Choose **Perfect Portrait** from the special edits part in guided mode.

- **Enhance the texture of the skin.**
  - o To give the skin a smoother appearance, click the **Smooth Skin button**. The smoothness effect can be adjusted by dragging the Strength slider.
  - o For more clarity, click **Increase Contrast.**
- Choose Features to modify Lips, Eyes, Nose, Face Shape, and Face Tilt for a chosen face with the use of the sliders that are available.
- **Get the facial features enhanced.**
  - o Click on **Remove Blemishes** to correct minor errors.
  - o Select **Whiten Teeth** to make your smile more radiant.

- You can see that the person's face is highlighted in a circle in the Open Closed Eyes window's box, indicating that the face has been identified in the image.

  (Optional) The Try Sample Eyes list displays a few samples for you to view. You can select a face that resembles the main image quite a bit. Photoshop Elements replaces the closed eyes in the main image with the selected face.
  - To make the eyes brighter, click **Brighten Eyes.**
  - To make the eyebrows and eyelashes darker, click **Darken Eyebrows.**
- **Get special touch-ups added.**
  - Select **Add Glow.** Modify the adjuster until you get the preferred effects.
  - Choose **Slim Down** to ensure that the face you have chosen looks slimmer.
- **Once you have been able to get the needed result, choose Next to make a choice of the next stage;**
  - **Save - Save / Save As** Use one of the available types to save the newly created image.
  - **Proceed with editing - In Fast / In Proficient:** Select whether you want to work in Advanced or Quick mode to continue editing the image.
  - **Share via Twitter / Flickr:** Select one of the social media or sharing options that Photoshop Elements offers to post your photo online.

Photomerge Guided Edits

In this section, you will learn about the various ways by which you can merge pictures in guided edits;

Paste between photos with Photomerge Compose

With the Photomerge Compose tool, you can swap out parts of an image. One way to do this would be to pick a person from one picture and add them to another. Two photos are required: a source and a destination. To achieve the most natural result, you can cut a section of the source image, paste it into the destination image, and then make adjustments to its color and proportion.

- After choosing two images from the Photo Bin, select **Photomerge > Photomerge compose.**

- To transfer an object or person into the picture editing area, drag the image you wish to work with. Next, select an option using one of the Selection tools, then click the **Next button**.
- The previous step's selection gets pasted into the image you want to transfer the selection to. Make sure the pasted information is proportionate to the rest of the picture by dragging the coach markings to resize and move the selection with the mouse. **Next should be clicked.**
- Now make sure that the pasted content's color and tonal values match the remainder of the image. Aim for the highest degree of natural selection. Click **Auto Match Color Tone** to do this task automatically in one step.

Combine the best-lit elements from two photos with Photomerge Exposure

To effectively handle scenarios in photographs with exposure issues, use Photomerge Exposure. To obtain a correctly exposed picture, you might combine two images into one. For instance, if you want the ideal image to have the following characteristics and it already has a window in the background:

- A clear view of the landscape outside the window.
- A decent exposure to the room's darker furnishings.

You frequently get either overexposed scenery outdoors the window or inadequately exposed objects within the room in such a situation.

Follow these steps to guarantee that you capture the ideal shot:

- **Take many exposures of the same scene, if possible. Take pictures with the least amount of shake and at various exposure values for the best results. For instance:**
  - To correctly expose the subject (the items inside the room), you can use the flash on two or more of the photographs.
  - After that, you can snap one picture without using the flash to correctly expose the background, which is the view outside the window.
- Get a perfectly exposed picture created by blending the pictures together. For you to have a photo well exposed, Photomerge exposure facilitates blending the two pictures together.

Automatic Photomerge Exposure

Using the Photo Bin, you can choose and deselect the necessary photos from the Elements Organizer.

- Select **Photomerge > Photomerge Exposure** in the Guided room, and then take one of the following actions:

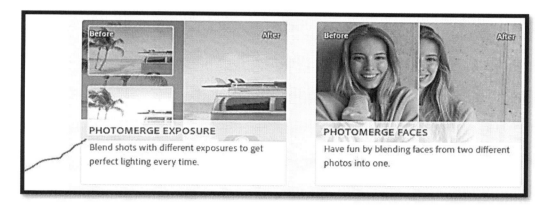

- ○ Choose **two to ten photographs (minimum required) in the Elements Organizer**. Then, in the Guided room, select **Photomerge > Photomerge Exposure.**
- ○ Use **File > Open to open the necessary files.**
  - ■ To see every file that has been opened, choose **Show Open Files in the Photo Bin.**
  - ■ Choose **as many as two or up to ten images within the Photo Bin**.
  - ■ Select **Photomerge > Photomerge Exposure** in the Guided Room.

Once done, Photoshop Elements will show the chosen pictures.

- Choose **Automatic in the Photomerge Exposure.**
- **Make a choice of any of the following choices;**
  - ○ **Simple Blending**: You cannot adjust the Photomerge Exposure parameters with this option. By choosing this option, the combined photo will only be shown.

- Smart Blending: By choosing this option, you can use the sliders to change the parameters. Depending on the parameters you choose, you can view the finished image. **You can change the following configurations:**
  - **Highlight**: gives you the option to change how many details are highlighted.
  - **Shadows**: lets you adjust the shadows' brightness and darkness.
  - **Saturation**: allows you to adjust the color's intensity.

Manual Photomerge Exposure

- Select **Photomerge > Photomerge Exposure** in the Guided room, and then take one of the following actions:
- Choose **Photomerge > Photomerge Exposure** after selecting at least two and as many as ten photographs in Elements Organizer.
- Open **File > Open** to view the necessary files.
  - To see every file that has been opened, choose **Show Open Files In The Photo Bin.**
  - Choose as many as two or up to ten images from the Photo Bin.
  - Select **Photomerge > Photomerge Exposure** in the Guided Room.

Photoshop Elements shows the chosen images.

- Click the **Manual option in the Photomerge panel.**
  The source photo is the first picture that appears in the Photo Bin. As the final photo, you can choose an image from the Photo Bin.
- Choose **the areas of the source image that are exposed:**
  - To paint the exposed areas of the source image, click the **Pencil Tool and move the cursor over them**. Alter the source image and, if needed, pick certain areas from it.
  - Select **the Eraser Tool**, and then paint over any areas you've decided to reveal with the mouse. This will deselect any areas that the Pencil Tool has selected.

Now, you may see a final image atop the one you originally chose, with various regions duplicated from several source photos.

- **Configure the subsequent choices;**

- ○ **Show Strokes**: make a click to display the strokes of your pencil in the source image.
  - ○ **Show Regions**: select to show the chosen areas in the final picture.
- **Additionally;**
  - ○ Use the Opacity Slider to adjust the transparency of these chosen areas so they correctly blend in with the background.
  - ○ To make the blended edges smoother, choose Edge Blending.

Note that only the parts of the source image that have been chosen for the Opacity Slider to impact are those that are visible. If you would like to alter the transparency of the areas you selected from the other photos, switch to a new source image. It retains the value assigned to a certain image.

- Click the **Alignment Tool** after selecting the **Advanced Option** to adjust the alignment of many pictures. After positioning three markers in each of the source and final images, click **Align Photos**. Select **"Done"**

Combine photos with Photomerge Panorama

To combine many images, use the Photomerge Panorama Guided Effect. For the merging process to function optimally, the images need to share common, overlapping portions from the shot scene.

- From the Photo Bin, select **several images with overlapping material,** and then select **Guided Room> Photomerge > Photomerge Panorama.**

- Select **the pan motion/layout options for your photographs** in the Photomerge Panorama panel's Panorama options section. To view the various options, click the **triangle**.

  - o **Auto Panorama**: Depending on which layout creates a superior photo merge, Auto Panorama analyzes the original photos and applies either a perspective or cylindrical layout.
  - o **Perspective**: designates one of the source images—by default, the center image—as the reference image, resulting in a composition that is consistent. The remaining photos are subsequently altered (if necessary, moved, extended, or skewed) to match the overlapping content layer.
  - o **Cylindrical**: displays separate images on an unfurled cylinder, which lessens the "bow-tie" distortion that can happen with the Perspective layout. Content overlaps are still compatible. The central position is taken by the reference image. Wide panoramas are best created with this.
  - o **Spherical**: aligns and modifies the pictures as though they were meant to be used for spherical internal mapping. Use a set of 360-degree photos you've shot to create 360-degree panoramas. Additionally, you can utilize Spherical with other file sets to get beautiful panoramic effects.
  - o **Collage**: rotates or scales any of the source layers, aligns the layers, and matches any overlapping material.
  - o **Reposition**: matches overlapping content and align the layers; none of the source pictures are altered (stretched or skewed).

- To adjust the look of the generated panorama, select the **Settings checkboxes.**

  - o **Blend Images**: determines the best borders between the images in order to match the images' colors and construct seams based on those borders. Blend Images Together is turned off, and a straightforward blend of a rectangle is made. If you plan to manually adjust the mixing masks, this might be better.
  - o **Vignette Discarded**: eliminates darkened edges from photos that have been affected by incorrect lens shading or defects in the lens and applies exposure adjustment.
  - o **Geometric Distortion Correction:** this choice helps to compensate for barrel, pincushion, or fisheye distortion.

116

o **Content-Aware Fill Transparent Areas**: Replace any transparent portions with surrounding, comparable image material in a seamless manner.

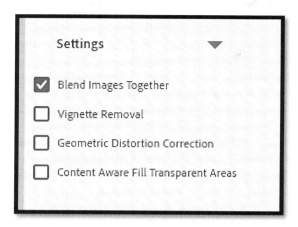

- Click on **Create Panorama** After analyzing the chosen pictures, Photoshop Elements initiates the panorama creation process.
- Photoshop Elements opens the newly created image in the Advanced view when it creates a panorama.

Activity

1. Move and scale objects in guided edits.
2. Change your picture to black and white.
3. Change your black-and-white picture to color.
4. Make fun and special edits to your photo.
5. Combine pictures with the use of picture Photomerge panorama.
6. Align your pictures for photo merging.

CHAPTER 5

GET TO KNOW THE PHOTOSHOP ELEMENTS TOOLBOX

The Tool Options

In both Quick and Advanced modes, Photoshop Elements offers you a toolkit to assist you in editing your photos. The toolbox contains tools for selecting, enhancing, drawing, and viewing images. There are a few simple-to-use tools in the Quick Mode toolbox. Zoom, Hand, Quick Selection, Eye, Whiten Teeth, Straighten, Type, Spot Healing Brush, Crop, and Move are the tools that are available in this mode.

The Color Picker

The color of an image's pixels can be altered using painting tools. Similar to conventional drawing tools, the Brush and Pencil tools apply color using brush strokes. Color is applied over huge regions using the Gradient tool, Paint Bucket tool, and Fill command. The colors already present in an image can be altered with tools like the Smudge, Blur, and Eraser tools. The ability to customize how a tool applies or alters color gives Adobe Photoshop Elements' painting capabilities immense power.

Applying color can be done in a variety of ways, including gradually, with soft edges, big brushstrokes, variable brush dynamics, varied blending qualities, and brushes with varying shapes. You can mimic the effects of an airbrush on paint. In this section, you will learn all you need to know about the use of the Adobe Color Picker. With the Adobe Color Picker, you can define colors numerically or choose from a color spectrum to choose the foreground or background color. Furthermore, you have the option to choose colors solely based on web-safe colors or colors based on RGB or HSB color models.

- To bring up the Color Picker, click **either the background or foreground color boxes in the toolbox.**

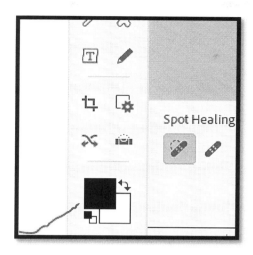

- Within the color field, click. The color is indicated in the color field by a circular marker, and the numerical values update to reflect the selected color when you click on it.
- To switch to a different color, **move the white triangles across the slider.**

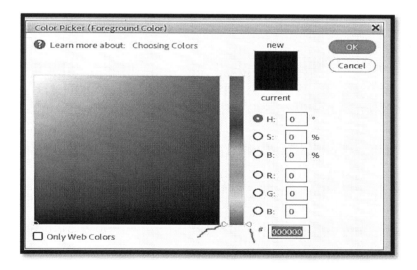

- **Alternatively, you can do any of the activities below to visually define a number:**

  - In the text box beneath the RGB values, type your color's hexadecimal value. (Web designers commonly utilize hexadecimal color values.)

- o Choose **a radio button for RGB color** and enter component values ranging from 0 to 255, where 0 represents no light and 255 represents the brightest light.
  - o Choose **a radio button for HSB color**, and then enter saturation and brightness as percentages and hue as an angle between 0° and 360° that represents a spot on the color wheel.
- The new color is shown in the top portion of the color rectangle located to the right of the color slider. The rectangle's bottom is where the original color is seen.
- To start coloring with the new color, click **OK.**

Please take note that if you can choose colors with the use of your system's built-in color picker or a plug-in color picker. Select **Preferences > General and then select the color picker.**

Color

Two color models are used in Adobe Photoshop Elements to modify color. The human visual system perceives color in terms of hue, saturation, and brightness (HSB), whereas computer monitors display color in terms of quantities of red, green, and blue, or RGB. An additional tool for understanding the connections between colors is the color wheel. Four image modes—RGB, bitmap, grayscale, and indexed color—that control how many colors are displayed in a picture are offered by Photoshop Elements. Hue, saturation, and brightness (HSB) are the three properties that the human eye uses to perceive color. In contrast, computer monitors use various amounts of red, green, and blue (RGB) light to display colors. The HSB and RGB color models are used in Photoshop Elements to choose and work with color. You can better comprehend the connections between colors by using the color wheel.

HSB model

The HSB model explains three basic properties of color based on how humans perceive color:

Hue: The color that an item transmits or reflects back. It is determined as a point on the conventional color wheel and given as a degree that ranges from 0 to 360. In everyday speech, hue is denoted by the color name, such as red, orange, or green.

Saturation: The color's intensity or purity. Saturation, often known as chroma, is the percentage ranging from 0 (gray) to 100 (totally saturated), which expresses the amount of gray relative to the hue. Saturation rises from the middle to the periphery of the conventional color wheel.

Brightness: The percentage indicating the color's relative lightness or darkness, often ranging from 0 (black) to 100 (white). Photoshop Elements does not allow you to generate or modify photos in the HSB mode, but you can use the HSB model when selecting a color in the Color Picker menu window.

RGB model

RGB (red, green, and blue) light can be mixed in different ratios and intensities to represent a wide section of the visible spectrum. The additive primary is these three hues. Red, green, and blue light are added to form white light. Two hues combine to become cyan, magenta, or yellow when they overlap. Monitors, video, and lighting all use the additive primary colors. Red, green, and blue phosphors, for instance, allow light to be emitted, which produces color on your monitor.

Color wheel

A useful tool for comprehending and remembering the relationships between colors is the color wheel. The primaries that add up are red, green, and blue. The subtractive primaries are yellow, magenta, and cyan. The complement of each additive primary, which is red-cyan, green-magenta, and blue-yellow, is located just across from it. Two additive primaries make up each subtractive primary, but not its complement. As a result, as you add more of a primary hue to your image, you also add less of its complement. Yellow, for instance, is made up of red and green light; blue light is absent from yellow. In Photoshop Elements, modifying yellow results in modifications to the color values in the blue color channel. You can take yellow out of your image by adding blue.

The Eyedropper/Sampler Tool

Without needing to choose a swatch, copying a color is made simple with the Eyedropper tool. It sets a new foreground or background color by sampling or copying the color of an area in your photo. The desktop of your computer, another open picture, or the current image can all be used as samples. To guarantee that the color is constantly accessible, you can include the sampled color in the Color Swatches panel. The region that the

Eyedropper tool samples can also be specified in terms of size. The eyedropper can be configured to sample the average color values of a 5 × 5 or 3 x 3 pixel areas beneath the cursor, for instance.

- From the toolbox, pick the **Eyedropper tool.**

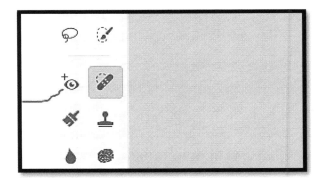

- (Optional) Select **an option from the Sample Size option** in the Tool Options bar to alter the eyedropper's sample size:
  - To find the exact value of the pixel you click, point to Sample.
  - To find the average value of the chosen number of pixels inside the region you select, use either the 3 By 3 Average or the 5 By 5 Average.
- Choose **the location of the color picker tool's sample source** from the Tool Options bar. Select **the Current Layer or All Layers option.**
- **Select a color by doing one of the following:**
  - Click t**he chosen color in your image to choose a new foreground color.** Click **inside your image and drag to select a color** that displays elsewhere on your computer screen.
  - You can use the **Alt-click (or Option-click on Mac OS) shortcut to select a different backdrop color from an image.**

The Eyedropper tool's foreground color box changes as you click and move it.

- Let go of the button of the mouse to choose a novel color.

Note: While using most painting tools, you can momentarily switch to the Eyedropper tool, which lets you swiftly change colors without having to select a different tool. All you have to do is press the Alt key (Mac OS: Option key). Let go of the **Alt key (or, in Mac OS, the Option key) after selecting your color.**

Choose a color from the toolbox

- **Take one of these actions:**

  - Click the **Default Colors** icon to make the foreground and background boxes black and white.
  - Click the **Switch Colors icon** to change the colors in the two boxes.
  - Select **a color from the Color Picker by clicking the uppermost color box** in the toolbox to alter the foreground color.
  - Click **the toolbox's bottom color box**, select **a color from the Color Picker, and adjust the background color.**

The Color Swatch panel

With the use of the Color Swatches panel (**Window > Color Swatches**), you can store the colors that you use most often whenever you happen to be taking pictures. The color of the background or foreground can be selected by selecting a color sample in the Color Swatches panel. You can create a customized swatch library by adjusting the colors, saving it, and then loading it again to use on a different picture. You can modify the Color Swatches panel's thumbnail presentation by selecting an alternate choice from the More menu. The Color Swatches panel allows you to add a lot of colors, but in order to get the most out of it, you need to control its size and arrangement. You can control panel size and group special or related swatches by creating libraries. The different swatch libraries are located in the Photoshop Elements installation folder\Presets\Color Swatches (or, on a Mac, Photoshop Elements installation folder\Support Files\Presets\Color Swatches) folder. Custom libraries can be created and then automatically added to the panel libraries pop-up menu by adding them to the Color Swatches folder.

Make a color choice with the use of the Color Swatches panel

- Select **Window > Color Swatches** if the Color Swatches window is not already open.

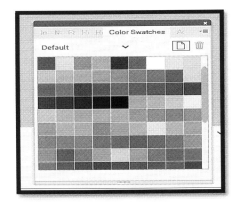

- (Optional) Select **a swatch library title** from the Swatches menu in the Color Swatches panel.
- **Take one of these actions:**
  - Choose **a color in the panel to make a choice of a foreground color.**
  - Ctrl-click **(or make use of the Command option with Mac) a color in the panel to make a choice of a background color.**

Add a color to the Color Swatches panel

You can save a color as a swatch in the Color Swatches window if it's a color you want to use frequently. The panel's color library is expanded using saved swatches. You have to save the complete library if you want to keep your custom swatches forever.

- In the toolbox, change the foreground color to the color you wish to add.
- **Select a task to complete in the Color Swatches panel:**
  - In the panel, choose the **New Swatch button located at the bottom**. A color swatch is added, which is given the automated label Color Swatch 1.

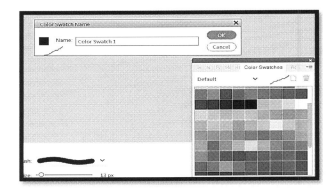

- ○ The More menu allows you to select **New Swatch.**
- ○ Click to add the color after putting the pointer over an empty area in the bottom row of the Color Swatches panel. The pointer then transforms into the Paint Bucket tool.
- Select **OK** after you have inserted a name for the new color.
- If the Save window appears, give the swatch library a new name and click **Save** if you are prompted to do so.

Save and make use of custom swatch libraries

- In the Color Swatches panel, perform any of the following actions:
  - Select **Store Swatches from the More menu** in order to store a library of swatches. Save the file to the Photoshop Elements\Presets\Color Swatches (For Mac, Photoshop Elements\Support Files\Presets\Color Swatches) folder in order for the set to show up in the panel's swatch libraries pop-up menu.
  - Click the **Load Swatches option in the panel's More menu** to pick and load a swatch library.

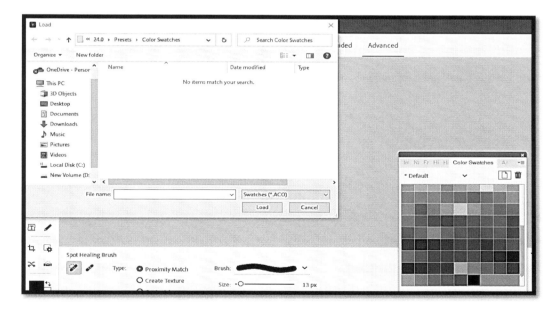

  - Select **a library by selecting Replace Swatches** from the More option in the panel. This will substitute the currently selected swatch library with the new library.

Delete a color from the Color Swatches panel

- **Take one of these actions:**
  - To confirm the deletion, move the color swatch to the panel's Trash icon and click **OK.**
  - Pick **a color in the Color Swatches window** after changing the pointer to a scissors icon by pressing the Alt (Mac OS) key.
- If you are asked to save the library, click **Save** after giving the library a name in the Save window's box.

Additional Foreground /Background color options

When filling selections with the Paint Bucket tool and painting with the Brush or Pencil tools, you apply the foreground color. The background color is the color that you apply using the Eraser tool to the Background layer. The two overlapping boxes at the bottom of the toolbox allow you to view and modify the colors of the foreground and background. The color of the backdrop is represented by the bottom box, and the foreground by the top box. The Gradient tool and certain special effects filters also combine the colors of the foreground and background. You can choose to alter the foreground or background color in the toolbox by making use of the Eyedropper tool, the Color Swatches panel, or the Color Picker.

About Blending Modes

Blending modes regulate how an editing or painting tool affects individual pixels in an image. **Visualizing the effect of a blending mode can be aided by using the following color schemes:**

- The original color of the image is known as the base color.
- The color that the painting or editing tool applies is known as the mixed color.
- The color that emerges from the blend is known as the outcome color.

You are at liberty to make a choice of any of the blending modes that can be found in the Tool options. Some of these modes are highlighted below;

Normal: applies paint or editing to each pixel to give it the desired color. This mode is the standard one. When working in bitmap or indexed-color mode with an image, normal mode is referred to as threshold.

Dissolve: applies paint or editing to each pixel to give it the desired color. Nevertheless, depending on the opacity at any given pixel location, the base color or the blend color will randomly replace the pixels to produce the desired color. Large brushes and the brush tool perform best in this setting.

Behind: only makes changes or paints on a layer's transparent areas. This mode is just like drawing on the back of transparent sections on a sheet of glass, except it only functions on layers where Lock Transparency is deselected.

Multiply: helps with the multiplication of the base color by the blend color after a thorough examination of the color data in each channel. There is always a darker hue as a result. Any hue can be multiplied by black to get black. Any color that is multiplied by white retains its original color. Using a painting tool, you can create progressively deeper hues by making successive strokes while painting with a color other than black or white. It's like sketching on a picture with several felt-tipped pens.

Color Burn: darkens the fundamental color to show the mixed color after examining the color data contained in each channel. There is no difference when white is blended in.

Darker burn: shows the lower value color after comparing the sum of all channel numbers for the base color and the blend. Darker Color obtains the result color by selecting the lowest channel numbers from both the base and blend colors; thus, it does not generate a third color, which can arise from the Darken mix.

Screen: looks at the color information of each channel, multiplies the base and blends colors' inverses. There is always a lighter color as a result. Black screening preserves color integrity. White is produced by screening with white. It has the same effect as superimposing several slides of photos on top of one another.

Lighter Color: displays the color with the higher value after comparing the total of all channel numbers for the base and blend colors. selects the highest channel numbers from the base and blends colors to create the result color, so it doesn't make a third color, which could come from the Lighten blend.

Soft Light: depending on the mixed color, either lightens or darkens the hues. It looks like a diffused spotlight was beaming on the picture. The picture is lightened if the blend color is less than 50% gray. The image gets darkened if the blend color is more than 50% gray. Pure black or white paint does not generate pure black or white; instead, it creates a noticeably darker or lighter area.

Hard Light: With respect to the blend color, this option either multiplies or screens the colors. It has the same effect as if the image were under a strong spotlight. The picture is lightened if the blend color is less than 50% gray. This is helpful for highlighting specific areas of an image. The image gets darkened if the blend color is more than 50% gray. This is helpful for enhancing an image's shadows. Pure black or white paint produces pure black or white.

Vivid Light: Depending on the blend color, burns or dodges the colors by adjusting the contrast. The image is brightened by reducing the contrast if the blend color (light source) is brighter than 50% gray. The image is made darker by boosting contrast if the blend color is less than 50% gray.

Linear Light: Depending on the blend color, burns or dodges the colors by adjusting the brightness. Brightness is increased to lighten the image if the blend color (light source) is brighter than 50% gray. The image is made darker by lowering the brightness if the blend color is deeper than 50% gray.

Pin Light: based on the color of the underblend, replaces the colors. Pixels darker than the blend color are replaced; pixels lighter than the blend color remain unchanged if the blend color (light source) is lighter than 50% gray. Pixels lighter than the blend color are replaced; pixels darker than the blend color remain unchanged if the blend color is more than 50% gray. This mode helps to enhance an image with special effects.

The Zoom Tool

With the use of this unique tool, you can easily magnify your image either more or less. Zoom In and Zoom Out are the relevant tools displayed in the Tool Options bar and each of them will be considered in this section.

Note: You can view different sections of a picture at varying magnifications using the Hand tool, Zoom tools, Zoom commands, and Navigator panel.

You have a few options for enlarging or decreasing your view. The zoom percentage is shown in the window's title bar (except when the current window is too small for the screen to accommodate).

Zoom in or out

- **Get any of the following done;**

    o   Click the **Zoom In or Zoom Out icon** in the Tool Options box after selecting the Zoom tool from the toolbar. To enlarge a portion, **click it**. With each click, the display is centered around the location where you click, and the image is magnified or reduced to the next predetermined percentage. The magnifying glass looks empty when the image reaches its minimum lowering level of 1 pixel or its highest magnification level of 3200%.

- ○ Within the Tool Options bar, drag **the Zoom slider**.
- ○ Select either **View > Zoom Out or View > Zoom In**.
- ○ Within the Tool Options bar, type the appropriate magnification degree in the Zoom text box.

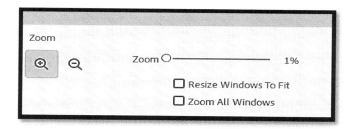

Display a picture at 100%

- Take one of these actions:
  - Double-click **the toolbox's Zoom tool**.
  - Select **the 1:1 button** in the Tool Options window after choosing either the Zoom or the Hand tool.

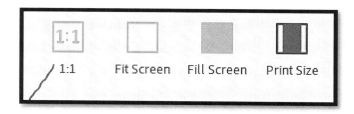

  - You may also right-click the picture and select Actual Pixels by selecting **View > Actual Pixels.**
  - In the status bar, type **100% and hit Enter.**

Fit a picture to the screen

- Take one of these actions:
  - Double-click **the toolbar's zoom tool.**
  - After choosing the Zoom or Hand tool, select the **Tool Options bar's** Fit Screen button. Alternatively, select **Fit On Screen with a right-click on the image.**

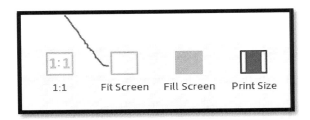

- Select **Fit On Screen under View**. These settings adjust the window size and zoom level to fill the available screen area.

Modify the size of the window while zooming

- Choose **Resize Windows to Fit** from the Tool Options bar while the Zoom tool is active. As you enlarge or decrease the image's view, the window resizes.

If you deselect **Resize Windows to Fit**, the window size remains fixed, independent of the image magnification. When working with tiled graphics or on smaller monitors, this can be useful.

Navigator panel

You can change the image's field of view and magnification using the Navigator panel. The magnification can be changed by dragging the zoom slider, typing a number in the text box, or clicking the **Zoom In or Zoom Out button**. To shift the view of a picture, drag the view box located in the thumbnail. The image window's borders are represented by the view box. You may also click to select the region of view by clicking on **the image's thumbnail.**

- Using the Navigator panel menu, select **Panel Options** to alter the view box's color. You can pick a custom color or select a color from the Color option by clicking the **color swatch** to launch the Color Picker. Select **OK.**

The Hand Tool

This is another tool that can be used to have a much wider view of the screen. With the use of the hand tool, you are able to move your picture in the Photoshop Elements workspace. You are also able to drag your picture with the use of this tool.

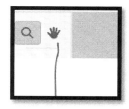

You can view different sections of a picture at varying magnifications when you make use of the Hand tool, Zoom tools, Zoom commands, and Navigator panel. You have a few options for enlarging or decreasing your view. The zoom percentage is shown in the window's title bar (unless the area of the window is too small for the screen to accommodate). Employ the window bars for scrolling or the Hand tool, then drag to pan across the image to view a different portion of it. The Navigator panel is also available for use. For the use of the hand tool, you can also follow the above-described settings for the zoom tool, they both work in tandem.

The Move Tool

In Photoshop Elements, the move tool is a very useful tool as it helps to drag objects or layers from one part of the window/screen to another.

Move a selection

You can cut and drag a pixel selection to an alternate location in the image with the use of the Move tool. The tool can also be used to copy or move selections within Photoshop Elements as well as to images in other programs that allow selections. There are times when you would have a quick need for you to make use of the Move tool and you have another being held down, all you have to do is simply hold down the Ctrl key. Note however that when you have the hand tool chosen, this technique will not work.

- Using a selection tool, make a selection in the Edit workspace, then choose the **Move tool within the toolkit.**

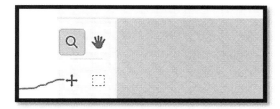

- Modify **the Move tool's options** in the options bar (optional).
- Drag **the selection** to a new location by moving the cursor inside the selection border. All of the pixel choices shift as you drag if you have numerous areas chosen.

Move tool options

In the options bar, you can alter the following configurations when you choose the **Move tool;**

- **Auto Select Layer**   Instead of selecting the layer that is presently chosen, it selects the highest layer that has pixels beneath the Move tool cursor.
- **Show Bounding Box** with this option you get to see the bounding box all about the image's selection or, if there isn't one active, the layer that is currently selected. You can adjust the selection or layer's size using the boxes on the sides and corners.
- **Show Highlight on Rollover** highlights specific layers when the mouse is moved over the picture. If there is a need for you to select and move a highlighted layer, click on it. When you roll over, layers that are previously chosen don't highlight.
- **Arrange menu** shifts the chosen layer ahead of, behind, or in between other levels. Bring to Front; Bring Forward, Send Backward, and Send to Back are among the available options. Selecting a layer and then selecting an item from the organize menu will organize the layer.
- **The align menu** makes the chosen layers aligned. Top edges, Vertical centers, Bottom edges, Left edges, Horizontal centers, and Right edges are among the available options. It is possible to simultaneously align many layers. Select a layer, press and hold the shift key, choose a different layer, and then select an option from the Align option to align the layers.
- **Distribute menu Spaces** chosen layered at equal distances. Top edges, Vertical centers, Bottom edges, Left edges, Horizontal centers, and Right edges are among the available options. Layers can be stretched out at the same time. You need to have at least three selected layers in order for this choice to be activated. Pick a layer, press down Shift, pick more layers, and then select a piece from the Distribute option to divide the layers apart.

Copy selections or layers

The Move tool and the Edit menu's Copy, Copy Merged, Cut, Paste, and Paste into Selection commands can be used to copy and paste selections. Remember that the copied data maintains its original pixel measurements when you paste a selection or layer between images of varying resolutions. The pasted section could look out of scale to the new picture as a result. To ensure that the source and destination photographs have the same resolution prior to copying and pasting, employ the

- **Image > Resize > Image Size command**.

Any selections you copy or cut are kept on the clipboard. In the clipboard, only one choice is kept at a time.

Copy selections with the Move tool

You transfer the selection from one open picture window to another when copying between photos and making use of the move tool to copy selections. When you drop the selection into the image window, a border appears to highlight the window.

- Choose **the area of the picture you wish to duplicate.**
- From the toolbox, choose **the Move tool in the Edit workspace.**
- When moving the selection you wish to copy and transfer, press **Alt (Option on Mac OS).**

- **One of the following actions can be taken to create more copies of the same selection:**
  - While moving the selection to each new position, hold **down Alt (Option on Mac OS).**
  - Press an arrow key while holding down **Alt (Option in Mac OS) to offset the clone by one pixel. (By moving and copying the pixels, this produces a blurred look.)**
  - Hit **Alt (Option in Mac OS) + Shift and an arrow key to offset the copied image by 10 pixels. (This does not clone the pixels; rather, it shifts them.)**

Copy a selection with the use of commands

- Employ the use of a selection tool to choose the area you would like to copy in the Edit workspace.
- **Do any of the following;**
  - To get the selection on the clipboard simply select **Edit > Copy.**
  - If you would like to have all the layers in the chosen area copied to the clipboard, click on **Edit > Copy Merged.**

Add to and subtract from a selection

To adjust the borders of an existing selection, you can add or remove elements from it. For instance, by removing a circular selection from within a circular selection, you may create a selection in the shape of a donut.

- **Choose a tool for selection and carry out one of the subsequent actions:**
  - To add to a selection, hold down **Shift (a plus sign shows next to the pointer); to subtract from a selection, hold down Alt (Option on Mac OS) (a minus sign shows next to the pointer)**. Next, pick the region that needs to be increased or decreased, then choose again.
  - Make another selection by clicking **Add To Selection or Subtract From Selection in the options box.**

The Marquee Selection Tools

There are basically two types of marquee tools; the Rectangular Marquee tool and the Elliptical Marquee tool. The Elliptical Marquee tool creates elliptical or circular selection boundaries, whereas the Rectangular Marquee tool creates square or rectangular selection borders.

Follow the set of instructions below to make use of these amazing tools;

- Make a preferred choice of the exact one you would like to use; either the elliptical or the rectangular.
- **In the Tool options bar, configure marquee tool options;**
  - Indicate if you want to choose an area where existing selections intersect, add to, remove from, or make a new selection.
  - Enter **a Feather value** to make the selection border softer and more indistinguishable from the surrounding area.
  - To make your selection's edges smoother, choose **Anti-aliased (Elliptical Marquee tool only).**
  - Select **Normal** to visually adjust the selection border's size and proportions; Fixed Ratio to establish the selection border's width-to-height ratio; or Fixed Size to set the height and width of the marquee from the Mode pop-up menu.
- Drag **the desired region into selection**. When dragging, keep the **Shift key pressed** to limit the selection marquee to a square or circle. After you start dragging, press **down Alt (Windows) or Option (Mac OS)** to move a marquee from the center. Holding down the spacebar while dragging with the selection tool allows you to move the marquee tool's selection border. Once the selection boundary is in the appropriate location, release the spacebar.

Lasso Selection Tools

With the use of the Lasso tool, you can draw freehand selection borders. You can make very precise and accurate decisions when you choose to make use of this tool.

- From the toolbox, choose **the Lasso tool.**

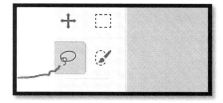

- **(Optional) In the Tool Options bar, configure the Lasso tool:**
  - o Indicate if you want to choose an area where other selections intersect, include an existing selection, deduct from an existing selection, or make a new selection.
  - o Enter **a Feather value** to make the selection border softer and more indistinguishable from the surrounding area.
  - o Choose **Anti-aliased** to soften the edges of your selection.

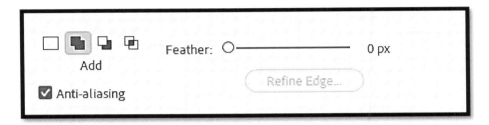

- **To create a boundary for a freehand selection, drag:**
  - o Release the mouse button, and then press **Shift to add to the selection. When the pointer switches to, drag**
  - o Release the mouse button, hit **Alt (or Option in Mac OS), and drag when the pointer switches to remove an item from the selection.**
  - o Holding down **the mouse button while pressing Alt (Option on Mac OS) will add straight-edge segments**. When the pointer shifts, release the button and click where you want the segment's end to be.
- Let go of the mouse icon to bring the selection border to an end. From the point at which you had to let go of the button of the mouse to the beginning of your selection, a straight selection segment is drawn.
- To fine-tune and increase the precision of your selection, click **Refine Edge**.

Quick Selection Tools

After you select or click-drag the desired region, the Quick Selection tool selects it based on similarities in color and texture. The Quick Selection tool produces a border quickly and logically, so you don't need to draw an exact mark.

- Choose the **Quick Selection Brush tool.**
- **Choose any of the subsequent options in the Tool Options bar;**

- **New Selection** with this choice, you will be able to draw a novel selection. Note that this is usually the default choice.
- **Add To Selection** With this choice, you can choose to increase an existing selection by adding to it.
- **Subtract from Selection** this choice allows you to remove from a selection that exists. Note that this choice is only always available after you have made a selection.

- Within the Brush Picker in the menu bar, select a brush. Use a bigger brush if you wish to choose a larger region. Use a smaller brush size for choices that are more accurate.
- Let go of the **mouse button** after clicking or clicking and dragging **over the region that encompasses the color spectrum of the object you wish to pick. The border of the selection emerges.**
- **Complete any of the following actions to get the selection refined;**
  - Click the **"Add To Selection" button** in the options bar,

  - Then **click or click and drag the desired region to add to the selection.**
  - Click or click-**drag across the region you wish to remove from the selection after selecting the Subtract From Selection button in the options box.**
  - Select the **New Selection button** in the menu bar to begin a new selection, then clicks or draw to designate the new selection area.

- Choose **Refine Edge** to create more adjustments to your selection and to ensure it is more precise.

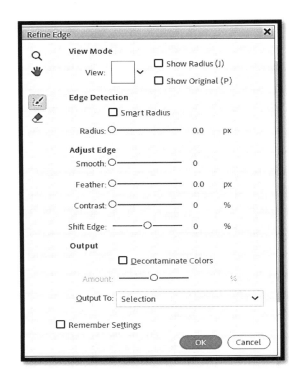

The Refine Selection Brush and Push Tool

By automatically recognizing the margins, the Refine Selection Brush makes it easier to add or delete areas from and within a selection.

Eye Tools: The Red Eye Removal Tool

Red eye is a typical problem that arises when the flash on your camera illuminates the retina of your photo subject. When shooting in a dark room, you will see it more frequently because the subject's iris is wide open. If the camera has a red-eye reduction feature, utilize it to prevent red-eye.

- o Choose **Automatically Fix Red Eyes in the Get Photos dialog box** to automatically fix red eyes when you import photos into the Elements Organizer. Using the Photo Browser, you may also eliminate red eyes from certain pictures.

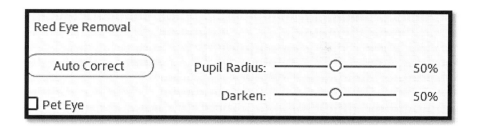

- Red eye can be fixed manually, navigate **to quick or Advanced mode and choose the Eye tool.**
- Configure **the Pupils Radius and Darken Amount in the options bar for tools.**
- **Choose from the following actions in the image:**
  - Click **on an eye's crimson region.**
  - Over the eye region, make a selection.

The eyes lose their redness when you let go of the mouse button. Moreover, you can use the Eye tool's AutoCorrect feature to automatically correct red eyes.

Open Closed Eyes

You can enable closed eyelids in your images by using the Open Closed Eyes function. The eyeballs in another picture on your computer or in the Elements Organizer collection can be used to open someone's eyes.

- In Photoshop Elements, **launch a photo.**
- **In either Quick or Advanced mode, do any of the following;**
  - After choosing the **Eye tool**, use the **Tool Options bar's Open Closed Eyes button.**
  - Open Closed Eyes by selecting **Enhance.**

It is evident from the Open Closed Eyes dialog that the person's face is highlighted in a circular manner to show that it has been recognized in the image.

- In the Try Sample Eyes list, a few examples are displayed to you. You have the option of selecting a face that resembles the main image. Photoshop Elements replaces the primary photo's closed eyes with the selected face.
- **Do any of the following;**
  - Choose a **Computer** to make a choice of a source picture from your computer.

o Select **Organizer** to make a choice of source picture from the Elements Organizer.

o Pick **Photo Bin** to make a choice of source pictures from files that are currently opened.

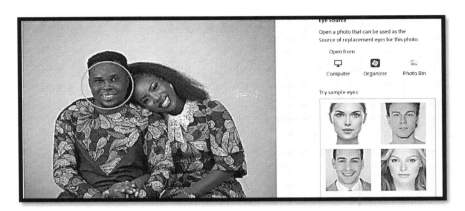

If you'd like, you can choose more than one source photo. Photoshop Elements replaces the closed eyes in the primary photo with faces from these source photos. To get the greatest results, you can test out several eye replacements. After you've chosen a face in the main image that needs its eyes opened, click on any of the faces in the source images. To get the best results, try several faces. If the skin tone in the source photo differs from the main photo, Photoshop Elements blends the skin tones together around the eyes.

- Choose **Before/After** for the compassion of results with the main picture.
- If you notice that you are not getting the desired results you can choose **Reset.**
- Select **OK.**
- Get the picture saved with the alterations.

The Spot Healing Brush Tool

Your images can be instantly enhanced using the Spot Healing Brush to eliminate blemishes and other defects. To remove flaws from an area, you can either drag or click once on the imperfection.

- Choose the **Spot Healing Brush tool.**

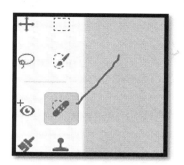

- Select **the brush size**. To cover the whole area with a single click, it is advisable to choose a brush that is somewhat larger than the region you wish to correct.
- In the Tool Options bar, select **one of the Type options listed below.**
  - **Proximity Match** finds an image region to utilize as a patch for the specified area by utilizing the pixels surrounding the selection's boundary. Try the Create Texture option under and then **Edit > Undo** if this solution isn't able to fix the problem to your satisfaction.
  - **Create Texture** creates a texture for the region to be fixed by using every pixel in a selection. Should the texture not function, attempt to drag across the region once more.

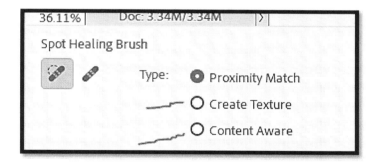

- Choose **the area you would like to fix in the picture or click-drag over a much wider area.**

What is Anti-Aliasing?

By reducing the contrast between the background and edge pixels, anti-aliasing smoothes down a selection's sharp edges. There is no loss of detail as just the edge pixels are altered. Cutting, copying, and pasting selections to generate composite images can benefit from anti-aliasing.

Content-Aware

Unwanted individuals or objects can be taken out of your pictures without damaging them. You can eliminate specific elements from a picture by using the Spot Healing Brush tool's Content-Aware option. Photoshop Elements employs a technique of comparing adjacent image elements to create a smooth selection that preserves important characteristics like object edges and shadows.

To get rid of anything unwanted:

- Choose the **Spot Healing Brush tool.**
- Under the Tool Options bar, choose **Content-Aware.**
- Overpaint the thing you wish to be taken out of the picture.

For small things, spot healing functions well. Make sure you are working with a high-end computer configuration if the image you are working on is huge and contains a large undesired object.

Try the following methods if you have trouble viewing huge images:

- One at a time, make tiny brushstrokes.
- Reduce the image's size.
- Restart the program and increase the RAM allotted.

The Healing Brush Tools

When you drag the Healing Brush over significant regions of imperfection, it fixes them. Items on a grassy field, for example, can be taken out of a background that happens to be uniform.

- Pick the **Healing Brush tool.**
- **Decide on a specific size of brush from the Tool Options bar and configure healing brush options;**
  - **The mode** determines how the pattern or source integrates with the current pixel structure. The original pixels are covered over by new ones in normal mode. The Replace mode maintains the texture and grain of the film at the brush stroke's edges.

- **The source** specifies the source that will be used to fix pixels. Samples make use of the current image's pixels. Pattern makes use of the pixels that you designate in the Pattern panel.
- **Aligned** retains the current sample point while constantly collecting pixels, even when the mouse button is released. Every time you stop and start painting again, deselect Aligned to keep utilizing the sampled pixels from the first sampling point.
- **Sample All Layers** To sample data from the current layer and below, all visible layers, or the current layer itself, select Sample All Layers.

- Place the cursor in any image that is opened then tap **Alt (Option in Mac OS)** and choose to get the data sampled. Unless one of the photos is in grayscale mode, the two pictures must be in the exact same color mode when you are applying a sample from one to another.
- To combine sampling data and existing data, drag the picture over the defect. Every time you let go of the mouse button, the sampled pixels blend in with the surrounding pixels.

Before making use of the Healing Brush tool, choose the region you wish to heal if the edges have a lot of contrast. To accurately follow the border of contrasting pixels, make your pick larger than the region you wish to heal. The Healing Brush tool's selection stops color bleeding from the outside when painting.

The Smart Brush Tools

The Detail and the Smart Brush tool helps to add color and tone modifications to particular regions of a picture with the use of the Smart Brush tool. These tools can also be used to apply specific effects. All you have to do is select a pre-made change and apply it. Adjustment layers are automatically created by both tools. This function preserves the original image layer, giving you more creative control over how you interact with your photos. No picture data is lost, so you may go back and make further changes. The Smart Brush tool similarly selects based on texture and color when you use it. The chosen area receives the change at the same time. Shadows, highlights, colors, and contrasts can all be changed. Give your image some color, add some texture, and experiment with other photo effects.

- Choose the **Smart Brush tool.**

- Using the Tools Options bar's preset drop-down menu, choose an effect, and then drag **your mouse over the image's objects to apply it.**

With a smart brush, you may apply different patterns and effects by selecting from a variety of predefined settings. Nevertheless, since the layer containing the effect is a pixel layer rather than an adjustment layer, you are unable to modify the effect's settings.

The following effects can be added to your photographs with the aid of the Textures presets:

- Improve uninteresting backdrops.
- Add a satin finish to the clothing and textiles in a picture.
- Include floral designs on the clothing in a picture.
- Designer patterns can be added to an image's backdrop or walls.

Similar to a painting tool, the Detail Smart Brush tool lets you apply adjustments to particular regions of the image. With its predefined pattern and effect options, this tool aids in fine-tuning specifics. It is more accurate to paint and apply the preset in smaller regions. To apply an effect, select it from the drop-down list and paint over the designated area. There are several different brushes available. The options bar contains brush size and shape settings.

It functions similarly to a Selection tool as well; to change the size and shape of the selection,

- Choose **Refine Edge in the menu of options. Click the Remove region from the Selection brush to eliminate a section from the selection.**

You can add to or take away from the regions that are being changed using both brush tools. Additionally, a photo can have multiple correction presets applied to it. Every preset adjustment is made to a separate layer of adjustment. The parameters for each adjustment can be adjusted independently. A pin shows up where the adjustment was originally made when it is made. For the particular adjustment, the pin serves as a reference. Applying a different adjustment setting results in the appearance of a new pin. This function facilitates the modification of a particular correction, particularly when using different adjustments.

- From the toolbox, choose **either the Smart Brush or the Detail Smart Brush tool.** Adjustment presets are displayed in a pop-up panel that opens.
- From the Tools Options bar's preset drop-down menu, choose **an effect.**
- **Optional: Modify the brush tool's dimensions and quality by doing any of the following actions:**
  - Open the **Brush Picker** from the options bar and change the settings if you choose to use the Smart Brush tool.
  - Using the Brush presets pop-up panel, choose **a preset brush tip if you used the Detail Smart Brush tool.** Next, modify the settings bar's brush size setting.
- In the image, paint or drag the tool. A color pin shows where you initially applied the brush tool once the correction is performed on its own adjustment layer.
- **Execute any of the following, if you choose to:**
  - Paint or drag the image to apply the current change to more sections of the picture. Verify that **Add To Selection is selected if needed.**
  - To erase portions of the present alteration, choose **Subtract From Selection and apply paint to the picture.**
  - Choose **New Selection**, pick a preset from the pop-up box, and then paint in the picture to make a new kind of correction.
  - Select **Refine Edges in the menu bar,** make any necessary adjustments in the dialog box, and then click **OK to smooth the selection's edges.**
- (Optional) If you have more than one adjustment, choose the adjustment you wish to change, add to, or subtract from by doing one of the following:
  - Press **a pin.**
  - Select **the modification from the menu at the bottom by right-clicking on the image.**

Modify Smart Brush tool correction settings

- **Take any of the subsequent actions:**
  - You can pick Change Adjustment Settings by **right-clicking on a pin or an active selection in the image.**
  - To access the particular adjustment layer, double-click **its layer thumbnail in the Layers panel.**
  - Tap **a pin twice.**
- Modify the configurations in the window and then select **OK.**

With Photoshop Elements, you can use the Smart Brush and Detail Smart Brush tools to perform a wide range of preset modifications. From the predefined pop-up window in the options bar, you select an adjustment. The Smart Brush predefined pop-up window can be customized, just like any other pop-up panel. To see the changes as a list or as thumbnails, use the panel menu. To make the picker float in the workspace where you want it, you may also drag it out of the menu bar. You can view all adjustments or just certain groups of changes by selecting from a menu located in the panel's upper-left corner. The changes include fixes and tone tweaks.

The Clone Stamp Tool

You can paint over things in your photo, eliminate image flaws, and replicate objects with the Clone Stamp tool, which uses an image sample as a paintbrush. Additionally, you can copy specific areas of one image to another.

- Press **S** to activate the Clone Stamp tool in Advanced mode, or choose **it from the toolbox's Enhance section.**

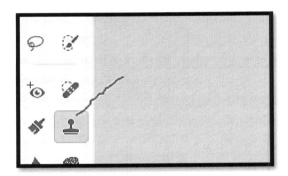

- **(Optional) Configure the options bar as follows:**

  - **Brush** configures the brush tip. Choose **a brush thumbnail by clicking the arrow close to the brush sample, and then pick a brush type from the Brushes pop-up menu.**
  - **Sample All Layers**   Choose Sample All Layers to sample (copy) data from every layer that is displayed. Deselect this option if you want to sample data from just the active layer.
  - **Size** configures the size of the brush in pixels. Move the Size slider, or insert a size in the text box.

- Opacity determines how opaque the paint you spread is. Paint stroke opacity can be reduced to reveal pixels beneath the stroke. You can input an opacity value or drag the slider.
- The mode determines how the pattern or source integrates with the current pixel structure. The original pixels are covered over by new ones in normal mode.
- Aligned irrespective of how many times you pause and restart painting, adjust the sampled area with the pointer when you start painting. This is the option you use when you want to remove undesired portions of a scanned shot, like a rip in the skyline or a telephone line. Every time you stop and start painting again, the Clone Stamp tool adds the sampled area from the original sampling point if Aligned is not chosen. To apply several copies of the same picture to different sections of the exact same picture or to a different image, deselect this option.

- **Choose Clone Overlay, and then configure the subsequent choices;**

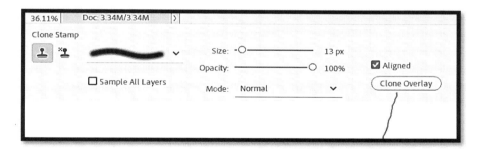

- **Show Overlay** To make the overlay visible inside the brush size, select Display Overlay.
- **Opacity** In the Opacity text box, type a percentage to adjust the overlay's opacity.
- **Clipped** Slide the Clipped option to enable overlay to the brush size.
- **Auto Hide** Click **Auto Hide** to have the overlay disappear while you work on the paint strokes.

- Point the cursor to the area of any open image that you wish to sample, then **click or press Alt (Option on Mac OS)**. As you paint, the tool replicates the pixels in your image at this sample location.
- **Take one of these actions:**

147

- o   To apply the tool's paint to the same image, **drag or click.**
- o   Use the tool to paint on the other specified image by **dragging or clicking.**

The Pattern Stamp Tool

Using the Pattern Stamp tool, you can create a design, or you can also use one of the pattern libraries to fill a selection or layer. You can choose from a variety of patterns in Photoshop Elements. You can design your own patterns to add personalization to your photos or to construct unique scrapbook pages. Created patterns can be stored in a library and subsequently loaded via the **Preset Manager or the Pattern pop-up panel** that shows up in the **Tool Options bar of the Paint Bucket and Pattern Stamp tools**. You may quickly utilize a pattern in several photographs by saving it.

Make use of the Pattern Stamp tool

Using your picture, a different one, or a predefined pattern, you can paint with the Pattern Stamp tool.

- ●   Choose the Pattern Stamp tool from the toolbox's Enhance section. (If it isn't visible in the toolbox, choose the **Clone Stamp tool and then click the Tool Options bar's Pattern Stamp tool icon.)**

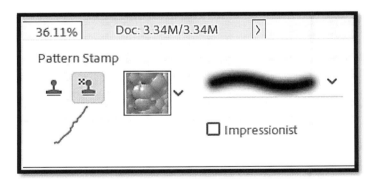

- ●   Within the Pattern pop-up panel located on the Tool Options bar, select **a pattern.** Choose **a library name from the panel option or select Load Patterns**, and then navigate to the library's folder to load more pattern libraries. Additionally, you can create your own pattern.

148

- To paint, drag **the Pattern Stamp tool** within the image after adjusting its settings in the Tool Options box. **Any of the subsequent Pattern Stamp tool settings can be specified:**

  - **Brush** configures the brush tip. Select a brush thumbnail by clicking the arrow close to the brush sample, followed by selecting a brush group from the Brush drop-down.
  - **Impressionists** uses paint daubs to apply the pattern, giving it an impressionistic look.
  - **The size** determines the brush's pixel size. You can enter a size in the text box or drag the Size slider.
  - **Opacity** determines the pattern's opacity when applied. A pattern stroke's underlying pixels can be seen when the opacity is set low. You can input an opacity value or drag the slider.
  - **Aligned** reproduces the pattern in a continuous, consistent way. From one paint stroke to the next, the pattern is in alignment. Every time you pause and resume painting, the pattern revolves on the pointer if Aligned is deselected.

Blur, Smudge, and Sharpen

The Blur Tool

By omitting details, the Blur tool softens sharp edges or portions of an image. Adding some blur to a cluttered background will help focus your subject more. Blur filters are another tool that you can utilize for this.

- Navigate to **Advanced mode;** choose **the Blur tool f**rom the section containing Enhance or you can choose to **Press R.**
- **Configure options in the options bar;**

  - **Mode** describes how the pixels you blur will mix together with the surrounding pixels in the picture.
  - **Brush**   The brush tip can be adjusted via the brush pop-up menu. To access additional brush shapes, navigate to the Brush drop-down menu within the pop-up window and choose a brush thumbnail.
  - **The size** determines the brush's pixel size. You can type in a measurement in the text box or drag the Size slider.

o **Sample All Layers** blurs every observable layer. Merely the active layer is blurred by the tool if this option is deselected.

- Move over the aspect of the image you would like to blur.

Blur filters

Gaussian Blur

A selection is rapidly blurred by a configurable amount using the Gaussian Blur filter. The term "Gaussian" describes the bell-shaped curve that Photoshop Elements produces after a weighted average is applied to the pixels. In addition to adding low-frequency detail, the Gaussian Blur filter can provide a hazy look. To control how far the filter looks for dissimilar pixels to blur, you can choose the blur radius in the filter parameters.

Lens Blur

You can utilize lens blur to create the illusion of a smaller depth of field, keeping some things in focus while blurring others in the picture. The image's focus and blurry areas are determined by the layer mask, stored selection, or transparency settings that are used. The iris shape you select determines how the blur manifests itself. The quantity of blades within an iris determines its shape. It is possible to rotate or curve the iris blades to make them more circular. Utilize the preview settings to observe how your photo is affected by adjusting the Lens Blur dialog's settings.

Radial Blur

The Radial Blur effect creates a gentle blur by getting to mimic the blur of a revolving or zooming camera. The amount of blur is adjusted using the Amount option. You can adjust the degree of rotation while spin blurs along concentric circular lines. You can set a number from 1 to 100 and zoom blurs along radial lines as if you were zooming in or out of the image. When it comes to smoother outcomes, blur quality varies from Draft (quick but grainy) to Good and Best (smooth but indistinguishable with the exception of a big selection). To set the blur's origin, drag the pattern inside the Blur Center box.

Smart Blur

With the Smart Blur filter, an image is exactly blurred. You can set the blur quality, threshold, and radius to control how far the filter looks for dissimilar pixels to blur. The threshold determines how different the pixels' values must be prior to them being deleted. Additionally, you can select a mode (Normal) for the complete selection or (Edge Only and Overlay Edge) for the edges of color transitions. Overlay Edge applies white and Edge only adds black-and-white edges when there is a strong contrast.

Surface Blur

An image is blurred with the Surface Blur filter, leaving the edges intact. This filter works well for eliminating graininess and noise while producing interesting effects. The size of the area sampled for the blur is specified by the Radius parameter. The degree to which the tonal values of nearby pixels must deviate from the value of the center pixel before they are included in the blur is determined by the Threshold option. The blur does not apply to pixels whose tonal value disparities are greater than the threshold value.

The Smudge Tool

The Smudge tool mimics the feeling of running a finger over paint that has been dampened. Where the stroke starts, the tool detects it and pushes the color in the direction you drag. You can smear the foreground color onto the image or distort the colors that are already present.

- Choose the **Smudge tool from the toolbox's Enhance section.** (If it is not visible in the toolbox, choose the **Blur or Sharpen tool, and then from the Tool Options bar, select the Smudge tool icon.)**
- To blur color, select an option in the Tool Options box and **drag it inside the image.**

You can choose to indicate the subsequent Smudge tool options;

- o **Strength** configures the amount of the smudge effect.
- o **Sample All Layers** Smudges with color from every layer that is visible. Only the colors from the active layer are used by the smudge tool if this option is deselected.

     o **Finger Painting** smears the color of the foreground at the start of every stroke. The smudge tool utilizes the color beneath the cursor at the start of each stroke if this choice is deselected.

The Sharpen Tool

To improve clarity or focus, use the Sharpen tool to focus on soft edges in a shot. A photo that has been oversharpened seems grainy. If you set the Strength value in the settings bar lower, you can prevent oversharpening. Initially, the sharpening should be kept mild and increased as needed by dragging over the area multiple times, each time increasing the sharpness. However, take note that the sharpening parameters in the Adjust Sharpness window are not accessible using the Sharpen tool or Auto Sharpen. The degree of sharpening that happens in shadow and highlight regions can be adjusted, as can the sharpening algorithm.

- Choose the **Sharpen tool.**
- Configure **your preferred choices in the options bar.**
- Move over the aspect of the picture you would like to have sharpened.

Precisely sharpen a picture

- Select **Enhance > Modify Sharpness.**
- Check the Preview box.
- To sharpen your image, select **any of the following settings, and then click OK.**
    - o **Amount** determines the degree of sharpness. To adjust the contrast between the border pixels and make the image appear sharper, type a value into the box or move the slider.
    - o **Radius** counts the number of pixels that surround the edge pixels that are sharpened. To modify the radius value, either type a number into the box or move the slider. Sharpening becomes more noticeable as the radius increases.
    - o **Remove** determines the algorithm that is used to sharpen the picture. The Unsharp Mask filter employs a technique known as Gaussian blur. Lens blur reduces sharpening halos and sharpens details more precisely by identifying edges and details in an image. Motion Blur works to lessen the blurry effects caused by moving subjects or cameras. Pick a blur choice from the selection that pops up.

○ **Angle** determines the motion direction for the Remove control's Motion Blur feature. To adjust the angle percentage to the left (counterclockwise) or right (clockwise), type a value in the box or slide the angle dial.

Unsharp Mask Filter

Sharpening edges in an image using a conventional film approach is replicated by the Unsharp Mask filter. Blur that is introduced during photography, scanning, resampling, or printing is corrected with the Unsharp Mask filter. It is helpful for photos that are meant to be viewed both online and in print. By using a threshold you choose, Unsharp Mask finds pixels that are different from surrounding pixels and raises the contrast of those pixels by the amount you provide. Lighter pixels get lighter and darker pixels get darker when they are adjacent within the given radius. On-screen, the Unsharp Mask filter's effects are noticeably more noticeable than in high-resolution published results. Try different parameters until you find the ones that work best for your picture if the printed output is the end destination.

- Choose **either a picture,** layer, or area in the **Edit workspace.**
- Select **Unsharp Mask from the Enhance section.**
- Choose the **Preview menu.**
- **Click on OK after you have been able to configure any of the following choices;**

○ **Amount** decides the amount of pixel contrast to be increased. In general, a number between 150% and 200% works best for printed high-resolution photos.

○ **Radius Indicates** how many pixels should be sharpened around the edges. Rounded corners, often between 1 and 2, are advised for high-resolution photos. A larger value sharpens a wider band of pixels, while a lower value simply sharpens the edges. A 2-pixel radius in a high-resolution printed picture indicates a smaller region, so this effect is considerably less obvious in print than on-screen.

○ **The threshold** establishes the minimum distance that distinct pixels must have from the surrounding region in order to be classified as border pixels and sharpened. Experiment with Threshold settings between 2 and 20 to avoid adding noise (in photographs with flesh tones, for example). All of the image's pixels are sharpened by the standard Threshold value of (0).

The Sponge, Dodge, and Burn Tools

The Sponge Tool

The sponge tool alters the color saturation of a particular place.

- Choose the **Sponge tool.**
- Configure **tool choices in the options bar;**

  - **Mode** raises or lowers the saturation of color. To increase the saturation of the color, select Saturate. Saturate boosts contrast in grayscale. To lessen the saturation of the color, select Desaturate. The desaturate function in grayscale reduces contrast.
  - **Flow** determines how quickly saturation changes. You can either input a number in the text box or drag the Flow pop-up slider.

- Move over the aspect of the picture you would like to alter.

The Dodge Tool

The image's darker and lighter parts can be adjusted with the Dodge and Burn tools. To bring out details in highlights and shadows, respectively, you can utilize the Dodge and Burn tools.

- Choose the **Dodge tool or the Burn tool**. You can look for the sponge tool if you are unable to locate these tools.
- **Configure tool choices in the options bar;**

  - **Range**: defines the tonal range of the image that the tool will work with. To adjust the midrange of grayscale, select Midtones; to adjust the dark sections, select **Shadows; and to adjust the light areas**, select **Highlights.**
  - **Exposure**: determines the tool's effect for each stroke. An elevated proportion amplifies the impact.
  - **Instructions:** Adjust the tool to a low exposure value and drag it multiple times over the region you wish to fix in order to dodge or burn it gradually.

- Move **over the aspect of the picture you would like to alter.**

The Brush Tools

Color can be applied in delicate or strong strokes with the Brush tool. It can be used to mimic airbrushing methods. (If it's not visible in the toolbox, choose the Color Replacement or Impressionist Brush tools, and then choose the Brush tool symbol in the Tool Options bar.)

- To paint a particular hue, first **set the foreground color.**
- Choose **the Brush tool** from the toolbox's Draw section.
- To paint, drag **the Brush tool within** the image after setting up the tool's parameters as needed in the Tool Options box.

You can choose to indicate any of the subsequent Brush tool choices;

- **Airbrush Mode** makes airbrushing possible. This option simulates classic airbrush techniques by adding progressive tones to an image.
- **Opacity** determines how opaque the paint you spray is. Paint stroke opacity can be reduced to reveal pixels beneath the stroke. You can input an opacity value or drag the slider.
- **Mode** describes how the paint you apply melds with the picture's existing pixels.
- **Tablet Choices if** you're using a pressure-sensitive drawing pad in place of a mouse, this setting configures the choices to be controlled with your stylus.

The impressionist Brush

The Impressionist Brush tool modifies the image's current colors and details to give the impression that it was painted with stylized brushstrokes. You may mimic the textures linked to painting in many artistic styles by playing with various styles, area sizes, and tolerance parameters.

- Choose the **Impressionist Brush tool** from the Tool Options bar while the Brush tool is chosen in the toolbox.
- To paint a picture, drag **a selection inside the Tool choices bar after setting the desired choices.**

    - **Mode** describes how the paint you apply integrates with the picture's existing pixels.

o **Advanced**   The brush stroke's shape is influenced by style. The brush stroke's size is controlled by area. There are more strokes when the area value is higher. Tolerance determines the minimum degree of color value similarity between neighboring pixels before the brush stroke affects them.

Brush Settings and options

By adjusting the rate at which the brush tool strokes fade off, you can replicate real brush strokes. You can choose which parameters, such as size, color, and dispersion, alter dynamically throughout a brush stroke. As you modify the brush dynamics settings, the brush changes are reflected in the brush icon in the Tool Options bar. After choosing a brush tool, choose Brush Settings (or Advanced, depending on the tool) from the Tool Options menu to adjust the brush dynamics.

- **Spacing** regulates the space between a brushstroke's brush markings. You can use the slider to input a value that is a % of the brush diameter or type a number to adjust the spacing. (Your changes to spacing are dynamically reflected in the brush icon in the Tool Options bar.)
- **Fade** determines how many steps need to be taken before the paint flow disappears. A paint stroke that has a low value will soon fade away, but a value of 0 has no fading effect. One mark on the brush tip corresponds to each phase. The range of possible values is 0 to 9999. For instance, if you enter 10 for Fade, it will fade in steps of 10. You might want to set a value of 25 or more for smaller brushes. In case the strokes disappear too soon, raise the values.
- **Hue Jitter** determines how quickly the stroke color changes from the background to the foreground. Switching between the two hues occurs more frequently at higher values than at lower ones.
- **Hardness** determines how big the hard center of the brush is. Enter a value as a percentage of the brush diameter by typing a number or by dragging a slider.
- **Scatter:** The distribution of brush marks inside a stroke is determined by brush dispersion. Higher numbers expand the scattering region, whereas lower values result in a denser stroke with less paint scattering.
- **Angle** describes the angle at which the long axis of an elliptical brush is offset from the horizontal. To indicate the desired angle, either type a number in degrees or drag the angle icon's arrowhead.

- **Roundness** describes the proportion of the brush's long to short axes. You can either move a dot in the angle symbol toward or away from the arrow, or you can enter a percentage. A circular brush has a value of 100%, a linear brush has a value of 0%, and elliptical brushes have an intermediate value.
- **Set this as a default this** option allows you to set the parameters that are now selected as your default settings. It is accessible for several tools that can have brush properties.

Adding a new brush to the brush library

- Choose the **Brush tool from the toolbox's Draw section.**
- Select the **arrow close to the Brush pop-up in the Tools Options bar to bring up the pop-up panel. From the Brush drop-down, select a category, and then pick a brush to edit.**
- To edit the original brush, click **Brush Settings** and move the sliders around.
- Choose the pop-up menu in the Brush pop-up window, then select **Save Brush.**
- Insert a name in the dialog box for Brush name and then select **OK**.
- If you would like to have a view of the updated set of brushes, re-launch Photoshop Elements.

Delete a brush

- Choose the **Brush tool from the toolbox's Draw section.**
- In the Tool Options bar, click **the arrow close to the brush sample to bring up the brush pop-up window.**
- **Take one of these actions:**
  - To erase a brush, click **it after changing the pointer to scissors by pressing the Alt key (or the Option key on a Mac OS computer).**
  - Select **Delete Brush** from the panel option after selecting the brush in the pop-up panel.
  - Pick Brushes from the **Preset Type list**, pick the brush from the available choices in the dialog box, and then click **Delete after selecting Preset Manager from the panel menu.**
- To have a brush saved, choose **Save Brush** from the click pop-up menu in the Brush pop-up.
- In the Brush Name dialog box, type a name and select **OK.**
- To view the updated brush set, restart **Photoshop Elements.**

Create a custom brush shape from a picture

To make a custom brush, choose a portion of a picture. The brush applies the foreground color to your image by using a grayscale version of that selection. For instance, you may paint a leaf in a fall hue after choosing it. With the Brush tool, you may also create a new brush shape. You can use a selection of the full layer to make a custom brush shape. The maximum size of a custom brush shape is 2500 pixels by 2500 pixels.

- **Take one of these actions:**

  - o Choose **a portion of the image to use as a custom brush**.
  - o Deselect everything to utilize the layer as a custom brush.
  - o Draw and choose **the brush with the use of the painting tools**. To create soft-edge effects, you can use either hard-edged or soft-edged strokes, or change the opacity of the strokes.
- Click on **Edit > Brush from Selection.**
- Give the brush a name then choose **OK.**

Tablet Settings

The majority of pressure-sensitive digitizing tablets, including Wacom tablets, are compatible with Photoshop Elements. Once your tablet's software control panel is installed, you can adjust the brush tool's attributes according to the selected tablet options and the pressure you put on your stylus.

- To control the Brush tool with pen pressure, select **it from the toolbox and then adjust the tablet settings in the Tool Options bar.**

To switch between mouse and pen mode;

- Choose **Wacom Tablet Properties after you have clicked on Start.**
- Make a choice of your preferred mode you would like to switch to.

The Eraser tool

The Eraser tool modifies the image's pixels by dragging over them. Erased pixels become transparent unless you're working in a layer with locked transparency or in the backdrop layer, in which case they change to the color of the backdrop. The transparency grid indicates pixels that are transparent.

- Choose the **Eraser tool from the toolbox's Draw section**. (If it isn't visible in the toolbox, choose the Magic Eraser or Background Eraser tool and then click the Tool Options bar's Eraser tool icon.)
- After adjusting the **Tool Options bar as needed, drag the cursor over the region you wish to remove**. Any of the subsequent Eraser tool parameters can be specified:
  - **Opacity**: specifies the erasure's strength. Pixels that are completely transparent on a layer and the background color of the Background layer are erased when the opacity of a layer is 100%. A reduced opacity paints a portion of the background color on the Background layer and erases pixels to limited transparency on a layer. (The Opacity option is unavailable if Block mode is used in the Tool Options box.)
  - **Type:** Brush mode allows you to generate soft-edged erasures by utilizing the brush tool's properties. Hard-edge erasures similar to a pencil are made in pencil mode. A 16-pixel square with a sharp edge serves as the eraser in block mode.

The Background Eraser Tool

Using the Background Eraser tool, you may quickly erase an object from its background by converting color pixels to transparent pixels. You can remove background fringe pixels while keeping the foreground object's boundaries with careful application. The tool's hotspot is shown by the tool pointer, which is a circle with a crosshair. Pixels inside the circle and with a color value equal to the pixel beneath the hotspot are deleted when you drag the cursor over them. The foreground item won't be erased if the circle overlaps it and doesn't contain any pixels that are comparable to the hotspot pixel.

- Choose **the layer that has the regions** you wish to remove from the Layers panel.
- Choose the **Background Eraser tool from the toolbox's Draw section**. (If it isn't visible in the toolbox, choose **the Magic Eraser or Eraser tool and then click the Tool Options bar's Background Eraser tool icon.)**
- After adjusting the Tool Options bar as needed, drag the cursor over the region you wish to remove. Don't aim to remove any regions with the tool's hotspot on

them. **Any of the subsequent Background Eraser tool parameters can be specified:**

- o **Size** pixel width of the brush.
- o **Tolerance** specifies the minimum color similarity between a pixel and the hotspot for the tool to have an effect on it. Erasure is restricted to regions that closely resemble the hotspot color when the tolerance is low. More colors are erased with a high tolerance.
- o **Brush Settings** defines the brush's settings, including diameter, hardness, spacing, and size. Either drag the Size sliders or type numbers into the text fields.
- o **Limits** To remove regions that have the hotspot color and are related to one another, select Contiguous. Any pixels inside the circle that resemble the color of the hotspot are erased by discontiguous.

The Magic Eraser tool

Using the Magic Eraser tool, all comparable pixels are altered when you drag them within a picture. The pixels become the color of the backdrop when working in a layer that has locked transparency; otherwise, they are erased to transparency. On the current layer, you have the option to remove all comparable pixels or just contiguous pixels.

- Choose the layer that has the area you would like to erase. When you choose a Background, it instantly becomes a layer anytime you make use of the Magic Eraser.
- Choose the **Magic Eraser tool from the toolbox by going to the Draw section**. (If it's not visible in the toolbox, choose the **Eraser or Background Eraser tool, and then click the Tool Options bar's Magic Eraser tool icon.)**
- **After adjusting the Tool Options bar as needed, click the layer's desired erasure region. Any of the subsequent Magic Eraser tool parameters can be adjusted:**
  - o **Tolerance**: specifies the color spectrum that will be removed. Pixels that are close in appearance to the pixel you select are erased when the tolerance is low. Pixels within a wider range are erased by a high tolerance.
  - o **Opacity**: specifies the erasure's strength. Pixels that are completely transparent on a layer and the background color of a locked layer are

erased when the opacity is 100%. On a locked layer, a lower opacity paints partly with the background color and erases pixels to limited transparency.

- o **Continuous**: Only the pixels that are next to the one you clicked are erased. To remove all pixels in the image that are similar, deselect this option.
- o **Anti-aliasing**: makes the area you're erasing appear more natural by smoothing its edges.

The Paint Bucket (Fill) Tool

When you click on pixels, the Paint Bucket tool fills in an area with a color value close to those pixels. A region can be filled with a pattern or the foreground color.

- Pick a color for the foreground.
- From the toolbox, pick the **Paint Bucket tool.**

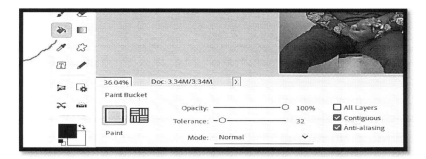

- Once the required settings have been made in the Tool Options menu, click **the area of the image that you wish to fill.**

You can also choose to make an indication of any of the following Paint Bucket tool choices;

- **Paint / Pattern** specify whether to use a pattern design (Pattern) or a foreground color (Paint) as the fill.
- **Opacity** determines how opaque the paint you apply is. Paint stroke opacity can be reduced to reveal pixels beneath the stroke. You can input an opacity value or drag the slider.
- **Tolerance** specifies the minimum degree of color similarity that filled pixels must have: high tolerance fills pixels with a wider variety of colors, while low tolerance fills pixels with color values that are extremely similar to the pixel you clicked.

- **Contiguous fills** neighboring pixels with comparable colors. To fill all identical pixels in the image—even ones that aren't touching—deselect this option. How comparable the colors must be is specified by the Tolerance parameter.

Fill a layer with a color or pattern

Rather than using a brush tool to apply a fill or pattern to your image, you can use a fill layer. You can modify the fill layer's mask to restrict the gradient to a specific area of your image, as well as the fill and pattern settings, to give yourself more versatility.

- Choose **a color for the background or foreground.**

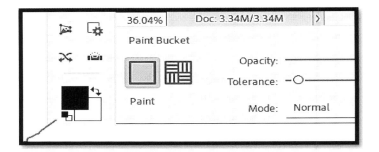

- Decide which space you wish to fill. In the Layers panel, select **the layer you want to fill in its entirety.**
- Select either **Edit > Fill Selection or Edit > Fill Layer.**

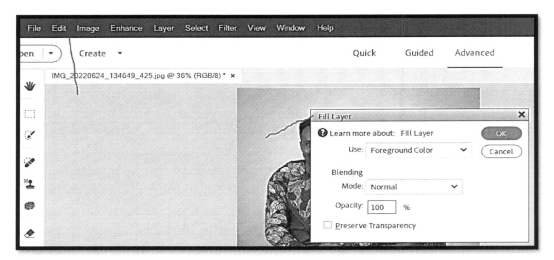

162

- Click **OK** after making your selections in the Fill dialog box.

  - ○ **Contents** Select a hue from the Utilize menu. Choose Color, and then use the Color Picker to choose a new color. Select Pattern to apply a pattern.
  - ○ **Custom Pattern** If you select Pattern from the Use option, this will indicate the pattern to be used. You have the option of making your own patterns or using ones from the pattern libraries.

The Gradient Tool

You can use the Gradient tool to choose an area and drag it within the image to fill it with a gradient. Both the gradient type and the distance between the beginning and finishing points—where you first push the mouse button and let go of it—affect how the gradient looks.

Go ahead to make a choice of any of the following gradient types in the Tool Options bar;

- **Linear gradient: a straight** line of shades connecting the beginning and ending points.
- **Radial gradient**: shades in a circular pattern from the beginning to the final area.
- **Angle gradient**: Colors in a counterclockwise circular motion surrounding the origin.
- **Reflected gradient**: shades with linear gradients that are symmetrical on both sides of the initial point.
- **Diamond gradient:** shades in the shape of a diamond that extends outward from the beginning. One of the diamond's corners is defined by the terminating point.

Libraries contain gradients. By clicking the menu and choosing a library at the bottom of the list, you can change which gradient library is displayed in the Gradient Picker menu. This option also allows you to save and load gradient libraries of your own. Gradients can also be managed with the Preset Manager.

Apply a gradient

- Use one of the selection tools to select the area you want to fill with the picture. If not, the entire active layer is filled with the gradient.
- Choose **the tool with a gradient.**

- To select the preferred gradient type, click the **Tool Options bar.**
- Using the Gradient Picker panel located in the Tool Options bar, select **a gradient fill.**
- (Optional) Using the **Tool choices bar, adjust the gradient choices.**
- Place the cursor where you want the gradient to begin in the image, then drag to specify the gradient's end. While dragging, keep Shift depressed to limit the gradient angle to a multiple of 45°.

Apply a gradient fill to the text

- Choose **the text that you like to fill in.**
- Select **Layer > Simplify Laye**r to create a bitmap image from the vector text. After you simplify the layer, you will not be able to change the text.
- To select the text, **Control-click (Command-click on Mac OS) the text layer's thumbnail in the Layers panel.**
- Get the **Gradient tool selected.**
- To select the preferred gradient type, click the **Tool Options bar.**
- From the Gradient Picker panel, select **a gradient fill.**
- To define the gradient's beginning and ending points, place **the pointer where you want them to be on the text and drag.**

Define a gradient

A gradient can be constructed by adding a color stop, dragging the color stop and the midpoint icon to establish the range between two colors, and adjusting the Opacity stops to the desired transparency.

- Choose the **Gradient tool from the Toolbox's Draw section**.
- Click the **Edit button** beneath the gradient sample to open the **Gradient Editor Dialog box.**
- Choose **a gradient** to serve as the foundation for your new gradient in the Gradient Editor Dialog box's Preset section.
- Double-click **the color stop** to select colors for your gradient, or click the color swatch to bring up the Color Picker. After selecting a color, click **OK.**

- Drag **a color's stop point left or right to change its placement.**
- Click **to define a new color and stop** beneath the gradient bar to add a new color to the gradient.
- Drag **the diamond beneath the gradient bar** to the left or right to change the position of the color transition midpoint.
- Click **Delete** to remove the color stops that you are altering.
- You can either drag the slider or input a percentage in the Smoothness text box to adjust the smoothness of the color transition.
- Drag the **Opacity stops** to adjust the gradient's transparency levels if desired.
- Give the new gradient a name, click **Add to preset,** and the gradient will be saved in the gradient presets.
- Press **OK.** The freshly made gradient has been chosen and is prepared for usage.

Specify gradient transparency

Every gradient fill has settings (also known as opacity stops) that regulate the fill's opacity at various gradient points. The gradient preview's transparency is shown by the checkerboard pattern. There must be two opacity stops in a gradient.

- Make a gradient.
- Select the left opacity stop above the gradient bar to change the gradient editor's initial opacity. When you edit the initial transparency, the triangle beneath the stop becomes black.
- **One of the subsequent actions will set the opacity:**
  - Enter a number between 100% (totally opaque) and 0% (completely transparent).
  - Using the Opacity slider, drag **the arrow**.
- Choose the right transparency stop over the gradient bar to change the endpoint's opacity. Next, modify the opacity as indicated in step 3.
- **One of the following actions can be used to change where the beginning or ending opacity is located:**
  - To move the matching opacity stop left or right, and drag it.
  - After choosing the matching opacity stop, enter a value in the Location field.
- **One of the following can be used to change where the midpoint opacity—the point halfway between the beginning and ending opacities—is located:**

- o Move the diamond to the left or right by dragging it above the gradient bar.
- o After choosing the diamond, type a value for Location.
- Click **Delete or drag the opacity stop** you are working on away from the gradient bar to remove it.
- Select **atop the gradient bar** to set a new opacity stop in order to add an intermediate opacity. After there, you can change and modify this opacity just like you would a beginning or ending opacity. You can either pick the stop and press the **Delete button** to get rid of an intermediate opacity, or you can drag its transparency stop up and off the gradient bar.
- Click **New** after entering a new name in the Name text box to save the gradient to the gradient presets. With the transparency level you choose, this generates a brand-new gradient preset.
- To choose the recently created gradient and close the dialog box, click **OK. Verify that in the Tool Options bar, Transparency is chosen.**

The Shape Selection Tools

To choose forms with just one click, utilize the Shape Selection tool. The Shape Selection tool will no longer choose a shape if you simplify the shape layer to turn it into a bitmap element; instead, utilize the Move tool. The Move tool can be used to relocate all of the shapes in a layer together if there are several shapes present. But you have to utilize the form Selection tool if you want to move a particular form within a layer.

- To choose shapes, employ the **Shape Selection tool.**
- Click the **shape to select it.**
- Drag **the shape to a new area to reposition it.**

Transform a shape

- Once you have chosen the **Shape Selection tool, choose the Show Bounding Box choice.**
- **Take one of these actions:**
  - To change a shape, click **on it, and then move an anchor to make the desired changes.**
  - After selecting the desired shape to modify, select **Image > Transform Shape and then select a transformation command.**

The Rectangle Tool, Ellipse Tool, and Rounded Rectangle Tool

Shapes in Photoshop Elements are vector graphics, meaning that rather than being composed of pixels, they are composed of lines and curves that are determined by their geometric properties. Because vector graphics are resolution-independent, they may be reproduced at any resolution and scaled to any size without sacrificing clarity or detail. They can be altered, resized, or moved without compromising the visual quality. Vector data is seen on the screen as pixels because computer monitors show images on a pixel grid.

Drawing a rectangle, square, or rounded rectangle

- Choose **between the Rounded Rectangle tool or the Rectangle tool.** Additionally, you can use the Tool Options bar to choose between the Rectangle and Rounded Rectangle tools.
- You can choose to configure the subsequent options in the Tool Options bar;

  - **Unconstrained** by dragging you will be able to configure the breadth and the height of a rectangle.
  - **Square** helps to have a square and rectangle constrained.
  - **Fixed Size** creates a rectangle with the precise dimensions you entered in the text boxes for the width and height.
  - **Proportional** creates a rectangle proportionate to the given parameters for Width and Height.
  - **From Center** draws a rectangle starting in the middle of the drawing area. Normally, a rectangle is created starting in the upper-left corner.
  - **Snap** snaps a rectangle's edges to its pixel boundary.
  - **Simplify** creates a raster graphic from the drawn shape. When a shape is transformed to raster form, it may appear pixelated and have jagged edges when it is shrunk or expanded.

- Move right within your picture to have the shape drawn.

Ellipse Tool

- Choose the **Ellipse tool right within the Edit workspace.**

- **You can get to configure the following options in the Tool Options bar;**

  - **Unconstrained** allows you to drag to adjust an ellipse's width and height.
  - **Fixed Size** creates an ellipse with the precise dimensions you entered in the text boxes for the width and height.
  - **Proportional** depending on the values that you enter in the height and width text fields, it draws a proportionate ellipse.
  - **Simplify** creates a raster graphic from the drawn shape. When a shape is transformed to raster form, it may appear pixelated and have jagged edges when it is shrunk or expanded.

- Move in your picture to create the ellipse.

The Polygon Tool

- Choose **the Polygon or the Star tool.**
- Configure the following options in the Tool Options bar;

  - **Smooth Corners** ensure that a polygon has smooth corners.
  - **Indent Sides By**   Indicates the extent of the indentations made by the star. This feature is exclusive to the Star tool.
  - **Smooth Indents** produces a polygon with a star form and smooth indents. This feature is exclusive to the Star tool.
  - **Simplify** creates a raster graphic from the drawn shape. When a shape is transformed to raster form, it may appear pixelated and have jagged edges when it is shrunk or expanded.

- Give a specific number of sides for the polygon in the Sides box.
- Move right within your picture to create the polygon of your choice.

The Line Tool

- Choose the **Line tool.**
- **Get to configure the following in the Tool Options bar;**

  - **The Arrowhead** creates an arrow-headed line. Choose At the Start, At the End, or At Both Ends to indicate which end the arrows are rendered on.

- Concavity specifies the degree of curvature at the arrowhead's widest point, the point where it hits the line. For the arrowhead's concavity, enter a value between −50% and +50%.
- Simplify creates a raster graphic from the drawn shape. When a shape is transformed to raster form, it may appear pixelated and have jagged edges when it is shrunk or expanded.

- Indicate the width of the line in pixels in the Width box.
- To create a line, move within your picture.

Typing Tools

An image can have text and shapes added to it in many colors, styles, and effects. To create and modify text, employ the Horizontal Type and Vertical Type tools. You can write paragraphs or just one line of text. To generate and modify text, employ the Horizontal Type () and Vertical Type () tools. A fresh text layer is created as you type new text. You can write paragraphs or just one line of text. When you enter single-line text, each line is independent of the next; as you modify it, a line's length increases or decreases but does not wrap to the following line. Press Enter to start a fresh line of text. The text of a paragraph is contained inside the borders you designate. A type tool enters edit mode when you click inside a picture, allowing you to enter and modify text. Choosing commands from the menu is only one of the operations you cannot do until you commit modifications to the type. When you see the Confirm and Reject buttons below the text, the Type tool is in edit mode.

Add text

- Choose either **the Vertical Type tool or the Horizontal Type tool from the toolbar.**

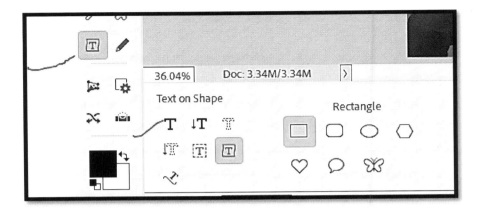

- **Take one of these actions:**

    - Tap **in the image** to set the type's insertion point in order to generate a single line of text.
    - Drag a rectangle to establish a textbox for the type in order to generate paragraph text.

The type baseline is indicated by the thin line that passes through the I-beam. The baseline designates the line that the type rests on in horizontal type and the central axis of the characters in vertical type.

- In the tool options bar, choose **type options like font, style, size, and color.**

- Enter the desired characters. To add a new line if you didn't create a textbox, hit **Enter.** The text shows up as a separate layer. In Advanced mode, hit **F11 to see the layers.**
- **One of the following actions will commit the text layer:**
    - Select **"Commit"** from the menu.
    - On the numeric keypad, press **the Enter key.**
    - Click **outside of the textbox in the image.**

o   Choose **an alternative tool from the toolbox.**

Type tool options

Configure the subsequent Type tool options from the options bar:

o   **Font Family** Sets the font family for newly created or updated text.
o   **Font Style** Apply font styles to newly created or existing text, such as bold.
o   **The size of the Font** sets the font size for newly created or updated text.
o   **The palette menu** adds a color to newly entered or chosen text.
o   **Leading the menu** establishes the distance between lines of fresh or chosen content.
o   **Tracking a**djusts the spacing between characters in newly entered or chosen text.
o   **Faux bold** gives fresh or old text a bold appearance. If the Font Style menu does not offer a real bold style for your font, use this option.
o   **Faux Italic** gives fresh or existing text an italicized look. If the Font Style menu does not offer an oblique or true italic style for your font, use this option.
o   **Underline** gives a new text or a portion of an existing text underlining.
o   **Strikethrough** inserts a line through a portion of an existing text or fresh text.
o   **Text Alignment** Indicates the text alignment. Text can be aligned left, center, or right if it is horizontally oriented. Top, center, or bottom for text-oriented vertically.
o   **Text Orientation Toggle** converts text from vertical to horizontal and from horizontal to vertical.
o   **Text in warp** Text on the chosen layer is distorted.
o   **Anti-aliased** uses anti-aliasing to create a more fluid appearance for text.

Using the Text on the Shape tool

- Press and hold the **Text on the Shape tool**. Press **Option and pick the current tool to swiftly switch to the text tool.**
- Choose **the form that you wish to add text to from the ones that are available.** To build the shape, drag the pointer over the image.
- Hover **your mouse cursor** over the path until the cursor icon turns to text mode in order to add text to the image. Press **the pointer to include text**. Text can be altered in the same manner as regular text.

- Once you've added text, select **commit**. It is necessary to write the text in certain forms. **The text shows a small arrow that you may move about the path or inside/outside by holding down the Ctrl key while clicking and dragging the mouse.** The text route can go both inside and outside of an area, and you can **drag the cursor into the area you've chosen.**

Using the Text on Selection tool

On the path's outline that was generated from a selection, add text. A selection is transformed into a path where content can be typed when it is committed.

- To use the **Text on Selection tool, choose it.** Tap **Option and press the current tool to swiftly switch the text tool.**
- To make the selection you want, point the cursor to the object in the picture and drag it around. The Offset slider allows you to change the selection's size. The selection is transformed into a path once you confirm it.
- Hover the mouse pointer over the path when the cursor icon changes to text mode to add text to the image. Press **the pointer to include text.** Once the text has been added, it can be edited just like any other text.
- Once you've finished adding text, select **Commit.** To resume your workflow, select **Cancel.**

Using Text on Custom Path tool

You can create and include text along the custom path.

- Choose the **Text tool on Custom Path.** Click **Option and press the current tool to swiftly switch the text tool.**
- Over the picture, create **a custom route.** From the tool options bar, **you can commit or cancel the created path to redraw.**
- In the tool options box, select **Modify to fine-tune or redraw the path.** To change the path, use the nodes that show up on it.
- Once a path has been created, you may add text by **clicking anywhere along the path. Text can be altered in the same manner as regular text.**
- Choose **Commit** after you have added a text.

The Pencil Tool

Hard-edged freehand lines can be created with the use of the Pencil tool.

- To paint a particular hue, first **set the foreground color.**
- Choose **the Pencil tool** from the toolbox's Draw section.
- To paint, drag **the Pencil tool into the image after adjusting its settings in the Tool Options window.**

Click **an image starting point to create a straight line**. Next, choose an ending point while holding down Shift. **Any of the subsequent Pencil tool parameters can be specified:**

- **The brush tip** decides the tip. Select a brush thumbnail by clicking the arrow next to the brush sample, followed by selecting a brush category from the Brush drop-down.
- **Dimensions** determine the brush's pixel size. You can enter a size in the text box or drag the Size slider.
- **Opacity** determines how opaque the paint you apply is. Paint stroke opacity can be reduced to reveal pixels beneath the stroke. You can input an opacity value or drag the slider.
- **Mode** describes how the paint you apply melds with the picture's existing pixels.
- **Automatic Erasure** The tool paints with the foreground color when you start sketching and drags over a region devoid of the foreground color. In other words, it only paints the foreground color if we start with a color other than the foreground color. Pencil colors with the background color when you click and paint over regions that contain the foreground color.

The Crop Tool

The area of a picture surrounding the selection is eliminated using the Crop tool. Crop the image to eliminate unwanted background elements and highlight the desired object. By default, the resolution of an image stays the same when it is cropped.

- Start by choosing **the Crop tool.**

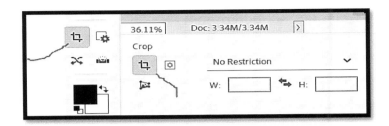

- Choose **an alternative crop ratio** from the list of options located on the left side of the Tool Options panel, or enter novel custom numbers in the Width and Height fields located in the options bar.

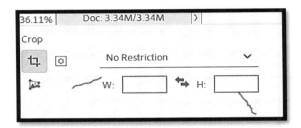

  - ○ **No Restrictions** enable you to resize the picture to any size.
  - ○ **Employ Photo Ratio** shows the photo's original aspect ratio after it is cropped. The values used for the cropped picture are displayed in the Width and Height boxes. You can adjust the image resolution using the Resolution field.

- Drag the desired portion of the image over. The crop marquee displays as a bounding box with controls at the corners and sides when you let go of the mouse button.
- **Alter the crop marquee by engaging in any of the subsequent choices;**
  - ○ Select **settings from the Tool Options panel's menu** on the left to alter the aspect ratio.
  - ○ The marquee can be moved with the arrow keys or **by placing the pointer within the bounding box and clicking and dragging.**
  - ○ Drag **a handle to change the marquee's size**. Holding Shift down while dragging a corner handle allows you to scale with proportions constraints when you select **No Restriction from the drop-down box.**
  - ○ Click the **Swap symbol in the options bar to switch the values for Width and Height.**

- Place the pointer outside the bounding box (it becomes a curved arrow) and drag it to rotate the marquee. (When an image is in Bitmap mode, the crop marquee cannot be rotated.)

Note: By adjusting the Crop tool options, you can alter the color and opacity of the crop shield—the cropped region that surrounds the image. To change the Color and Opacity values in the Crop Tool section of the Preferences dialog box, select **Edit > Preferences > Display & Cursors.** Deselect **Use Shield** if you would prefer not to see a colored shield when cropping.

- To complete the cropping, double-click **the bounding box or click the green Commit button in the marquee's lower-right corner.** Press **Esc or click the red Cancel icon to stop the cropping process.**

Crop to a selection boundary

The regions outside of the current selection are eliminated using the Crop tool. Photoshop Elements crops the image to the bounding box containing the selection when you crop to a selection boundary. (Selections with irregular shapes, such as those created using the Lasso tool, are cropped to fit inside a rectangular bounding box.) Photoshop Elements cropped the image by 50 pixels on each visible edge when you used the Crop command without first creating a selection.

- To choose the area of the image you want to save, use any selection tool, like the **Rectangular Marquee tool.**
- Choose **Crop > Image.**

Automatic cropping suggestions

One of the most important tools in the photo editing process is the Crop tool and technique. The Crop tool in Photoshop Elements 13 and later automatically presents four usable alternatives. Among these, you can select the ideal crop for your requirements. After choosing one of the four recommendations or ignoring them completely, you are free to crop as much as you like.

Using the automated cropping recommendations:

- Launch **Photoshop Elements and open a picture.**

- Click on **the Crop tool**. Within the Tool Options panel, four thumbnails representing the automated recommendations are available.
- Select **the thumbnail that appears to fit the best**. On the other hand, if you **choose a different aspect ratio from the Tool Options panel's drop-down list, you can view more options**.

Perspective Crop tool

When cropping an image, you can adjust its perspective with the use of the Perspective Crop tool. When you have a distorted image, this is helpful. When an object is photographed at an angle other than straight on or when a wide-angle lens is utilized to capture a significant portion of an object, distortion results. For instance, the edges of a tall structure appear closer together at the top than they do at the bottom when photographed from the ground.

- Open **Photoshop Elements and select an image**.
- Choose the **Perspective Crop tool in advanced mode from the toolbar's Modify section**.

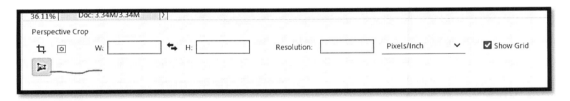

- To adjust the perspective of an object, create **a marquee or boundary around it, and then crop the image to fit within that area**.
- To change the marquee's shape, use the selection's corners. When the pointer turns white when you hover over a corner, clic**k to move it.**
- In the Tools Options panel, you **may also enter settings for the width (W), height (H), and Resolution fields. The finished image is resized to fit the given resolution, width, and height.**
- To **change the image's perspective and crop it to fit the marquee, click.**

The Cookie Cutter Tool

A photo can be cropped into any desired shape with the Cookie Cutter tool. To crop your photo into a certain form, select a shape and drag it over the image. To obtain the region you wish to crop, you can alternatively resize and shift the bounding box.

- Choose **the Crop tool when in the advanced mode**.
- In the Tool Options window, click the **Cookie Cutter symbol** and choose a shape. Choose an alternative library from the Shapes drop-down menu to view additional libraries.
- To choose a shape, **double-click on it.**
- To build the form border and transfer it to the desired spot inside the image, **drag it within the image.**
- For the cropping to be completed, choose the **Commit button or hit Enter. Press Esc or choose the Cancel button to stop the cropping process**.

The Perspective Tool

When cropping an image, you can adjust its perspective with the use of the Perspective Crop tool. When you have a distorted image, this is helpful. When an object is captured at an angle other than straight on or when a wide-angle lens is utilized to capture a significant portion of an object, distortion results. For instance, the edges of a tall structure appear closer together at the top than they do at the bottom when photographed from the ground.

- Open **Photoshop Elements and select an image**.
- Choose the **Perspective Crop tool in advanced mode from the toolbar's Modify section**.
- To adjust the perspective of an object, **create a marquee or boundary around it, and then crop the image to fit within that area.**
- To change the marquee's shape, use the selection's corners. When the pointer turns white when you hover over a corner, click **to move it.**
- In the Tools Options panel, you may also enter settings for the width (W), height (H), and Resolution fields. The finished image is resized to fit the given resolution, width, and height.
- To change the image's perspective and **crop it to fit the marquee, click.**

The Recompose Tool

The Recompose tool makes it easier to resize images intelligently without affecting key visual elements like people, buildings, animals, and more. When resizing an image, normal scaling transforms every pixel in the same way. Pixels in sections lacking significant visual content are impacted by recompose. You can upscale or downscale photographs with Recompose in order to adjust the orientation, fit a layout, or improve composition. Recompose lets you intelligently protect content while resizing images so that you may choose which sections to keep or eliminate. It is also possible to recompose without utilizing the safeguard regions feature. Drag the picture handles, for instance, to recompose a shot without designating any sections for removal or protection.

Recompose a photo in Guided mode

- To resize a photo, open it in the photo bin and choose the Guided option.
- Choose **Recompose under Special Edits > Guided.**

- Use the Protect brush to mark the areas that need to be protected. When you right-click on the image, you **can choose from the following modes**:
  - **Use Normal Highlight** Painting and this mode is comparable. List all the areas that need to be protected. For instance, painting or outlining the complete circle is necessary when using Normal Highlights to safeguard it.

178

- o **Use Quick Highlight**   It is possible to rapidly identify the areas that need to be protected. Around the topic to draw attention to the necessary areas. Trace the circle's perimeter, for instance, to emphasize the region inside the circle. The Quick Highlight feature makes sure that the circle's contents are designated as protected. The green places show the areas that are being marked for protection.
- Choose **Clear Protect Highlights** from the menu when you right-click the image to **remove portions of the undesired marked areas (green).**
- Using the eliminate brush tool, make a mark on the unimportant parts that you wish to eliminate. The locations designated for removal are shown in red.
- Choose **Clear Remove Highlights** from the menu when you right-click the image to remove portions of the undesired marked areas (red).
- To recompose your photo, drag **the image handles or choose a size from the Preset drop-down menu.**

Recompose a picture in advanced mode

- To resize an image, open it in the photo bin, choose Image > Recompose, or use the Recompose tool.
- **Use the Protect brush to mark the areas that need to be protected. When you right-click on the image, you can choose from the following modes:**
  - o Employ standard highlight
  - o Apply Fast Highlighting
- **To remove portions of the undesired marked regions (green), do one of the following:**
- Use the **Eraser tool to erase**.

- Click **the photo with a right-click, and then choose Clear Protect Highlights**.
- Using the eliminate brush tool, make a mark on the unimportant parts that you wish to eliminate. The locations designated for removal are shown in red.
- **To remove parts of undesirable highlighted regions (red), take one of the following actions:**
  - Use the **Eraser tool to erase.**
  - When you do a right-click on the image, choose **Clear Remove Highlights.**
- Move the handles of the picture to have your picture Recomposed. Choose the **Commit Current Operation symbol** when you are done.

Recompose options

When you are making use of the recompose tool, below are some of the options you can also choose to make use of;

- **Size** allows for the definition of the size of the brush.
- **Preset** is used to indicate the desired ratio to be used while resizing. The Preset operates based on the aspect ratio of the image rather than its size. For instance, when you resize an image, the preset ratio of 3x5 is used. Holding down the Shift key, move the corner handles to resize the image with the same ratio. The Preset menu now includes a preset that crops the image to a 16:9 aspect ratio.
- **Threshold** The Recompose threshold is set with this. When the threshold is set to 100%, a 100% Recompose is indicated. The Recompose tool behaves similarly to the Transform tool if it is set to 0%.
- **Highlight Skin Tones** emphasizes and distinguishes skin tones for safety. Skin tones can be retained in certain areas. To see the recommended skin tones region, choose the Highlight Skin Tones icon. Use the Protect Eraser tool or right-click the picture and choose Clear Protect Highlights to remove the skin tone-containing areas that have been recognized.
- **Swap height and width are** used to switch the height and width values that are given. As an illustration, you have entered the numbers H: 10 and W: 15. If you want to adjust the height and width, click the Swap symbol. H: 15 and W: 10 are the updated values.

The Straighten Tool

An image that is not perfectly aligned can be caused by a camera shake. For instance, the horizon in a sunset photo could not be exactly horizontal. You may realign the image in Photoshop Elements so that the horizon is completely horizontal. The Straighten tool (P) can be used to realign an image either horizontally or vertically. Additionally, you have the option to automatically crop or resize the canvas to allow for image straightening.

- To draw a line along the horizon (when visible) in Quick mode, select the Straighten tool (P). Create a line that you believe needs to depict the photo's horizontal axis when it is not visible. Based on the choice you selected, the picture is straightened and any resulting empty edges are immediately filled.

Manually straighten a picture in advanced mode

- Choose **the Straighten tool.**

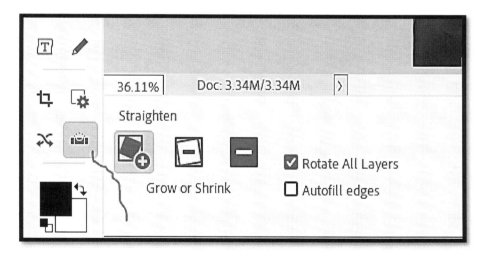

- **Make a choice from the choices that are available;**

    o **Grow or Shrink Canvas To Fit** fits the rotating image on the canvas by resizing it. Corners of the image fall outside the current canvas upon straightening. There are vacant background patches in the straightened image, but no pixels have been cropped.

- o **Crop to Remove Background** removes any white background from the photograph by cropping it after it has been straightened. There are some clipped pixels.
- o **Crop to Original Size** maintains the original image's dimensions on the canvas. The image has been straightened, however, some pixels have been cropped and there are blank background patches.

- **Get any of the following done to have the picture straightened;**

  - o Draw a horizontal line parallel to an edge to align horizontally. One could imagine, for instance, a train with its horizon misaligned. Parallel to the train, draw a horizontal line.
  - o Draw a vertical line parallel to an edge to align vertically. One could imagine, for instance, an incorrectly positioned tower. Draw a line parallel to the tower that is vertical.

Fill Empty Edges Instantly

As opposed to filling in translucent pixels or background color, the Straighten tool now includes an improved option that intelligently and automatically fills the boundaries with pertinent image data. The only modes that support the Autofill edges feature are Grow or Shrink and Original Size. Choose Autofill edges before you draw a line to activate picture straightening. Any spaces left around the margins of the picture when you create the line are immediately and wisely filled in.

- Select **Image > Rotate > Straighten Image** to automatically straighten the picture while maintaining the canvas surrounding it. There are vacant background patches in the straightened image, but no pixels have been cropped.
- Select **Image > Rotate > Straighten And Crop Image** to automatically straighten and crop the image. While there are no blank backdrop patches in the straightened image, some pixels have been cropped.

Manually straighten a picture in Quick mode

- Choose **the Straighten tool.**
- **Make a choice from the available choice buttons;**

  - **Maintain Canvas Size** fits the rotating image on the canvas by resizing it. Corners of the image fall outside the current canvas upon straightening. There are vacant background patches in the straightened image, but no pixels have been cropped.
  - **Maintain Image Size** resizes the picture to get rid of any backdrop that is left unfilled after straightening. There are some clipped pixels.

- **Get any of the following done in order to have the picture straightened;**

  - Draw a horizontal line parallel to an edge to align horizontally. One could imagine, for instance, a train with its horizon misaligned. Parallel to the train, draw a horizontal line.
  - Draw a vertical line parallel to an edge to align vertically. One could imagine, for instance, an incorrectly positioned tower. Draw a line parallel to the tower that is vertical.

Activity

1. Add foreground and background to your photo.
2. Zoom your picture with the use of the Zoom tool.
3. Move your picture with the use of the move tool.
4. Refine your selection with the use of the edge selector.
5. Sharpen your picture with the use of the sharpening tool.
6. Erase a part of your picture with the use of the erase tool.
7. Type a message on your picture with the use of the type tool.
8. Crop a part of your picture with the use of the crop tool.

CHAPTER 6

SELECT AND ISOLATE AREAS IN YOUR PHOTOS

Why select and isolate?

Take a brief look at selections, including their definition, functions, and the things they enable editors to accomplish. With the use of selections, you can focus on specific areas inside an image. This could entail separating an individual or object from the background, focusing on a certain hue, or separating a particular aspect of the scene, such as the sky or clouds. These can be edited separately from other scene elements by being isolated. In order to place an individual in a completely different background and setting, we can even shift a selection from one picture to another. Selections can range widely in complexity and come in a multitude of varieties, notwithstanding their helpfulness. Photoshop includes nearly a dozen tools to build them, so this should come as no surprise.

Feathering

Anti-aliasing or feathering can be used to soften a selection's sharp edges. By reducing the contrast between the background and edge pixels, anti-aliasing smoothes down a selection's sharp edges. There is no loss of detail due to the fact that only the edge pixels are altered. Cutting, copying, and pasting choices to produce composite images is a valuable application of anti-aliasing. Elliptical Marquee, Magnetic Lasso, Polygonal Lasso, Lasso, and Magic Wand tools allow you to choose anti-aliasing.

The Anti-Alias option must be selected before the selection can be made; anti-aliasing cannot be added to an already-made selection.

- Choose the **Magic Wand, Lasso, Elliptical Marquee, Magnetic Lasso, or Polygonal Lasso tool from the Edit workspace**.
- Go to the settings bar and select **Anti-aliased.**

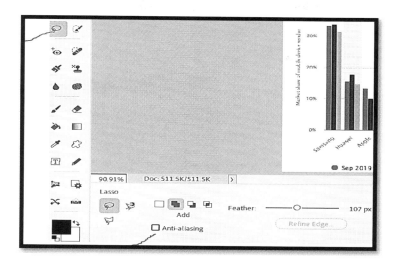

- In the image window, make a selection.

Blur the edges of a selection by feathering

- Feathering a selection helps soften its sharp edges. Feathering creates a transition in between the selected pixel and the surrounding pixels to soften edges. The selection's edge may lose some information as a result of this blurring.
- Using the Elliptical Marquee, Rectangular Marquee, Lasso, Polygonal Lasso, or Magnetic Lasso tools, you can make a selection with feathers. Using the Select menu, you may also feather an already-existing selection. You can drag, cut, copy, or fill in the selection to see the feathering effects.

Define a feathered edge for a selection tool

- **Choose from the following actions in the Edit workspace:**
  - To specify the breadth of the feathering, select any lasso or marquee tool from the toolbox and enter a value for the Feather in the options bar. At the selected border is where the feathering starts.
  - Choose **a soft-edged brush** within the brushes pop-up panel in the menu bar by selecting **the Selection Brush tool.**

185

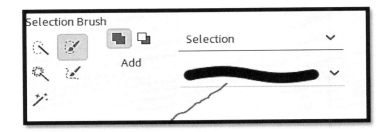

- Select **something in the picture window.**

Define a feathered edge for an existing selection

- Make a selection in the **Edit workspace by using a selection tool from the toolbox.**
- Choose **Feather under Select.**
- In the Feather Radius text box, enter a number between 2 and 250, then click **OK.** The feathered edge's breadth is determined by the feather radius.

Select Subject, Background, or Sky

With only one click, you can instantly choose the Subject, Sky, or Background in your picture. Photoshop Elements recognizes the Subject, Sky, or Background in your shot using Adobe Sensei AI technology*.

To view the possibilities for one-click selection, take the following actions:

- To open the specified photo, choose **File > Open or Open in the Quick or Advanced workspace.**
- Either of the following workflows can be used to access the one-click selection options:
  - Choose **Subject, Background, or Sky from the choices under the Select menu.**

○ Select **any tool from the Tools panel to begin the selection process**. Then, use the action bar to select an option from Subject, Sky, or Background.

- Give Photoshop Elements a few moments to choose the Subject, Sky, or Background from your image automatically. The choice will be shown as a marching ant or dotted line in motion.

Refine the edge of your selection

The Refine Edge dialog box in Photoshop Elements allows you to refine your selection by selecting a piece of an image, right-clicking on the selection, and selecting Refine Edge from the context menu. Using **Select > Refine Edge** is another way to bring up the Refine Edge dialog.

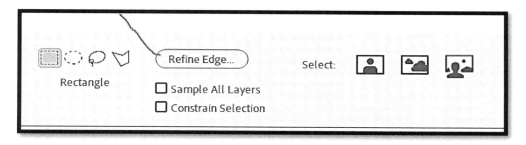

- On a Mac, select **a section of a picture, Control-click the selection**, then select **Refine Edge to launch the Refine Edge dialog box.**

  o **View Mode** Select a view mode for your selection from the View pop-out menu. F will cycle through the available modes.

  o **Show Radius** shows the radius of the edge refinement.

  o **Refine Radius and Erase Refinements** Adjust the boundary precisely where edge refining takes place. Press E to easily switch between the tools. Press the bracket keys to adjust the brush size. Note: To add tiny details to the selection, brush over sensitive regions like fur or hair.

  o **Smart Radius** automatically modifies the radius to account for both soft and hard edges present in the border area. If the border has a consistent hard or soft edge, or if you would prefer more exact control over the Radius setting and refining brushes, deselect this option.

  o **Radius** establishes the dimensions of the selection boundary where edge refinement takes place. For edges that are sharp, use a short radius, and for softer edges, a large one.

  o **Smooth.** smoothes out the selection border's uneven patches, or "hills and valleys," to produce a more rounded appearance.

  o **Feather** softens the change in pixel values between the selected and adjacent areas.

  o **Contrast** Soft-edged transitions along the selection boundary become increasingly abrupt as they are increased. Refinement tools and the Smart Radius option work better most of the time.

  o **Shift Edge** soft-edged borders can be moved outward with positive values or inside with negative ones. You can help eliminate undesired background colors from the selection edges by shifting these borders inward.

  o **Clear the Colors** substitutes the surrounding completely chosen pixel's color for the color fringes. The softness of selection edges determines how strong color replacement is.

  o **Amount** alters the level of decontamination and fringe replacement.

  o **Output To** decide whether to create a new layer or document or to use the refined selection as a selection or mask on the active layer.

Edit and Refine Selections

One of the most important aspects of editing is selecting. The Refine Selection Brush tool is a feature of Photoshop Elements. This tool uses automatic edge detection to assist you in adding or removing areas to and from a selection. The tool's cursor is a pair of concentric circles. The outer circle shows the region to search for an edge, while the inner circle represents the brush's size.

To refine the selection of a picture;

- Launch **a picture in Quick/Advanced mode.**
- Choose the **Refine Selection Brush tool.**

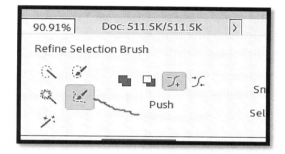

- From the four modes that are available (Add, Subtract, Push, Smooth), choose the **Add mode.**

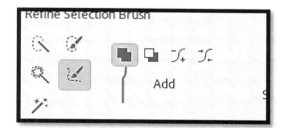

- To make accurate and well-chosen selections on an image, press and hold the cursor over it. The selection starts to expand inside the cursor's concentric circles. Observe a region with a lighter color at the increasing selection's outside edge. This is the Selection Edge that will assist you in choosing exactly what you want.

- o Selection Edge (the area in the accompanying image that is enclosed by areas B and C)
- o The Selection Edge slider sets the size of the Selection Edge. To achieve the desired effect, play about with the hardness and softness of this parameter.

- In the Selection Edge region, all textures, including hair, fur, and grass, is meticulously recorded.

    - o Hover the mouse pointer over the selection's edge until the cursor changes to the Selection Edge cursor mode in order to capture more of the small details. In this mode, select and paint regions that have fine details with the tool.
    - o When you move the inner, dark gray part of the pointer over the edge of a selection, the cursor changes to this mode. Additionally, the Selection Edge slider parameter controls the size of the darker area of the cursor. More space can be painted over in a larger scenario.

- Until the regions you want to choose are chosen, keep choosing new regions and honing the edges you've chosen. View the information that you are able to capture by using an alternative overlay option.
- Proceed with the experimentation and execute Step 6, adjusting your selections and using the **Refine Selection Brush tool Subtract, Push, and Smooth modes.**

Defringe a selection

A selection that is moved or pasted includes some of the pixels that surround the selection border. A fringe or halo around the selection's edges may be the result of these extra pixels. When the Defringe Layer command is executed, any pixels that possess fringes are replaced with neighboring pixels that have pure colors (i.e., no background color). For instance, when you move the selection while selecting a yellow object on a blue background, a portion of the blue background moves with the object. The yellow pixels in the Defringe Layer take the place of the blue ones.

- A selection can be copied and pasted into an existing or new layer.
- Select **"Enhanced > Adjust Color > Defringe Layer."**
- Enter the number of pixels you want to replace surrounding the object in the Defringe dialog box. A value of one or two ought to be adequate.

- Press **OK.**

Cut and paste a selection into another photo

The Move tool and the Edit menu's Copy, Copy Merged, Cut, Paste, and Paste into Selection commands can be used to copy and paste selections. Remember that the copied data maintains its original pixel dimensions when you paste a selection or layer between images of varying resolutions. The pasted section can look out of proportion to the new image as a result. To ensure that the source and destination photographs have the same resolution before copying and pasting,

- Use the **Image > Resize > Image Size command.**

Any selections you copy or cut are kept on the clipboard. In the clipboard, only one selection is kept at a time.

Copy a selection using commands

- Using a selection tool, choose the area you wish to copy in the Edit workspace.
- Take one of these actions:
  - To copy the selection to the clipboard, select **Edit > Copy.**
  - To copy every layer in the chosen region to the clipboard, select **Edit > Copy Merged.**

Paste one selection into another

To insert copied content or clipboard content inside a selection, use the Insert Into Selection command. By using this command, you may make the most of the elements that are present in the specified area and avoid the pasted image from appearing flat and artificial. For instance, to keep the reflection in a pair of sunglasses, use the Hard Light blending mode at 85% opacity. This method of employing blending modes requires you to make a new layer and paste the selection onto it.

- To copy a portion of a photo to paste, use the **Copy command in the Edit workspace.**
- Select **the picture that you wish to paste the copied image into**.
- Select **Paste Into Selection under Edit**.
- Drag the copied image to the desired spot while keeping your cursor inside the selection boundary.

191

- To commit the edits after you're happy with the outcome, deselect the copied image.

Note: Only the chosen boundary contains the duplicated photo. The duplicated image can be moved inside the border; but, it won't be seen if it is moved entirely outside of it. When a different tool is chosen, **hold down Ctrl (Command on Mac OS) to bring up the Move tool. (The Hand tool is incompatible with this technique.)**

Fill or stroke a selection

Fill a layer with a color or pattern

Rather than using a brush tool to apply a fill or pattern to your image, you can use a fill layer. You can modify the fill layer's mask to restrict the gradient to a specific area of your image, as well as the fill and pattern settings, to give yourself more versatility.

- Choose **a color for the background or foreground.**

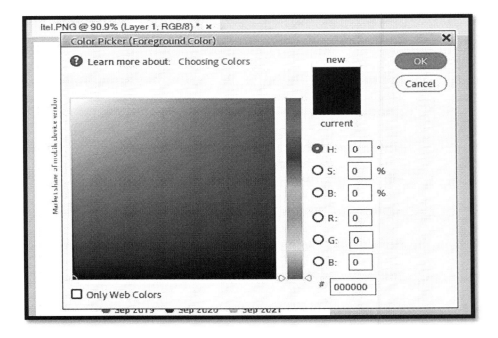

- Decide which space you wish to fill. In the Layers panel, select **the layer you want to fill in its entirety.**
- Select either **Edit > Fill Selection or Edit > Fill Layer.**

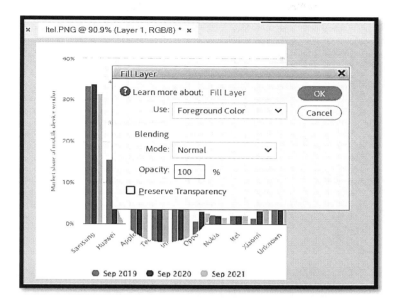

- Click **OK** after making your selections in the Fill dialog box.

    o **Contents**   Select a hue from the Utilize menu. Select Color, and then use the Color Picker to choose a new color. Select Pattern to apply a pattern.
    o **Unique pattern**   If you select Pattern from the Use option, this will indicate the pattern to be used. You have the option of making your own patterns or using ones from the pattern libraries.
    o **Mode** describes how the color pattern you use melds with the image's existing pixels.
    o **Opacity** determines the color pattern's opacity before application.
    o **Preserve** Transparency only occupies opaque pixels.

Stroke objects on a layer

A selection of a layer's contents can be automatically surrounded with a colored outline using the Stroke command. You need to convert it to a standard layer before you can apply an outline to the backdrop. The whole layer is outlined since there are no translucent pixels in the background.

- Choose **a region** inside the picture or a layer within the Layers window.
- Select **Stroke (Outline) Selection under Edit.**

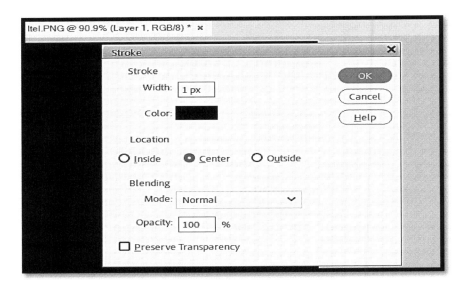

- To add the outline, select o**ne of the following options in the Stroke dialog box, and then click OK.**

  o **Width** Indicates how wide the outline with a firm edge is. Pixel values can vary from 1 to 250.

  o **Color** determines the outline's color. To choose a color in the Color Picker, click the color swatch.

  o **Location** indicates whether the outline should be centered on the selection or layer boundaries, outside, or inside of them.

  o **Mode** describes how the paint you apply melds with the picture's existing pixels.

  o **Opacity** determines how opaque the paint you apply is. You can drag the slider by clicking on the arrow or by entering an opacity value.

  o **Maintaining transparency** only makes strokes in a layer's opaque pixelated sections. This option isn't available if there is no transparency in your image.

Activity

1. What is feathering?
2. Cut and paste a selection into another picture.
3. Fill or stroke a selection.

CHAPTER 7
RESIZE YOUR IMAGES

Image Resizing

The quantity of pixels along a picture's width and height is its image size, also known as its pixel dimensions. For instance, a picture taken with your digital camera can be 1500 pixels in width and 1000 pixels in height. These two metrics establish the file size and show how much image data is there in a picture. The quantity of picture data in a specific space is called resolution. In pixels per inch (ppi), it is expressed. The resolution increases with the number of pixels per inch. In general, the quality of your printed image improves with increased resolution. The resolution of an image controls how finely detailed it appears. A digital image doesn't have a set physical output size or resolution, even though it contains a certain quantity of visual data. An image's physical dimensions vary when its resolution is altered, and vice versa when its width or height is altered. In the Image Size window that opens (choose **Image > Resize > Image Size)**, you can observe how image size and resolution relate to one another. The other two numbers adjust in tandem with a change in one.

You can keep the aspect ratio (the proportion of picture width to image height) constant by using the Constrain Proportions option. The picture does not resize or stretch if you choose this option and alter the image's resolution and size. You can alter an image's size without altering its resolution by using the Resample Image option. Resample the image if you need to print at a certain resolution, or at a resolution that is higher or lower than what the present version permits. However, resampling can result in a loss of image quality.

About monitor resolution

Pixel measurements are used to characterize the resolution of your monitor. For instance, if the resolution of your display is 1600 x 1200 and the pixel dimensions of your photo are the same, the photo will fill the screen at 100%. The pixel dimensions of the picture, the monitor's size, and the resolution setting all affect how large an image appears on the screen. You can deal with photographs of any pixel size with ease in Photoshop Elements because you can adjust the image magnification on the screen. A photo's expected display resolution should be taken into account when preparing it for onscreen viewing.

Display the image size of an open file

- The file data box at the lower part of the file can be clicked and held. The image resolution (PPI), number of color channels, and width and height of the image (in pixels and the unit of measurement currently chosen for the rulers) are all displayed in the box.

View the print size on the screen

- **Take one of these actions:**

  - Select **Print Size under View**.

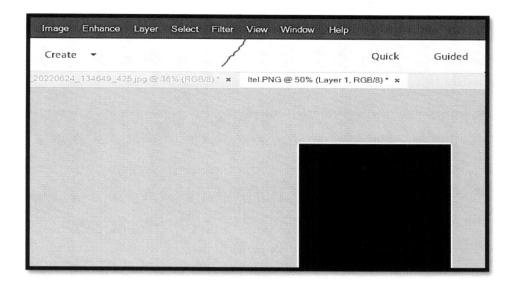

- Choose **Print Size in the Tool Options window after selecting the Zoom or Hand tool.**
- The image's magnification is changed to show its approximate printed size, as indicated in the Image Size dialog box's Document Size section. Remember that the size of the onscreen print depends on the resolution and size of your monitor.

Change print dimensions and resolution without resampling

If the image is being sent to a print shop that needs files to be at a specified resolution, you may need to adjust the print dimensions and resolution. You do not need to follow this process if you are printing straight from Photoshop Elements. Instead, Photoshop Elements applies the proper image resolution based on the size you select in the **Print dialog box.** Note however that there is a need for you to resample the image if you want to modify the print dimensions or resolution alone, keeping the overall pixel count proportionately the same.

- Select **Image > Resize > Scale.**
- Verify that the Resample Image option is deactivated. If this option is deselected, the image may not maintain its current proportions but you can adjust the print

dimensions and resolution without altering the overall amount of pixels in the image.

- Choose **Constrain Proportions** to keep the aspect ratio as it is. When you adjust the height using this option, the width is immediately updated as well.

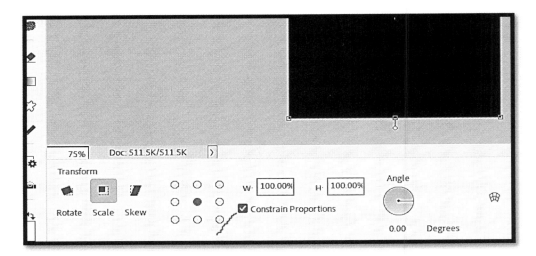

- Change the height and width values under Document Size. Select **a different unit of measurement if you'd like.**
- Change **the value entered for Resolution**. Select **a different unit of measurement if preferred,** and then click **OK**.

If you need to go back to the initial values shown in the Image Size dialog box, make use of **Alt (Option in Mac OS)** + choose **Reset**.

Resample an image

Resampling is the process of altering an image's pixel dimensions. An image's resampling alters not only its screen size but also its quality and printed output, namely the resolution and dimensions of the image printed. Image quality can be lowered by resampling. Information is eliminated from the image when you downsample, or reduce the amount of pixels in it. The image loses some sharpness and detail as you upsample, or increase the number of pixels in it. New pixels are created based on the color values of existing pixels. Scan or produce a picture at the resolution needed for your printer or output gadget to save upsampling. Resample a copy of your file if you wish to see how altering pixel dimensions will appear on screen or in print proofs at various resolutions.

- Pick **Image > Resize > Image Size**.
- Choose **Resample Image, and choose an interpolation choice**;

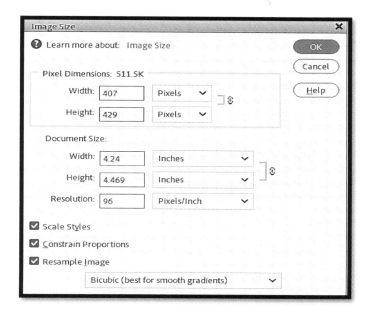

Nearest Neighbor Quick, but not as accurate. It is advised to use this technique to maintain sharp edges and create a smaller file for illustrations with non-anti-aliased edges. Nevertheless, this technique may result in jagged edges, which show up when scaling or warping an image or applying several adjustments to a selection.

Bilinear this option produces medium quality.

Bicubic is slow, but actually much more precise, giving rise to the smoothest tonal gradations.

Bicubic Smoother employ this option when you have to make images bigger.

Bicubic Sharper Utilize while shrinking an image's size. This technique keeps the details in an image that has been resized. It might, however, over-sharpen certain portions of the picture. Try using Bicubic in this situation.

- Choose **Constrain Proportions** to keep the aspect ratio as it is. When you adjust the height using this option, the width is immediately updated as well.
- Enter the **Width and Height values in Pixel Dimensions**. Select **Percent** as the unit of measurement to input numbers as percentages of the current dimensions. The image's new file size is displayed next to Pixel Dimensions, with the previous file size enclosed in parenthesis.
- Choose **OK** to later the pixel dimensions and get the image resampled.

Downsample and use the Unsharp Mask (**Enhance > Unsharp Mask**) to get the best results in creating a smaller image. Increase the resolution of the scan to create a larger image.

Maximum image size limits in Photoshop Elements

The largest image size that can be used with Adobe Photoshop Elements is specified in this section. The maximum dimensions of an image are different for the Organizer and Editor. For the Organizer and Editor, there are additional differences in what may be done with an image that exceeds the maximum dimensions. By changing an entry in the Windows registry, you can override the Organizer's limit.

Maximum image size limit in the Editor

An image's maximum dimensions in Photoshop Elements are restricted to 30,000 pixels by 30,000 pixels via the Editor. An image that exceeds the limit cannot be opened or created in the Editor.

Maximum image size limit in the Organizer

The maximum size of an image can be limited by Photoshop Elements' Organizer depending on the RAM that is installed on your computer. The restriction was put in place to stop Photoshop Elements from trying to use more RAM than is necessary, which could slow down the application or make it seem to freeze when dealing with really big photos. If an image is larger than the allowed amount, you can still import it into an Organizer catalog, but the Organizer won't show you a thumbnail for it when you import it or show it in a slideshow or other production. Additionally, the Organizer will display the error notice "Unable to print [filename], Adobe Photoshop Elements will skip printing this file" if you attempt to print the image. The image can be viewed and edited in the Editor by selecting Edit > Go To Full Edit, provided that it does not exceed the Editor's maximum image dimensions of 30,000 by 30,000 pixels.

The table below lists the maximum dimensions for images. Multiplying an image's width by height in pixels yields the image's dimensions. Open the image in Photoshop Elements Editor to determine its width and height in pixels. Then, **select**:

Examine the figures in the Pixel Dimensions box by selecting **Image > Resize > Image Size.**

Amount of RAM Installed	Image Dimensions Limit
Less than 512 MB	18 megapixels (18,874,368 pixels)
512 MB to 1 GB	36 megapixels (37,748,736 pixels)
1GB to 2GB	54 megapixels (56,623,104 pixels)
More than 2 GB	72 megapixels (75,497,472 pixels)

For PSD files including layers, the Organizer has an additional image size limit. The Organizer won't provide a thumbnail for a layered PSD file if its size is larger than half of the typical image size limit. The Organizer limits layered PSD files because drawing layers takes more memory than drawing flattened (non-layered) files.

Canvas Resizing

The workspace surrounding an already-existing image inside the image window is called the canvas. It is an image's entire editable region. Any side of an image has the ability to change the canvas's size.

The newly added canvas appears in the Background layer's presently selected background color (by default) or the canvas extension color that was chosen in the Canvas size window. The additional canvas is transparent in other layers.

- Select **Image > Resize > Canvas Size**.

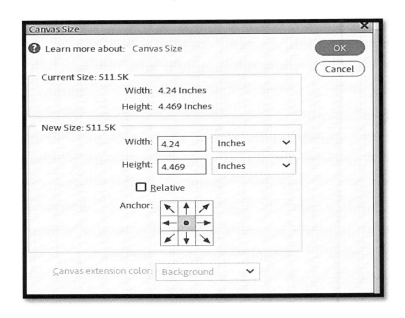

- **Take one of these actions:**
    - Enter **the new canvas's full measurements in the Width and Height fields**. Select the desired unit of measurement using the drop-down menus next to it.
    - Choose **Relative and input the desired amount** to enlarge or reduce the canvas's size. To make the canvas smaller, use a negative number. To expand the canvas by a given measure, such as two inches on each side, use this option.
- To select a desired place on the canvas, click **an arrow on the Anchor icon.**
- Select **a color from the Canvas Extension Color menu and click OK to modify the color of the newly added canvas.**

Activity

1. Resize your image.
2. Resize your canvas.

CHAPTER 8
FIX AND ENHANCE YOUR PHOTOS

Auto Fixes

In this chapter, you will learn about the various auto-fixes that can be done when you are editing your pictures.

Auto Smart Tone

The Auto Smart Tone tool adjusts your image's tonal value using a clever algorithm. Your photo is corrected with the Auto Smart tone feature. To further fine-tune the results, you can also move the joystick control around the picture. Photoshop Elements assesses the tone of the area that is being sampled when you move the joystick over various areas of your image. The entire picture is then given a tone adjustment. As a result of this, when you modify the joystick to different areas of the image it will yield various outcomes. The entire image in the picture (below) brightens when the joystick is moved toward the brighter areas, such as the grass or the sky. The pictures in the upper-right and lower-right corners clearly show this.

Apply Auto Smart Tone to a picture

- Choose **Auto Smart Tone** from **Enhance** when you have an image opened. Once done, a standard tonal correction will then be added instantly.

- To adjust the final image, move the joystick control that appears on the picture.

- View the thumbnail pictures that show up at each of the four edges of the picture to get a perfect idea of how the image will look when you get to shift the joystick control in a particular way.

Auto Smart Tone Learning

You have the option to choose Learn from this Correction while utilizing the Auto Smart Tone feature. Photoshop Elements continues to learn from all of your editing actions when you choose this option. The tonal ranges of an image, both before and after you use the Auto Smart Tone tool, are used by the algorithm to learn. This aids in improving the automatic tonal recommendations for a fresh image made by the Auto Smart Tone feature. As a result of this, every time you utilize the feature on an image, the computer will instantly make recommendations for tone treatment (joystick control location) based on the adjustments you have made to earlier photographs. It gets increasingly adept at taking a guess at the kinds of adjustments you would like to see made to a new photograph the more tones you correct through this function. This learning is used by the feature to provide you with comparable adjustments on similar types of photographs. In the Preferences menu, select **General > Reset Auto Smart Tone Learning** to undo the learning that the Auto Smart Tone feature has collected from your usage and actions as you might have a need for the algorithm to learn a different kind of tonal treatment.

Adjust Color

To add to having to eradicate dust spots and other flaws, Photoshop Elements offers various tools and commands that can be used for adjusting your photographs' color, sharpness, and tonal range. Depending on your needs and level of experience, you can choose to work in any one of three modes.

- **Quick** If the experience you have with digital images is limited, you should start repairing photos in Quick mode. Numerous fundamental tools for adjusting lighting and color are included.
- **Guided** If you're not familiar with Photoshop Elements or digital imaging, you can utilize Guided Edit to guide you through the color correction process. This is also a wonderful method to improve your process comprehension.
- **Advanced** If you have experience working with photographs, you will discover that the most powerful and adaptable image-correction environment is offered by the advanced mode. It includes tools to rectify image faults, make selections, add text, and paint on your images, in addition to lighting and color correction commands.

You may choose to alter the image pixels directly when making use of certain adjustment commands. Alternatively, you can use adjustment layers to quickly and easily make nondestructive changes until your image looks perfect. When you use the Smart Brush and Detail Smart Brush tools in this mode, an adjustment layer is immediately created for the correction you are applying.

Camera Raw The Camera Raw window allows you to open and edit raw files if you shoot digital photos in the raw format supported by your camera. You can improve the photographs by simply adjusting the color and exposure because your camera hasn't processed the raw files yet. It's rare that you'll need to use Photoshop Elements for additional modifications. Save camera raw files in a compatible file format before opening them in Photoshop Elements.

Correct color in Quick Mode

Many of Photoshop Elements' fundamental photo-fixing functions are neatly grouped together in Quick Mode. Restrict the number of color and lighting adjustments you make to a shot when working in Quick mode. In a photo, what you usually just use is one of the auto controls. Give a try to another control by clicking the **Reset button** if the first one doesn't yield the desired results. Whether or whether you have used an auto control, you can still modify your image with the slider controls. Apply the Sharpening adjustment to an image last.

- **Take one of these actions:**
  - Once a picture is open, select **Quick.**
  - When in Quick mode, you can retrieve any photographs you have saved in the Photo Bin.
- (Optional) Make a pick from the menu (found in the bar above the open image) to set the preview choices. You can get the preview configured to display the image both before and after you make a correction, or it can display the two previews side by side (horizontally or vertically).
- (Optional) You can choose to zoom, reposition, and crop the image with the use of the tools in the toolbox. In addition, you can also add text to the picture, adjust red eyes, whiten teeth, and make a decision.
- Click the **Rotate button** that can be found on the taskbar to rotate the image to the left in 90° steps in a counterclockwise direction. Click **the arrow close to the Rotate button, and then press the Rotate right button to rotate the image in a clockwise manner.**

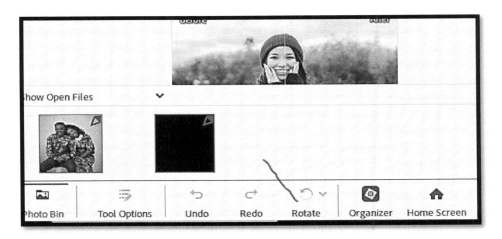

- Choose **an image-correcting control** (such as Balance, Color, or Lighting). Select the corresponding tab to adjust that feature of the image if control has other options (for example, the Color control comprises the Saturation, Hue, and Vibrance tabs).
- **To add a fix, get any of the following done;**

- Use the sliders to make the required adjustments, then preview the changes on the picture or enter a value in the text box adjacent to the sliders.
- To see a preview of the photo alteration, move the mouse pointer over the thumbnails. To temporarily apply the change to the image, click the **thumbnail.**
- Use a preview as a starting point for fine-tuning an image by clicking and holding **the mouse icon** on a preview thumbnail, then **dragging the cursor left or right.**

- **Do any of the following to undo a fix or reset the picture;**
  - Use **Ctrl-Z** to undo the correction that was done while you were still in control, or select **Edit > Undo**.
  - Click **Reset** to remove all of the picture's corrections. The image is brought back to its original form at the start of the editing session.

Fix Photos with touch-up buttons

In the Modify panel, the touch-up buttons can be accessed with ease in Quick mode. You can make edits and alterations to specific areas of an image by using these buttons. The same layer is altered with the use of the Eye, Spot, and Healing Brush tools. A new adjustment layer is created and worked on by the Whiten Teeth tool. A new layer for modifications is also created using the text tools. Consequently, several tools do not alter data on the image layer indefinitely. Adjustment settings are always modifiable without causing any degradation to the source image. The Smart Brush tool's modifications are applied using the Whiten Teeth and Touch Up buttons.

- **Do any of the following in the Quick mode;**
  - To eliminate red eyes from a picture, make use of the **Eye tool**. Red eyes are eliminated from people's flash images with this tool. You can either click the Auto button in the settings bar or drag the tool around an eye in the image that needs to be fixed.
  - If you would like to include a whiter teeth effect in a photograph, click the Whiten Teeth button. Drag **the desired tooth-brightening area of the image into the window.**

- **You can get any of the following done if you happen to have carried out Whiten Teeth adjustment;**

  - By selecting the **Add to Selection button** and dragging the image in, you can apply the change to other areas of the picture.
  - By selecting the **Subtract from Selection button** and dragging the image in, you may take away the modification from certain areas of the picture.

Correcting color in advanced mode

If you have experience working with photographs, Photoshop Elements provides you with the most robust and adaptable image-correction environment. It has various tools for repairing image flaws, choosing objects, painting your photos, and adding text, in addition to lighting and color correction commands. Some of the adjustment commands allow you to operate directly on the image pixels for alterations. As an alternative, you can also use adjustment layers to quickly and easily make nondestructive changes until your image is perfect. As you apply a correction, the Smart Brush and Detail Smart Brush tools automatically build an adjustment layer.

- **Specify a color management option** this option helps to specify the options for the management of colors.
- **View the picture at 100% and crop, if need be** Examine the image at 100% zoom just before the application of any color adjustments. Photoshop Elements shows the image as realistically as possible at 100%. Additionally, you can look for visual flaws like scratches and dust accumulation. If you want to clip the file, do so right away to make sure the histogram only uses pertinent data and to lower the amount of RAM needed. To ensure that you crop a well-centered selection, you might want to use the Zoom tool to zoom out before cropping an image to maximize the view.
- **Check the scan quality and tonal range** this option takes a swipe at the histogram of the picture in order to have an evaluation as to if the image has just enough details for the production of output with high quality.
- **Resize your picture, if need be**. If you plan to utilize your image in another project or application, resize it to the appropriate size. Generally, you don't need to scale it if you plan to print it or utilize it in a Photoshop Elements project.

- **Adjust the highlights and shadows** Adjust the values of the image's extreme highlight and shadow pixels (sometimes referred to as the tonal range) to start making repairs. The greatest amount of detail is achievable across the entire image when an overall tone range is set. Setting the white and black points, or highlight and shadow, is the term for this procedure.
- **Adjust the color balance** you can repair oversaturated or muted colors, as well as undesired color casts, by adjusting the image's color balance after correcting the tonal range. A few auto commands in Photoshop Elements allow you to adjust color and tone range simultaneously.
- **Make other special color adjustments** after you've adjusted your image's general color balance, you may optionally make changes to bring out the colors. For instance, if you want the colors in your image to be more vibrant, you can boost the saturation.

About Histograms

The histogram can be used to examine the tone distribution of the image and determine whether any corrections are necessary. In a bar chart, a histogram displays the distribution of an image's pixel values. The picture shadow values, starting at level 0, are displayed on the left side of the chart, while the highlight (level 255) is displayed on the right. The total number of pixels in a level is shown on the chart's vertical axis. The Histogram panel (F9) allows you to see the histogram of an image. Additionally, the Levels and Camera Raw dialog boxes offer histograms. As you work, you can update the histogram to observe how your changes are affecting the tonal range. Click the **Cached Data Warning symbol to update the data on the histogram.**

The visual detail in the shadows or highlights may be clipped—blocked up as pure black or even pure white—if a lot of pixels are grouped together close to the shadow or highlight ends of the chart. You won't be able to retrieve this kind of image very well. To achieve a better tonal range, you might have to consider rescanning the image if it is a scanned one. Verify whether your exposure is accurate using an image histogram if your digital camera is capable of displaying one, and change it if needed. If there are any pixels missing from the highlights and shadows, the histogram can indicate that the image is not utilizing the entire tonal range available. Stretching the tone range of an image with a limited range can be fixed by using one of the **Enhance > Auto commands** or the **Levels command.**

Preview changes

Adjust Hue/Saturation

The Hue/Saturation command modifies the color, hue, and lightness of an image as a whole or of its individual color components. To add special effects, color a black-and-white image (like a sepia effect), or alter the color range of a specific area of an image, use the Hue slider. To adjust the vibrancy or mutedness of colors, make use of the Saturation slider. For instance, you can choose to saturate the colors in a landscape to give it a pop of color. Alternately, subdue an eye-catching hue, such as a striking red shirt in a photograph. If there is a need for you to lighten or darken a section of an image, you can use the Lightness slider in conjunction with the other modifications. Due to the fact that this modification lowers the overall tone range, be careful not to apply it to the entire image.

Change color saturation or hue

- **Take one of these actions:**
    - Select **Hue/Saturation beneath Adjust Colour under Enhance.**

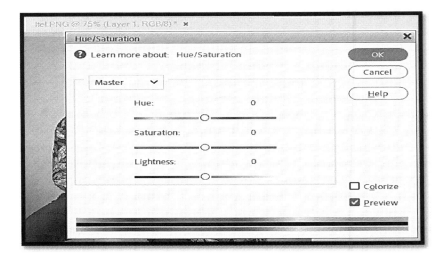

    - Either open an existing Hue/Saturation adjustment layer or select **Layer > New Adjustment Layer > Hue/Saturation.**
    - The colors on the color wheel will be represented by the two color bars that can be found in the dialog box. The color prior to the adjustment is

displayed in the upper bar, and the effect of the adjustment on all hues at full saturation is displayed in the lower bar.

- Select **the colors** you want to change from the Edit drop-down menu:
  - To instantly change all of the hues, select **Master.**

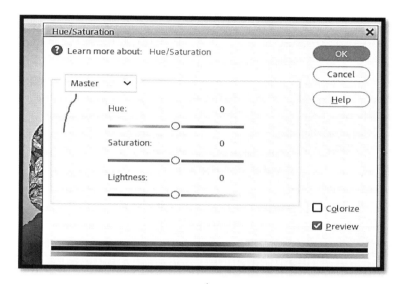

- Select **the desired color adjustment from among the available preset color ranges**. You can modify any range of colors by dragging the adjustment slider that appears between the color bars.
- To adjust Hue, either input a value or move the slider until the desired colors are displayed. The text box's values indicate how many degrees the pixel has rotated from its original color around the color wheel. Clockwise rotation is indicated by a positive value, and counterclockwise rotation by a negative value. The possible values are −180 to +180.
- Enter **a number for saturation, or drag the slider to the right to raise it or to the left to lower it. The range of values is −100 to +100**.
- Enter **a value for Lightness, or drag the slider to the left to decrease it, or to the right to increase it.** The range of values is −100 to +100. When applying this slider to the full image, proceed with caution. It will narrow the image's overall tone range.
- Choose **OK.** Or, if you would like to cancel your alterations and commence all over again, hold down Alt (Option in Mac OS), and then select **Reset.**

Modify the range of Hue/Saturation sliders

- **Take one of these actions:**
  - Select **Hue/Saturation under Adjust Hue/Colour beneath Enhance**.
  - Either open an existing **Hue/Saturation adjustment layer or select Layer > New Adjustment Layer > Hue/Saturation.**
- Make a choice of an individual color from the Edit menu.
- **Adjust the adjustment slider by doing any of the following:**
  - Without changing the range, you can modify the degree of color fall-off by dragging one of the triangles.
  - You can change the range by dragging one of the gray bars without changing the degree of color fall-off.
  - To choose a new color region, drag **the gray center portion of the adjustment slider.**
  - The color component's range can be changed by dragging one of the vertical white bars adjacent to the dark gray center portion. The color fall-off is reduced by increasing the range and vice versa.
  - **Ctrl-drag the color bar (Command-drag on Mac OS) to move it along with the adjustment slider bar.**
  - The name adjusts to reflect if you move the adjustment slider to fall into a new color range. For instance, the name becomes Red 2 if you select Yellow and adjust its range to land in the red portion of the color bar. Up to six of the distinct color ranges (such as Red 1 through Red 6) can be changed into variations of the same color range.
- Select the color picker and click **the image to modify the range by selecting colors from the image.** To increase the range, use the color picker + tool; to decrease it, use the color picker - tool. You may also use Shift to increase the range or Alt (Option in Mac OS) to decrease it when the color picker tool is selected.

Replace Color

An image's exact color can be changed with the Replace Color command. It is possible to adjust the substitute color's hue, saturation, and lightness.

- Select **Enhance > Adjust Color > Replace Color.**

- **Choose a setting for the image thumbnail's display:**
  - Selection shows the mask in the preview box, **resembling a black-and-white copy of the image.**
  - Image opens the preview box with the image displayed. When you have a small screen or are working with a magnified image, this option comes in handy.
  - After selecting the desired color for the picture or preview box, click the **color picker button**. The color picker + and − tools can be used to add and delete colors, respectively, to prevent them from altering.
  - You can adjust how much the selection includes related colors by using the Fuzziness slider.
  - Select a new color by doing one of the following:
    - Drag **the sliders for Hue, Saturation, and Lightness, or type values into the text boxes.**
    - Click the **Results box, use the Color Picker to select a new color, and then click OK.**

213

- Click on **Reset after you have held down Alt (Option in Mac OS) to cancel all of the changes you have made and begin again.**

Adjust Color Curves

By modifying the highlights, mid-tones, and shadows in each color channel, the Adjust Color Curves command enhances the color tones in an image. This command can be used to correct photographs in shots that have silhouettes due to intense backlighting or that have slightly washed-out objects from being too close to the camera's flash. You can compare and select several tonal presets in the Adjust Color Curves dialog box. Choose a style from the drop-down menu in the Choose A Style box. Adjust the highlights, shadows, and midtone brightness and contrast to fine-tune the adjustment.

- Choose **an image to open in Photoshop Elements.**
- Use one of the selection tools to pick out the section or layer of the image that needs adjustment. (If no selection is made, the image as a whole is adjusted.)
- Select **Adjust Color Curves under Enhance > Adjust Color.**

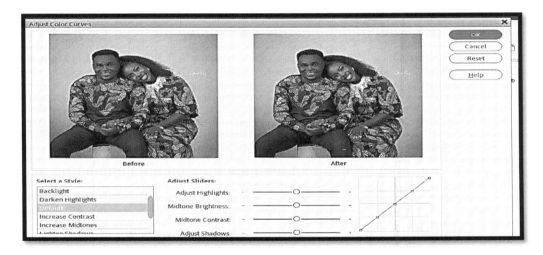

- Choose **a style (Backlight or Solarize are two examples).**
- The Shadows, Midtone Contrast, Highlights, and Midtone Brightness sliders can all be adjusted.
- Click **OK** to make the necessary adjustments to your image. Click **Reset to undo the change and begin again**. Press **Cancel to dismiss the Adjust Color Curves dialog box.**

214

Adjust Color for Skin Tone

To bring out more natural skin tones, use the Adjust Color for Skin Tone command to adjust the overall color of a shot. Photoshop Elements modifies the skin tone in an image by clicking on a specific section of skin, along with all other colors in the image. To get the desired final color, manually tweak the red and brown colors independently.

- Select the layer that requires adjustment after opening the picture.
- Select **Enhance > Color Adjustment > Color Adjustment for Skin Tone**. Click on **a skin region.**

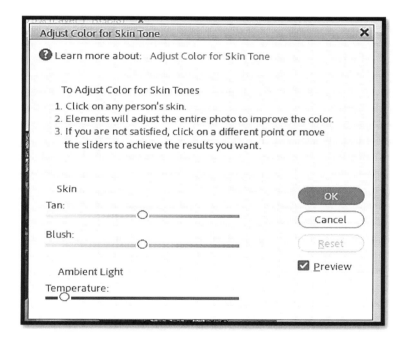

- Photoshop Elements automatically modifies the image's color. Alterations could be minute.
- **Move any of the following sliders in order to get the correction fine-tuned;**
  - **Tan** helps to increase or reduce the amount of brown in skin tones.
  - **Blush** also helps with the increase or decrease of the amount of red on skin tones.
  - **Temperature** modifies the whole color of skin tones.
- Choose **OK** when you are done, or you can also choose to cancel the alterations you must have made and commence all over again by choosing **Reset.**

Adjust Lighting

In Quick mode as well as advanced mode, Photoshop Elements offers multiple automated lighting and color correction instructions. Your selection of command will rely on what your image requires. Every auto command has an experimentation option. If the command's outcome doesn't suit your needs, you can attempt a different one by selecting **Edit > Undo**. Usually, using many auto commands to fix an image is not necessary.

- Use one of the selection tools to choose and modify a specific region of the image. The change is applied to the entire image if no selection is made.
- **Select a command from the Enhance menu, such as**
  - **Auto Smart Fix** enhances the detail of the shadows and highlights and, if required, adjusts the overall color balance.
  - **Auto Levels** modify an image's overall contrast and maybe its color. Try using this command if your image has a color tint and requires additional contrast. The way Auto Levels functions is that it maps each color channel's lightest and darkest pixels to black and white separately.
  - **Auto Contrast** modifies an image's overall contrast without changing its color. Use if the colors are correct but the image needs additional contrast. Highlights look lighter and shadows seem darker when using auto contrast, which maps the image's lightest and darkest pixels to white and black.
  - **Auto Color Correction** identifies the image's highlights, midtones, and shadows to adjust color and contrast instead of focusing on specific color channels. It uses a preset set of settings to set the white and black points and neutralize the mid-tones.

Brightness/ Contrast

It is recommended to apply the Brightness/Contrast command to specific areas of an image. This command can be used to minimize contrast in an image or to modify the brightness of the entire image. For tone modifications, the Levels and Shadow/Highlight instructions are preferable.

- **Take one of these actions:**
  - To directly modify image pixels, select **Enhance > modify Lighting > Brightness/Contrast.**

- To modify a layer, select **Layer > New Adjustment Layer > Brightness/Contrast.**

- Click **OK** after dragging the sliders to adjust the brightness and contrast. You can drag the level to the right or left to make it higher or lower. The figure to each slider's right indicates the brightness or contrast value.

Shadows/Highlights

- Click on **Enhance > Adjust Lighting > Shadow/Highlights**.

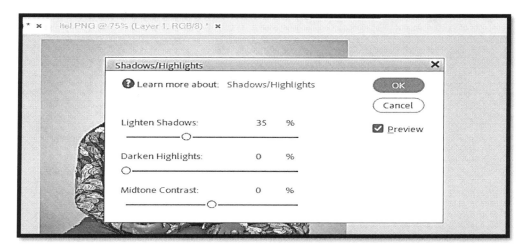

- Move any of the adjustment sliders or insert values in the text boxes, and then choose **OK.**
  - o **Lighten Shadows** enhances the gloomy portions of your picture and brings out more of the shadow detail that you managed to capture.
  - o **Darken Highlights** increases the amount of highlight detail that was recorded in your picture and darkens the sections of your picture that are bright. The regions of your picture that are pure white have no detail and are unaffected by this change.
  - o **Midtone Contrast** Modifies the middle tones' contrast by adding or subtracting. If the contrast of the image is off after adjusting the highlights and shadows, use this slider. Holding down Alt (Option on Mac OS) will cause the image to revert to its appearance when you first access the dialog box. Choose the Reset button.

Levels

- **Get any of the following done;**

  - o Select the option **Enhance > Adjust Lighting > Levels**...

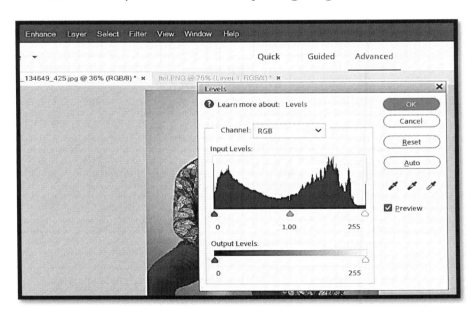

  - o Either select **Layer > New Adjustment Layer > Levels or open an already-existing adjustment layer called Levels.**

- From the Channel menu, select **RGB**. Any changes you make impact the red, green, and blue channels when the display is set to RGB. The gray channel is the only one present in an image that is grayscale.
- By sliding the black and white Input Levels sliders (the left and right sliders immediately beneath the histogram) to the edges of the first set of pixels on each end of the histogram, you may adjust the shadow and highlight values. Input Levels 1 and 3 text boxes also allow you to directly enter values.

Drag the **Shadow slider (represented by Alt on Mac OS)** to observe which regions will be cut to black (level 0). Move the Highlight slider (Option on Mac OS) to see which sections will be trimmed to white (level 255). Individual channel clipping is indicated by colored sections.

- Move the gray Input Levels (middle) slider to change the middle tones' brightness without changing the values of the shadows or highlights. Additionally, you can type values directly into the Input Levels text box in the middle. (An unadjusted midtone value of 1.0 indicates the current value.) Press **OK**. The Histogram panel shows the effect of the adjustment.

Convert to Black and White

Precisely convert to black and white

You can select a particular conversion style to be deployed to the image using the Convert to Black And White command. The Remove Color command, on the other hand, instantly turns everything to black and white for you. ou can compare and select from various conversion settings in the Convert To Black and White dialog box by using the available picture styles. Use the provided sliders to fine-tune the conversion after selecting a style.

- Launch a picture, and choose an area or layer to have it converted. The whole image will be converted if you do not make a specific selection of an area or layer.
- Select **Enhance > Convert To Black and White.**

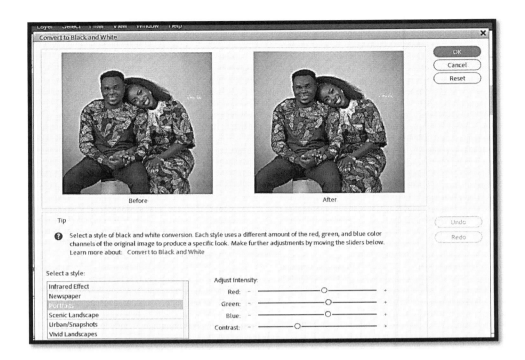

- Choose **a style (Portraits or Scenic Landscape, for example) that corresponds with the content of the picture.**
- To change the contrast, blue, green, or red, drag the Adjustment Intensity sliders.
- Click **OK** to transform your image. You can also click Reset to undo your changes and begin again. Click **Cancel to exit the Convert to Black And White dialog box.**

Automatically convert to black and white

By giving each RGB pixel in an RGB image an equal red, green, and blue value, the Remove Color command turns the image into black and white. Every pixel's total brightness stays constant. The Hue/Saturation dialog box's Saturation value of -100 is equivalent to using this command.

- Use one of the selection tools to choose and modify a specific region of the image. The change is applied to the entire image if no selection is made.
- Select **Enhance > Modify Color > Eliminate Color.**

Add custom presets for black-and-white conversion

By altering a particular text file, you can manually apply custom presets to the black-and-white converter.

- Once Photoshop Elements is closed, open **the folder containing the bwconvert.txt file:**
  - **Windows**: [Directory for installing Photoshop Elements]\Necessary*bwconvert.txt*
  - **Mac OS**: Show Package Contents can be selected by command-clicking Adobe Photoshop Elements. Mac OS: /Applications/Adobe Photoshop Elements/Support Files/Adobe Photoshop Elements Editor.app/Contents/Required/bwconvert.txt. Go to the Required/Contents folder.
- Using a plain text editor, open **the bwconvert.txt file (such as Notepad).**
- Include your new preset and provide it with a distinct name, adhering to the same naming rules as the presets that are already in the file.
- Conserve **the original filename while saving the file.**
- To view the presets, launch Photoshop Elements and select **Enhance > Convert To Black And White.**

Add color to a grayscale image

A grayscale image can be fully colored, or specific regions can be colored in different hues. For instance, you could choose to color someone's hair brown, then after making another choice, add pink to their cheeks.

- To work on an adjustment layer, select **Enhance > Adjust Color > Adjust Hue/Saturation or Layer > New Adjustment Layer > Hue/Saturation.**
- Click on **Colorize.** Photoshop Elements changes the image to match the current foreground color's hue if it isn't black or white. Every pixel's brightness value remains constant.
- If you'd like to choose a different color, use the Hue slider. To change the saturation, use the Saturation slider. Next, press **OK.**

Colorize Photo

- Launch a picture in Photoshop Elements.

221

- Select **Enhance > Photo Colorization. Alternatively, you can hit Alt+Ctrl+R (Windows) or Option+Command+R (macOS).**

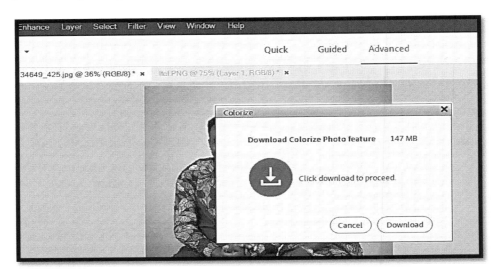

- Within the Colorize Photo workspace after downloading, a preview is created. The panel on the right will display four color choices. Select **the option that best suits your needs.**
- Select **OK** or choose **Reset** if you would like to go back to the initial picture.

Change colors in certain regions of a picture

- Launch **Photoshop Elements and open a photo.**
- Select **Enhance > Photo Colorization. Alternatively, you can hit Alt+Ctrl+R (Windows) or Option+Command+R (macOS).**
- Toggle the **Manual setting on the right panel.**
- Use t**he Magic Wand or Quick Selection Tools** in the right panel to select the areas you want to alter the color.
- To mark the region you want to recolor, click **the Droplet tool** and add the droplet to the selection. Several droplets can be added, depending on your requirements.
- A customizable palette of colors is shown in the Color Palette for every droplet. All you have to do is click on the color you want from the Color Palette after selecting a droplet (chosen droplets have a blue edge).

    o To choose a preferred color, you can also utilize the icon or the vertical slider in the All Applicable Colors window.

- ○ The Color Palette samples are accompanied by the most recent color used. This allows you to choose the color that was previously used.
- ○ To see the outcome without droplets, turn off the **Show Droplets toggle.** You can use the Before-After toggle to view both the original and altered photos. Click **Reset** to restore the original photo and undo all modifications.

- Once you are sure you are content with the outcome, choose **OK.**

Haze Removal

The damping effect that climate or environmental factors have on your images—especially landscape photos—can now be eliminated. The masking effect that haze, fog, or smog produces can be lessened by using the Auto Haze Removal option.

There are basically two ways by which you can remove haze in Photoshop Elements;

Auto Haze Removal

- Launch **a picture in Photoshop Elements,** in either the Quick or Advanced modes.
- Click on **Enhance > Auto Haze Removal with the picture opened.**

;

- In Photoshop Elements, open **an image in the Enhanced or Quick rooms.**
- Select **Enhance > Eliminate Haze**.
- To attain the required degree of haze removal, adjust **the sensitivity and haze reduction sliders.**
- To have a perfect view of the effectiveness of the feature of haze reduction on your picture, employ the use of the Before / After toggle icon.
- When you have completed all the necessary things, choose **OK**. Choose **Cancel** to cancel **Haze Removal edits** to the picture.

Unsharp Mask

Sharpening edges in an image using a conventional film approach is replicated by the Unsharp Mask filter. Blur that is introduced during photography, scanning, resampling, or printing is corrected with the Unsharp Mask filter. It is helpful for photos that are meant to be viewed both online and in print. By using a threshold you choose, Unsharp Mask finds pixels that are different from surrounding pixels and raises the contrast of those pixels by the amount you provide. Lighter pixels get lighter and darker pixels get darker when they are adjacent within the given radius. On-screen, the Unsharp Mask filter's effects are noticeably more noticeable than in high-resolution printed output. Try different parameters until you find the ones that work best for your image if the printed output is the end destination.

Smooth Skin

You can make people look their very best with the use of automatic skin smoothing in portraits.

Below is just how you can go about it;

- Launch **a picture in Photoshop Elements**.
- Click on **Enhance then choose Smooth Skin.**

- The face in your picture will instantly be chosen in the dialog box for smooth skin. Note however that if the picture contains more than a single face, all the faces detected will be highlighted. All you have to do is choose the face you would like to adjust.
- Move the **Smoothness slider** to get the effect you really want.

224

- Make use of the Before/ After switch to have another look at the changes you have made.
- Choose **Reset** to go back to the picture you have not edited (initial picture).
- Once you are content with the outcome, pick **OK.**

Adjust Facial Features

Face-aware technology is used by the Adjust Facial Features workflow to recognize and modify a person's facial features in a picture. Simple sliders can be used to raise or decrease the influence of facial characteristics like the jaw, nose, lips, and eyes in a portrait photo.

- Launch a picture in Photoshop Elements. Note however that if you would like Adjust Facial Features to work adequately, make sure that there are one or more faces in your picture.
- Choose **Adjust Facial Features after you have selected Enhance.**

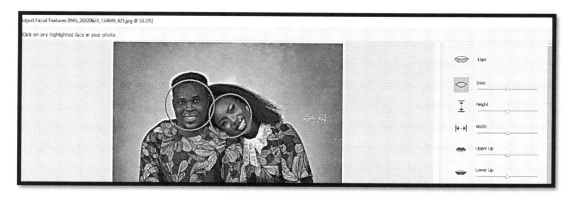

- The person's face is highlighted in a circle in the Adjust Facial Features dialog box, signifying that the face-aware feature has identified a face in the image.

Note: Multiple faces in the image? Photoshop Elements will display numerous circular highlighters that detect faces in the image if there are multiple faces present. To change a face's features, click **on one of the rings or faces.**

- **For a chosen face, you can choose to alter these features with the use of the sliders that are available;**

225

Feature	Characteristics
Lips	Smile, Height, Width, Upper lip, Lower lip
Eyes	Height, Width, Size, Tilt, Distance
Nose	Height, Width
Face Shape	Width, Forehead height, Jawbone shape, Chin height
Face Tilt	Angle, Left-Right, Up-Down

- Double-click the slider to return adjustments to a specific attribute. Changes made to that attribute are deleted.
- **Take one of these actions:**
  - Click **Reset** to remove the changes you have made to your facial characteristics.
  - Click **OK** to apply the changes made to the face features.

Shake Reduction

A photograph will become blurry due to a camera shake if the photographer or the camera shakes while being taken. Maintaining high shutter rates to prevent camera shake isn't always feasible. When shooting in low light, it could be necessary to keep the shutter open for a prolonged period of time, which could cause blur from shaking. Additionally, if the photo is shot while driving, the vibration from an uneven road may cause the image to appear blurry. There are two ways to lessen shake-induced blur in a photo: automatic and manual.

Automatic Shake Reduction

- Launch **a picture from the Photo Bin.**
- Click on **Enhance > Auto Shake Reduction.**
- If you are not content with the outcome, choose **Enhanced > Automatic Sake Reduction to get the process executed once more.**
- If for any reason you cannot get a shake reduction with the use of the automatic mode, give reducing shake with the manual option a try.

Manual Shake Reduction

- Select **a picture to open from the Photo Bin.**
- Select **Shake Reduction under Enhance.**
- Photoshop Elements creates a **Shake Region** on the image and begins analyzing the area for shake when the Shake reduction dialog opens. Shake correction is performed to the entire image after analysis is complete.
- The shake threshold can be adjusted using the Sensitivity Slider. The resulting image might be better if the sensitivity is increased.
- A Shake Region can be moved around by using the pin located in its middle. A **Shake Region** can be moved, and when you do, the image is optimized once again and the area beneath the region is reanalyzed for shake adjustments.
- If you would like to analyze the picture and get blurriness reduced more, include more Shake Regions;
  - **Get any of the following done;**
    - Make use of the mouse to draw a rectangular shape on any aspect of the picture.
    - Choose the **Shake Region in the Shake Reduction window.**
  - Employ the use of the sensitivity slider in order to get the shake threshold varied. The new Shake Region will then be analyzed and the corrections will be included instantly.
- **If you would not like to make use of a Shake Region;**
  - Click **the pin to show that the Shake Region** is temporarily excluded from being utilized for photo analysis.
  - Shake Regions can be deleted by **selecting the region's pin and then clicking the delete icon in the Shake Region's upper-right corner.**
- Employ the **Before / After** toggle button to swiftly see the initial picture and the shake-corrected picture in use at the moment.

- Choose **OK** to proceed.

Work with Adjustment and Fill Layers

You can play with color and tonality with adjustment layers without having to change an image's pixel composition permanently. An adjustment layer can be compared to a veil that colors the layers behind it. An adjustment layer's functionality can be changed, but by default, it affects all layers below it. A white box that represents the adjustment for that layer appears in the Layers panel when you create an adjustment layer. You can fill a layer with a gradient, solid color, or pattern using fill layers. Fill layers don't have an impact on the layers underneath them, in contrast to adjustment layers. A fill layer needs to be simplified and converted into a standard layer before you can paint on it. You can move and reposition adjustment and fill layers in the same way that you do image layers, and they share the same opacity and blending mode settings. Adjustment and fill layers are titled according to their type by default (e.g., invert adjustment layer and Solid Color fill layer).

Creating adjustment layers

- Choose the topmost layer you would like to affect in the Layers panel.
- Make any selection if you would like to have the effects of the adjustment layer confined to a chosen area.
- **Take any of these actions;**
  - Click the **Layers panel's Create New Fill or Adjustment Layer button** to make changes to every layer below the adjustment layer. Next, select a type of adjustment from the list below. (Fill layers, not adjustment layers, are the first three choices in the menu.)
  - Select **Layer > New Adjustment Layer> [adjustment type] to modify a single layer or several layers underneath the adjustment layer. Click OK after selecting Use Previous Layer to Create Clipping Mask from the New Layer dialog box.**
  - **Levels** this choice helps with the correction of tonal values in the picture.
  - **Brightness/ Contrast** this choice helps to lighten or darken the picture.
  - **Hue/Saturation** this option helps to modify the colors in the picture.
  - **Gradient Map** maps pixels to the color in the chosen gradient.
  - **Photo Filter** this choice alters the color balance and color temperature of the picture.

228

- o **Invert** this option helps with the production of a picture negative effect through the creation of a negative based on the values of the brightness of the picture.
- o **Threshold** this option renders the image in monochrome with no gray hence you will be able to find the lightest and darkest parts.
- o **Posterize** gives a picture a flat, poster-like appearance by lowering the number of brightness values, or levels, and consequently the number of colors.
- Click **OK** after selecting your settings in the dialog box. When you choose in step 3 to Use Previous Layer to Create a Clipping Mask, the adjustment layer and the layer just below it are grouped together, and the effect is limited to the group.
- Press **Alt (Option on Mac OS)** and move the pointer across the line separating the group's bottom layer from its layer below to add more layers to the group. When the pointer splits into two circles that overlap, **click.**

Create fill layers

- Choose **the layer that the fill layer ought to be placed atop in the Layers panel.**
- Make a selection to limit the fill layer's effects to a specific area.
- **Take one of these actions:**
  - In the Layers panel, choose the **Create New Fill or Adjustment Layer button and select the fill type you wish to create**. (The panel's first three options are for fill layers; the remaining options are for adjustment layers.)
    - Select **[fill type] under Layer > New Fill Layer. Click OK in the New Layer dialog box.**

Solid Color with this choice you are able to create a layer that is filled with a solid color selected from the **Color Picker.**

Gradient generates a gradient-filled layer. From the Gradient menu, you may select a predetermined gradient. Click **the color gradient** to modify the gradient in the Gradient Editor. To change the gradient's center, drag inside the image window.

Additionally, you can designate the gradient's form (Style) and application angle (Angle). Choose Align with Layer to compute the gradient fill using the bounding box of the layer, Dither to lessen banding, and Reverse to reverse its orientation.

The pattern produces a layer that is covered in patterns. Select **a pattern by clicking on it** and a pop-up panel will appear. Scaling the pattern is possible, and you can select Snap to Origin to align its origin with the document window. Choose **Link with Layer** to indicate that the pattern follows the Fill layer wherever it goes. With this option chosen, the Pattern Fill dialog box will open and you may drag within the image to reposition the pattern. After making changes to the pattern settings, choose the New Preset option to create a new preset pattern.

Edit an adjustment or fill layer

- **Get to do any of the following to launch the adjustment or fill options dialog box;**
  - Click **twice on the adjustment or fill layer's leftmost thumbnail** in the panel containing layers.
  - Choose the layer in the panel and select **Layer > Layer Content options.**
- Complete the alterations you need to make and select **OK.**

Merging adjustment layers

Adjustment or fill layers can be merged in multiple ways: with the layer behind it, with other selected layers, inside its own group, with connected layers, and with all other visible layers. Nevertheless, you are unable to use a fill or adjustment layer as the base or target layer in a merge. The modifications are reduced in complexity and applied permanently to the merged layer when you merge an adjustment layer or fill the layer with the layer underneath it. Beneath the merged adjustment layer, the adjustment no longer has an impact on any other layers. A fill layer can also be simplified into an image layer without having to be merged. You don't need to merge adjustment layers in order to save file space because filling layers with masks (the layer's rightmost thumbnail in the Layers panel) and adjustment layers that only contain white values don't contribute a lot of data to the file.

Edit the layer masks

A layer mask obscures portions of a layer or the layer as a whole. A mask can be used to reveal or conceal areas of an image or effect. An adjustment layer's adjustment effect is applied to all underlying layers when its layer mask (right thumbnail) is fully white. Paint the matching region of the mask black if you wish to avoid applying the effect to specific areas of the underlying layers. The mask delineates the filled-in region within a fill layer when it is affixed to it.

- In the Layers panel, pick **the adjustment or fill layer.**
- Choose **any painting or editing tool or the Brush tool.**
- **To see the layer mask, use these methods:**

- To see just the mask, **Alt-click (or, on Mac OS, Option-click) the thumbnail of the layer mask (the one on the right). To view the other levels again, Alt-click (or Option-click on Mac OS) the thumbnail once more.**
- Hold down **Alt+Shift (Option+Shift on Mac OS) and click the thumbnail of the layer mask (the rightmost thumbnail) to view the mask in a red masking hue.** To turn off the red display, hold down **Alt+Shift (Option+Shift on Mac OS) and click the thumbnail once more.**
- Choose **the matching pixels if you want to limit editing to a portion of the mask.**

- **Modify the layer mask;**
    - Apply black paint to the layer mask to erase portions of the adjustment effect or fill.
    - Use white paint to add areas to the fill or adjust the effect on the layer mask.
    - Gray paint can be used on the layer mask to partially remove the adjustment effect or fill so that it appears in varying degrees of transparency. (From the Swatches panel, select a gray shade by single-clicking the foreground color swatch in the toolbox.) Your choice of gray paint tones will determine how much of the impact or fill is eliminated. Lighter tones produce more opacity, while darker shades have more transparency.

Activity

1. Adjust the hue/saturation in your picture.
2. Remove color in your photo.
3. Adjust the color curves in your picture.
4. Modify the facial features in your picture.
5. Modify the sharpness of your picture.

CHAPTER 9
WORK WITH PHOTOSHOP ELEMENTS LAYERS

How layers work

Layers are clear sheets of glass that are stacked and allow you to paint images on them. A layer's transparent sections let you look through them to the layers below. Each layer can be worked on separately, and you can experiment to get the desired look. Up until the layers are combined (merged), each one is separate. The Background layer, which is the bottommost layer in the Layers panel, is always locked (protected), thus unless you turn it into a regular layer, you are unable to modify its opacity, blending mode, or stacking order. Layers are helpful given that they let you add elements to a picture and work on them separately without erasing the original. You have the ability to modify color and brightness, add special effects, rearrange the content of a layer, set opacity and blending settings, and more for every layer. Additionally, you may use layers to construct web animations, link layers so you can work on them at the same time, and modify the stacking order.

Layers are organized in the Layers panel, which you should keep visible whenever you're working with Adobe Photoshop Elements. With a single look, you can see the active layer (the chosen layer that you are editing). You can connect layers, so they move as a unit, helping you manage layers. Merging layers that you're done editing will reduce the file size. The Layers panel is a crucial source of information when editing photos. You can also use the Layer menu to work with layers. Ordinary layers are pixel-based (image) layers. There are a number of other layer types you can use to create special effects.

Fill layers this is a type of layer that has a color gradient, solid color, or pattern. Adjustment layers this type of layer allows the fine-tuning of color, brightness, and saturation without having to make any permanent alterations to your picture until you either flatten or collapse the adjustment layer. Type layers and shape layers permit you to produce text and shapes using vectors. Painting on an adjustment layer is not possible, but painting on its mask is. Fill and text layers need to be converted into standard picture layers before you may paint on them.

Select a layer to edit

Only the active layer is impacted by any changes you make to an image. Make sure the right layer is chosen when modifying an image if you don't get the desired effects.

Execute one of these actions:

- Choose **the name or thumbnail of a layer from the Layers window.**
- **Holding down the Ctrl (or Command in Mac OS) key while clicking each layer will select multiple layers.**

Show or hide a layer

The eye icon in the leftmost column of the Layers panel indicates that a layer is visible. The layer is not visible when a line crosses the eye symbol.

- In case the Layers panel isn't open already, select **Window > Layers**.

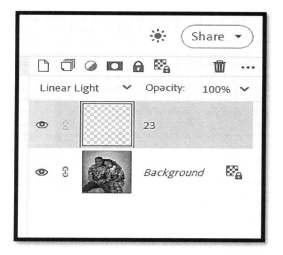

- **Take one of these actions:**

Tap the eye icon to make a layer hidden. The layer is hidden when a line crosses the eye icon. To display the layer, select the eye column once again.

- You can reveal or hide many layers by dragging through the eye column.

- Alt-clicking (Option-clicking on Mac OS) the layer's eye symbol will show only that layer. To view all the layers, repeat the Alt-click (or Option-click in Mac OS X) in the eye column.

Lock or unlock a layer

To safeguard the contents of a layer, you can lock it completely or partially. A lock icon displays to the right of the layer name when it is locked and editing or deleting the layer is not possible. You can reposition locked layers in the Layers panel's stacking order, with the exception of the Background layer.

Choose the layer within the Layers panel, and then take one of the subsequent actions:

- To lock all layer attributes, select the **Lock all pixels icon in the Layers panel**. To unlock them, click **the button once again.**
- To prevent painting in the transparent portions of the layer, hit the **Lock Transparency icon in the Layers window**. To unlock, click **the icon once more.**

Delete a layer

Your image file will get smaller if you remove any layers that you are not using.

- In the Layers panel, select **the layer.**
- **Take one of these actions:**
  - In the Layers panel, select the **Delete Layer icon.** In the dialog box that appears, select **Yes to proceed with the deletion.** Click the **Delete icon while holding down the Alt (Option on Mac OS) key to dismiss this dialog box.**
  - Click **Yes** after selecting **Delete Layer** from the Layer menu or the Layers panel More menu.

The Layers panel

From the top layer to the lowest Background layer, all of the layers in an image are listed in the Layers panel (**Window > Layers**). The Layers panel can be dragged out and tabbed with other panels when working in the Custom Workspace in Advanced mode. The layer that is currently being worked on, or the active layer, is easily distinguished by being highlighted. To ensure that the changes and edits you make impact the appropriate layer, keep an eye on which layer is active when working on a picture. As an illustration, confirm that you are viewing the active layer if you select a command and nothing appears to happen. You can create, hide, link, lock, and delete layers, among other things, by using the panel's icons. Your modifications only impact the highlighted, chosen, or active layer, with a few exceptions. The panel displays the list of layers along with a thumbnail, title, and one or more symbols that provide details about each layer:

- **Eye:** this means that the layer can be seen. Choose the eye to either show or conceal a layer. When the layer is concealed the icon will have a slant line over it. Note however that when a layer is hidden, it cannot be printed.
- **Padlock**: this means that the layer is locked.
- **Brown box**: The image was imported from Adobe Photoshop and has layer groups. Layer groups are not supported by Photoshop Elements, and they are shown collapsed. To get an editable image, you have to make them simpler.

Adding layers

In the Layers panel, newly added layers show up above the layer that is chosen. You can use any of the following techniques to add layers to an image:

- Make fresh, empty layers or apply layers to selections.
- Transform an image into a normal layer and back again.
- Selects can be pasted into a picture.
- Make use of a shape tool or the Type tool.
- Make a copy of an existing layer.

An image can have up to 8000 layers, each with a different opacity and blending mode. Memory limitations, however, might reduce this upper bound.

Create and name a new blank layer

- **Get any of the following done;**
  - Choose the **New Layer button** in the Layers panel to create a layer with the default name and parameters. The final layer is named based on the order in which it was created and uses Normal mode with 100% opacity. (Double-click the newly created layer and type a new name to rename it.)
  - Either select **Layer > New > Layer or select New Layer** from the Layers panel menu to create a new layer with a name and settings. After entering a name and selecting other settings, click **OK.**

The new layer will then instantly be chosen and it will also be shown in the panel that is at the top of the layer that was chosen last.

Create a new layer from part of another layer

A portion of an image can be moved from one layer to a newly made one while maintaining the original.

- Make a selection and choose an already-existing layer.
- **Select from the following options:**
  - ○ To transfer the selection to a new layer, pick **Layer > New > Layer Via Copy.**
  - ○ To cut and paste the selection onto a new layer, choose **Layer > New > Layer via Cut.**

The chosen area is positioned in relation to the image boundaries in a new layer.

Convert the Background layer into a regular layer

The layer at the bottom of an image is called the background. The Background layer, which typically (though not always) holds the actual image data of a photo, is layered with other layers. The Background layer remains locked at all times to safeguard the image. It must first be converted into a standard layer if you wish to alter its opacity, blending mode, or stacking order.

- **Take one of these actions:**
  - ○ In the Layers panel, double-click the **Background layer.**
  - ○ Select **Layer > New > Background Layer.**
  - ○ To preserve the original Background layer and generate a duplicate as a new layer, choose the Background layer and select **Duplicate Layer from the Layers panel flyout menu.**

Note: Regardless of how you convert the layer, you may make a duplicate copy of the converted Background layer by selecting it and selecting Duplicate Layer from the Layer menu.

- Give the new layer a name.

Note: Erased areas turn transparent when you drag the Background Eraser tool over the Background layer, which instantly transforms it into a regular layer.

Make a layer the Background layer

If the image already contains a Background layer, you cannot convert a layer to become the Background layer. In this instance, the Background layer needs to be changed from its current state to a standard layer first.

- Choose **your preferred layer in the Layers panel.**
- Pick **Layer > New > Background from Layer.** The background color fills any translucent portions in the original layer.

Simplify or Flatten a Layer

By converting it to an image layer, you can make a smart object, frame layer, type layer, shape layer, solid color layer, gradient layer, pattern fill layer, or a layer group imported from Photoshop, simpler. Before you may use the painting tools to edit or add filters to these layers, you must first simplify them. On simpler layers, however, the type- and shape-editing capabilities are no longer available.

- In the Layers panel, choose a type layer, shape layer, fill layer, or Photoshop layer group.
- **Simply either the layer or the imported layer group;**
  - In the Tools Options box, pick **Simplify** if you chose a shape layer.
  - Select **Simplify Layer from the Layer menu** or the Layers panel flyout option if you have chosen a type, shape, fill, or Photoshop layer group.

Copy layers from one image file to another

Any layer can be copied from one image to another, even the Background layer. Remember that the largest printed copy of the layer is limited by the resolution of the destination image. Additionally, you might not expect the cloned layer to seem larger or smaller if the pixel size of the two photos differs.

- Launch both pictures you would like to make use of.
- Pick the preferred layer you would like to copy in the Layers panel of the source image.
- **Take any of these actions;**
  - To pick every pixel in the layer, pick **Select > All. Then, select Edit > Copy.** After that, select **Edit > Paste** after making the destination picture active.

- o Drag **the layer name into the destination picture from the source image's Layers panel.**
- o Drag the layer from the source image to the image's destination using the Move tool (pick section of the toolbox).

In the Layers panel of the destination image, the cloned layer is visible above the active layer. A portion of the layer is visible if the layer you are dragging is bigger than the final image. Other parts of the layer can be dragged into view using the Move tool.

Move the content in a layer

Like layered photos behind glass, layers are similar to that. In order to modify the amount of content that is visible in a layer with respect to the layers above and below, you can "slide" that layer.

- In the Layers panel, select all of the layers and then click on the **Link Layer symbol of any one layer to move multiple levels at once.**
- Choose the **Move tool** from the Tools panel's Select section.
- **Take one of these actions:**
  - o To move the chosen layer or layers to the desired location, drag within the image.
  - o To move a layer in 1-pixel intervals, use the keyboard's arrow keys; to move a layer in 10-pixel increments, use Shift and an arrow key.
  - o To move a layer or layers straight up or down, straight to either side or on a 45° diagonal, hold down **Shift while dragging.**

Change the stacking order of layers

A layer's appearance relative to other layers is determined by their stacking sequence.

It is necessary for the Background layer to always be at the bottom of the stack. You must first turn the Background layer into a regular layer before you can move it.

- Choose one or more layers from the Layers panel. Holding **down the Ctrl key while clicking each layer will select multiple layers.**
- **One of the following actions will alter the stacking order:**
  - To reposition a layer, drag **it up or down the Layers panel.**

- Select **Bring To Front, Bring Forward, Send Backward, or Send To Back after selecting Layer > Arrange.**

Link and unlink layers

Layers that are linked allow their contents to be moved together. Additionally, all related layers can be copied, pasted, merged, and transformed at the same time. One associated layer may need to be edited or moved at some point. To operate on a single layer at a time, you can easily unlink the layers.

- One of these techniques can be used to connect layers:
    - Select a layer and then click the **layer's link symbol.**

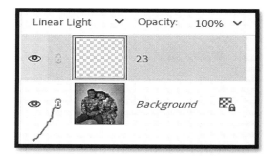

- Choose the levels that you want to connect. Holding **down Ctrl (or Command in Mac OS) while clicking the layers you wish to pick allows you to select many layers at once. Select any layer by clicking its link symbol.**
    - When you have many layers selected, use the **right-click menu to choose Link Layers.**
- **Get any of the following done in order to unlink layers;**
    - Select **the link symbol** of a layer to have a layer unlinked.
    - Right-click and **choose the Unlink Layers menu if you would like to unlink more than one layer**.

Merge layers

Layers can significantly increase an image's file size. An image's file size is decreased by merging its layers. Only when you have completed modifying layers to produce the desired image should you merge them. Only visible layers, only linked layers, only one layer with its sublayer, or only selected layers can be merged. It is also possible to combine the contents of every visible layer into a chosen layer without removing the other visible layers (this does not result in a smaller file size). You can flatten an image once you've finished working on it. All visible layers are combined, all hidden layers are removed, and transparent regions are filled with white during flattening.

- Navigate to the Layers panel and ensure that an eye symbol is shown close to each of the layers you would like to merge.
- **Take any of the subsequent actions;**
  - Select **multiple layers by clicking on each while holding down the Ctrl (or Command on Mac OS) key to merge the chosen layers.** Using **a right-click, select Merge Layers.**
  - Pick the **uppermost layer in a pair and pick Merge Down from the Layer menu or the Layers panel flyout menu to combine it with the lowermost layer.**
  - Select **Merge Visible** from the Layer menu or Layers panel flyout option to combine all visible layers. First, hide any layers you wish to keep separate.
  - Choosing **Merge Linked** from the Layer menu or Layers panel flyout option after selecting **one of the linked layers will merge all visible linked layers.**

Merge layers into another layer

You can make use of this technique when there is a need for you to keep the layers you are merging intact. The result will then become a merged layer and all the initial layers.

- Make sure the eye icon is visible (not crossed) for the layers you do want to merge, and click **the icon next to any layers you don't want to merge (the icon appears with a line across it).**
- Choose **a layer to combine all visible layers into**. In the Layers panel, you have the option to either choose **an already-existing layer or create a new layer to combine.**
- Using the Layers menu or the Layers panel More menu, select **Merge Visible while holding down the Alt key (Option in Mac OS). A copy of every layer that is visible is combined into the chosen layer by Photoshop Elements.**

Flatten an image

Photoshop Elements flattens an image by combining all visible layers into the backdrop, which significantly reduces the file size. When an image is flattened, all hidden layers are removed, and any transparent regions are filled with white. Generally speaking, you should wait to flatten a file until you've completed modifying each layer separately.

- Verify that the layers in your image that you wish to maintain are visible.
- From the **Layers panel more menu or the Layers menu,** select **Flatten Image.**

Note: If you select Document Sizes from the status bar pop-up option at the bottom of the image window, you can see the difference between the layered file size and the flattened file size of your image.

Transform and warp a layer

By dragging control points, you can use the Warp command to change various elements, including text, shapes, and images.

- Select **Warp under Image > Transform.**

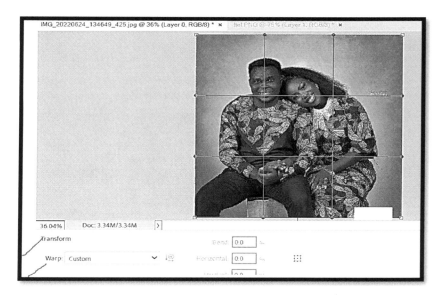

- **Take one of these actions:**

- To apply warp presets to the inserted items, select a warp style from the Warp pop-up menu located in the Tool Options bar.
- You can manually modify the geometry of a placed item by dragging its control points, a section of the mesh or bounding box, or a section inside the mesh.

- **You have the following options in the Tool Options bar:**
  - Select **a warp style** from the Warp menu and click the **Change The Warp Orientation button in the Tool Options bar to adjust its orientation.**
  - Fill in the values in the Tool Options bar's Bend (set bend), Horizontal (set horizontal distortion), and Vertical (set vertical distortion) text boxes to determine the amount of warp using numbers. If the Warp pop-up menu is set to None or Custom, you are unable to enter numerical numbers.
- **Do any of the subsequent actions;**
  - Choose the **Commit button** or tap enter **to commit the transformation.**
  - Choose the **Cancel button,** or tap **Esc to cancel the transformation.**

Activity

1. Choose a layer to edit.
2. Simplify or flatten a layer.
3. Merge one layer into another.
4. Transform and warp a layer.

CHAPTER 10
CREATE AND EDIT TEXT

Text in an image

Text can be edited and layer commands applied to it once a text layer has been created. In text layers, you can add new text, edit existing text, and remove text. All text receives the characteristics of any styles that are applied to a text layer. A text layer's orientation can also be altered, from vertical to horizontal. The type lines run from top to bottom in a vertical text layer. The type lines run from left to right in a horizontal text layer.

- **Get any of the following done;**
  - Choose either the **Vertical or Horizontal Type tool (or the Move tool and double-click the text).**
  - Choose **the text layer from the Layers panel when in the Advanced mode.**

The Type tool adapts at the insertion point to the layer's orientation when you click inside an already-existing text layer.

- **Place the insertion point in the text and get any of the following done;**
  - To configure the insertion point, click.
  - Choose the character or characters that you wish to alter.
  - Type text whatever you like.
- **Commit the text layer by doing any of the following;**
  - Choose the **Commit button in the options bar.**
  - Select **in the image.**
  - Choose **a different tool in the toolbox.**

Choose characters

- Choose **a tool for typing.**
- Either click in the text flow to choose a text layer automatically, or **pick the text layer in the Layers panel.**
- After placing the insertion point in the text, choose **between the following actions:**
  - Drag **to pick a character or several.**
  - To pick only a single word, **double-click.**

- To select a line of text in its entirety, **triple-click.**
- To pick a range of characters, click **a place in the text and then Shift-click.**
- To pick every character in the layer, select **Pick> All.**
- Holding down **Shift while pressing the Right or Left Arrow key allows you to choose characters with the arrow keys.**

Choose a font family and style

A typeface is a collection of characters that have the same weight, breadth, and style, whether they are letters, numbers, or symbols. You have the option to choose a font on its own, as well as the font family (like Arial) and typeface. A type style is a variation of a single typeface within a font family (bold, italic, regular, etc.). Depending on the font, different type styles are possible. Bold and italic variants can be applied in faux (false) versions of fonts that don't have the desired style. A computer-generated font that mimics the appearance of a different typeface design is called a faux font.

- Pick one or more characters whose font you wish to alter if you are editing already written text. Using the buttons and choices in the options bar, you can alter the font type, style, size, alignment, and color of every character in a layer, including those that are selected.
- Make your selection from the Font Family pop-up menu in the options bar.
- **Try a few of the following:**
    - Select **a font type** from the choices bar's Font type pop-up menu.
    - Click **any or both of the faux bold and faux italic buttons** if the font family you choose does not include these styles.

You can alter the type color before or after you input text, but it takes the color of the current foreground into account when you enter a type. You can alter the color of a layer's entire text or just certain characters while modifying text layers that already exist.

Choose a font size

The size of the type in the image is determined by its type size. The font's actual size is determined by the image resolution. In a 72 ppi image, a capital letter in 72 pt text is around one inch high. Because pixels in higher-resolution photos are packed closer together, a particular letter point size decreases with increasing resolution.

- When altering pre-existing text, choose one or more characters whose sizes you wish to adjust. Choose **the text layer in the Layers panel to adjust the size of every character within it.**
- Choose from the **Vertical Type and Horizontal Type tools**.
- Enter or choose a **new Size value in the options bar**. A size bigger than 72 points can be entered. The default unit of measurement is applied to the value you input. Enter the unit (in, cm, pt, px, or pica) after the value in the Size text box to use a different unit of measurement.

Points are the type's default unit of measurement. On the other hand, the Units & Rulers panel of the Preferences dialog box allows you to modify the measurement unit. After selecting **Edit > Preferences > Units & Rulers, choose Type and choose a unit of measurement.**

Change text color

The type color can be altered either before or after the text is entered. You can alter the color of a layer's entire text or just certain characters while modifying text layers that already exist. A gradient can also be applied to text within a text layer.

- **Get any of the following done;**
  - Choose **a type tool** to alter the color of text prior to you choosing it.
  - Choose **a type tool** and then move to choose the text to alter the color of the text currently in use.
- Click the **Color menu** in the options bar to select a color from a list of color swatches. Click **to choose a color and add it to the palette.**

Apply style to text

Text can be given effects. You can apply any effect from the Effects panel to text within a layer.

- Write and commit the text to which you wish to apply a style when working on fresh work. Next, choose **a preset from the Tool Options bar's options.**
- Choose **a layer that has text on it if there is any already.**
- Double-click **the thumbnail of a style you wish to apply to the text in the Effects panel after opening it.**

Other transform options

You can warp type to take on different shapes by distorting it into the form of an arc or a wave, for example. You cannot distort individual characters; warping affects every character in a text layer. Faux bold text cannot be warped either.

- In the Edit workspace, choose **a text layer.**
- **Get any of the following done;**
    - ○ Choose **a type tool, and select the warp button in the tool options bar.**
    - ○ Click on **Layer > Type > Warp Text.**

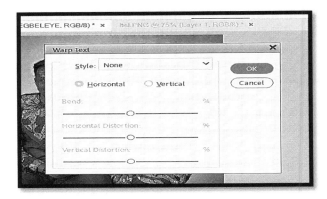

- The Style pop-up menu allows you to select a warp style. The basic form of the twisted text is determined by the style.
- Choose **between a horizontal and vertical orientation for the warp effect.**
- (Optional) Enter **values for extra warping settings to regulate the warp effect's perspective and orientation:**
    - ○ Bend to indicate the amount of warp.
    - ○ Utilize Horizontal Distortion and Vertical Distortion to add perspective to the warp.
- Choose **OK.**

Activity

1. Insert text into your image.
2. Warp a text in an image.

CHAPTER 11

ADD PHOTO EFFECTS AND FILTERS

The Filter / Adjustment menu

Filters can be used to retouch or clean up images. Furthermore, you can apply special art effects or use distortion effects to make original changes utilizing filters. Some of the filters from third-party developers can actually be accessed as plug-ins in addition to those from Adobe. These plug-in filters show up at the lower part of the Filter lists after they are installed.

Below are the three ways by which you can apply filters;

- **Filter menu** here you have all of the filters available and you will be able to apply these filters individually.
- **Filter Gallery** shows a thumbnail representation of each filter's capabilities, similar to the panel. You can apply specific filters more than once and apply filters cumulatively using the Filter Gallery. To get the desired effect, you can also reorganize the filters and modify the parameters of each filter you've used. The Filter Gallery is frequently the greatest option for applying filters because of its extreme flexibility. But not every filter in the Filter menu is present in the Filter Gallery.
- **Filters panel** shows a brief description of each filter's capabilities that is shown in the Filter menu. You can apply separate filters to a picture in the Advanced view using the Filters panel.

With the use of the following information, you can have an adequate understanding of the process of adding filters to your pictures;

- Have a clear view of the outcome of the filter. Having to filter a huge image can take a lot of time. Using the Filter Gallery to preview the filter's effects is faster. The majority of filters also allow you to preview the results in both the document window and the Filter Options dialog box. At that point, you may decide whether to use the filter or abort the process without wasting any time.
- Only the active portion of an image is usually affected by filters. Only the active, visible layer or a specific portion of the layer is impacted by filters.

- Not all photographs can be processed by filters. Certain filters cannot be applied to grayscale photos, and none can be applied to bitmap or indexed-color images. A lot of filters don't function with 16-bit photos.
- It is possible to reapply the prior filter. The Filter menu's top row displays the most recent filter you used. To further improve the image, you can repeat it using the same parameters as before.

Tips for creating visual effects with filters

With the use of the techniques below, you can achieve nice visual outcomes with the use of filters;

- **Highlight the filter's edges**. Feathering the selection before applying the filter allows you to soften the edges of the filter effect when you're applying it to a selected area.
- **Apply filters one after the other to create effects.** To create an effect, you can add filters one at a time or to multiple layers consecutively. The effect can be blended by selecting various blending modes in the Layers window. A layer needs to have pixels in order to be visible and affected by a filter.
- **Construct backgrounds and textures**. You may create a range of backdrops and textures by using filters on grayscale or solid-color photos. Then, you can make these textures blurry. Applying certain filters (like the Glass filter) to solid colors yields interesting results, whereas others have little to no visible effect at all. You may use Add Noise, Chalk & Charcoal, Clouds, Conté Crayon, Difference Clouds, Glass, Graphic Pen, Mezzotint, Note Paper, Pointillize, Reticulation, Rough Pastels, Sponge, or Underpainting for these kinds of hues. Any of the filters in the Texture submenu are also available for use.
- **Boost the uniformity and quality of the images**. By using the same filter on every image in a series, you can improve or mask flaws in the photos or create a uniform appearance.

Apply a filter

- **Make a choice of the aspect of the picture you would like to add the filter;**
  - After deselecting any chosen areas, choose **the layer in the Layers panel to apply a filter to the entire layer.**
  - Select **an area with any selection tool to add a filter to a part of a layer.**
- **Make a choice of how you would like to add a filter;**

o To access the Filter gallery, navigate to **Filter > Filter Gallery,** pick a category, and then click **the filter you wish to use.**

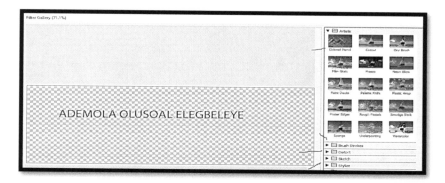

o Double-clicking the desired filter in a category after choosing **Window > Filters will bring up the Filters panel.**

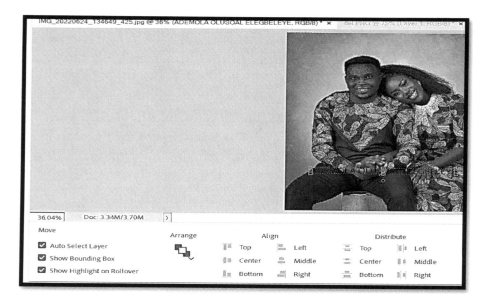

o To utilize the Filter menu, select **Filter, then pick a submenu, then select the desired filter.** A Filter Options dialog box opens when ellipses (†) are placed after a filter name.

• Insert values or choose options if you see a dialog box.

- Choose the Preview option to get a preview of the filter in the document window, if it is available. To preview the filter, use one of the following techniques, based on the filter and the manner in which you are utilizing it:
  - To **zoom in or out of the preview window, use the + or - buttons underneath it.**
  - To select a zoom percentage, click **the zoom bar (where the zoom percentage shows).**
  - To center a particular portion of the image in the preview window, click and **drag within the window**.
  - To conceal the filter thumbnails, click the **Show/conceal button** located at the top of the dialog box. The preview area increases while the thumbnails are hidden.
  - To remove a filter's effect from the preview image, click **the eye icon next to the filter.**
- If there are any sliders in the dialog box, you can see a real-time preview (real-time rendering) by holding down **Alt (Option on Mac OS) and dragging a slider.**
- To center a certain portion of the picture in the preview window, click on **the image window. (Not every preview window may be compatible with this.)**
- If you are making use of the Filter Gallery, or the filter opens in the Filter Gallery, ensure you take any of the subsequent actions and choose OK;
  - To apply an extra filter, click the **New Effect Layer button** located at the bottom of the dialog box. To apply numerous filters, you can add more effect layers.
  - Drag the name of a filter to a different location in the list of deployed filters at the dialog box's bottom to rearrange the filters that have been applied. You can drastically alter the appearance of your image by rearranging the order of the filters.
  - By choosing the filter and selecting the **Delete Effect Layer option**, you can remove applied filters.
- If you happen to be making use of the Filter panel, ensure you do any of the following and choose OK;
- To add a filter to your photo, click on it.
- You can perform any of the following if it is possible.
  - Sliders can be used to change the filter's intensity.

- To add more effects, click the **Apply More button**. A few one-click filters, including Blur, are available.
- Certain filters allow for more customization. Select the **"Advance Options"** option. To change the filter that is applied to the photo, move the sliders and choose other settings in the dialog box.

The Filter Gallery

Filters can be added again and cumulatively with the use of the Filter Gallery (**Filter > Filter Gallery**). To get the desired effect, you can also reorganize the filters and modify the parameters of each filter you've used. You have a great deal of control over how each filter affects your image because you may apply multiple filters to it using the Filter Gallery dialog box. Due to its versatility and ease of use, the Filter Gallery is frequently the greatest option for applying filters. Not all filters, nevertheless, can be accessed using the Filter Gallery. Certain commands can only be accessed individually through the Filter menu. Additionally, unlike the Effects panel, you are unable to apply Styles and effects from the Filter Gallery.

Improve performance with filters and effects

There are certain filters and effects that require a lot of RAM, particularly when used on high-resolution photos. These methods can help you perform better:

- Experiment with the settings and filters on a small portion of the picture.
- Examine the filters and settings on a scaled, smaller version of your photo. Once you are happy with the outcome, reapply the filter on your original image using the same parameters.
- Before applying the filter or effect, free up memory by erasing the undo history, the clipboard, or both. Select **[command] > Edit > Clear.**
- To free up additional RAM, close **other programs**.
- Modify the filter settings to reduce the complexity of memory-intensive filters. Stained glass, glass, ripple, scatter, sprayed strokes, chrome, cutout, and splatter are among the memory-intensive filters. (For instance, enlarging the cell size will simplify the Stained Glass filter). To make the Cutout filter less difficult, either decrease Edge Fidelity or raise Edge Simplicity.)

The Effect panel

You can choose to apply picture effects from a single location in the Effects panel. The Effects panel can be found in both Quick and Advanced mode on the taskbar by default. It shows previews of the artwork or effects that you can apply or add to a picture. A menu of category choices and related subcategories is provided in the majority of sections. You can select effects from three different categories: Color Match, Classic, and Artistic.

Classic Effects

Use the Classic effects in Photoshop Elements to improve your images. In the Quick and Advanced modes, select your preferred effect from the 11 Classic effects available.

To add a Classic effect to your picture, follow these steps:

- Launch **Photoshop Elements and open a photo.**
- To choose from 11 traditional effects in Quick mode, select **Effects.** To choose from more than thirty classic effects in the Advanced mode, select **Effects > Classic.**

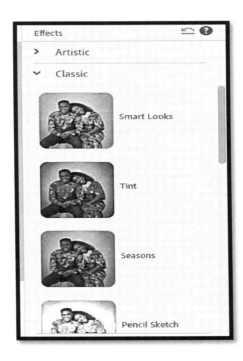

- To apply a Classic effect to your photo, choose **your favorite**.
- Choose **Advanced** to recompose the entire image or specific portions of it. To recompose a shot, you can utilize the **Brush in Tool Options** to mask off desired areas. Additionally, Size and Opacity can be defined.
- To save the picture, choose **File > Save As**. To post it on social media, **choose Share.**

Artistic Effects

You can easily add effects to your images that are modeled after well-known paintings or prominent art movements with just a single click. You can also apply one of the incredible artistic effects to all or portions of your shot, and you can quickly edit the results to get the precise appearance you desire. Both the Quick and Advanced modes allow you to utilize artistic effects.

Get any of the following done if you feel you would like to add an effect that is quite artistic to your picture;

- Navigate to either the Quick mode or advanced mode then choose O**pen to add a picture of your choice.**
- To make your preferred choice from diverse artistic effects, choose **Effects and Artistic in the panel on the right side.**

- Make your preferred choice of any Artistic effect to add to your picture.
- **Get any of the following done;**
  - State **Intensity**.
  - By choosing **Preserve original photo colors**, you can save the original colors of the image.
  - You have the option to take away the picture's creative effect from the topic or background.
  - Choose **Advanced** to recompose the entire image or specific portions of it. To recompose a shot, you can utilize the **Brush in Tool Options** to mask off desired areas. Additionally, the **Size and Threshold** can be defined.
- You can choose to pick **Share** so as to spread it on various social media platforms or you can also click on **File > Save As.**

Photo Effects

You can easily create various appearances for your photographs with photo effects. Select a subcategory from the Effects panel, such as Panels, Textures, Vintage Photo, Monotone Color, and Faded Photo.

- **Frame** A frame generates a drop zone where you can simply add or modify content. You can also choose to apply a range of effects to the boundaries of a chosen layer, or to a piece of a layer.
- **Image Effects Add** effects to a duplicate of a chosen layer. When an image is applied with the Blizzard effect, it appears as though snow is falling. The image is transformed into a striking neon picture using the Neon Glow effect. To blur an image or soften colors, apply image effects like Oil Pastel or Soft Focus. Additionally, you can mix and match image effects; however, you could be asked to flatten layers first.
- **Textures** Add layers of texture to a picture. One can opt to apply a texture as a background to a brand-new, blank image or apply a texture to an already-existing image. You may make visually engaging and appealing images by layering photographs and experimenting with opacity and other layer techniques.

It is worth taking into consideration that many photo effects add filters with values that are modified.

Color Match

With the use of the color match, you can choose to select from pre-made presets or upload your own image. Further adjustments can be made to brightness, saturation, and color. Examine the Quick and Advanced versions of the Color Match effect.

Applying Color match effect in Quick mode;

- In opening the photo you want to apply the effect to, either pick **File > Open or click the Open button.**
- Select from **pre-made settings in the Color Match section of the Effects panel.**

It is worth taking into consideration the fact that color match effects do not work with each other, and as layers are not added, any presets applied to the primary input photo will be replaced by the effect of another preset.

One of the following two methods can be used in the addition of one preset over another:

- When using the next preset, save the result of the previous one and use it as the input photo.
- In Quick mode, apply the **first preset > Change to the Advanced mode**. In the Advanced mode, use the Quick mode result as your input photo and choose the preset you want to use.

- Depending on your requirements, you can choose to fine-tune the Saturation, Brightness, and of course the Hue much more.
- You can choose **Share** if you would like to send this to various social media platforms and if not, simply click on **File > Save As** to have the picture saved.

Application of color matches effect in Advanced mode;

- To open a picture over which you want to apply the effect, choose **File > Open or click the Open button.**
- Change **the mode to Advanced.**
- You can use one of the presets that are already included in the Effects panel, or you can use a photo of your own as a Custom preset by choosing **the Import photo button in the advanced mode.**

Note: A Custom preset can be used as long as the application is running because it is saved for the duration of the launch session. It is deleted when relaunching the program in order to make disk space available. Even though you can bring in the Custom preset more than once in a single launch session, only the Custom preset that you applied most recently will be retained and used for the duration of the session. Every time you import a new Custom preset, the one that was previously imported will be replaced.

- Depending on what you really need, you can adjust your photo's brightness, hue, and saturation further.
- To save the picture, choose **File > Save As**. To post it on social media, choose **Share**.

Render Filters

Cloud

The Clouds filter has the ability to produce a soft cloud pattern with the use of inconsistent values that vary between the foreground and the background color in the toolbar. To bring up a much-starker cloud pattern, press down Alt and Option in Mac OS and then select **Filter > Render > Clouds.**

Difference Clouds

Applying the Difference Clouds filter multiple times results in rib and vein patterns that mimic a marble texture. Initially, the image is partially inverted in a cloud pattern;

subsequent applications yield a cloud pattern made of randomly produced values that fluctuate between the foreground and background color in the toolbox.

Fibers

The Fibers filter uses the colors of the background and foreground to simulate woven strands. The Variance option lets you adjust how the colors change; a low value produces longer color streaks, while a high value produces extremely short strands with a more variable color distribution. The appearance of each fiber is set by the Strength option. Short, stringy fibers are produced by a high setting, whereas spread-out fibers are produced by a low setting. You can choose to randomize the pattern's appearance until you find one that you like. The active layer's image data is replaced with fibers when the Fiber filter is applied.

Lens Flare

The lens flare filter mimics the refraction of light that occurs when intense light is shone into a camera lens. The lens type allows you to adjust the flare's brightness, location, and form. To adjust the flare location, click on the dialog box's preview pane.

Texture Fill

The Texture Fill filter employs a grayscale Photoshop image as a texture for a picture.

Adjustment Filters

Equalize filter

By applying the Equalize filter, one can more evenly represent the complete range of brightness levels in a picture by redistributing the pixel brightness values. Photoshop Elements determines the composite image's brightest and darkest values when you use this command. Then it remaps them so that the black value is represented by the darkest value and the white value by the brightest value. Next, Photoshop Elements shares the intermediate pixel values uniformly throughout the grayscale by equalizing the brightness.

- Choose either an image, layer, or area.
- Click on **Filter > Adjustments > Equalize.**

257

- If you chose a portion of the image, choose what you would like to equalize in the dialog box, and choose OK;
  - o Equalize Selected Area Only in order to distribute just the pixel selection in an even manner.
  - o Equalize the Entire Image Based On the Selected Area in order to evenly distribute all image pixels depending on the ones that are in the selection.

Gradient Map filter

The Gradient Map filter maps the grayscale range of a picture to the colors of an indicated gradient fill.

- Choose **an image, layer, or area.**
- **Do any of the following;**
  - o Select **Gradient Map under Filter > Adjustments.**

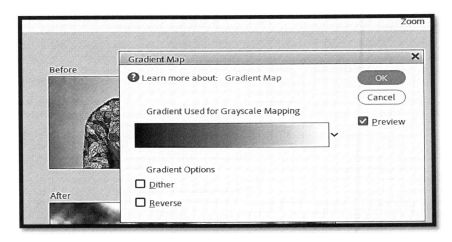

  - o To create a new Gradient Map adjustment layer or open an existing one, use the Layers panel or Layer menu.
- **Choose the gradient fill that you wish to apply:**
  - o Click **the triangle t**o the right of the gradient fill that is visible in the Gradient Map dialog box to select from a selection of gradient fills. Click **in a blank space of the dialog box to dismiss the list after choosing the preferred gradient fill.**
  - o Click **the gradient fill** to make changes to the gradient fill that is currently shown in the Gradient Map dialog box. Next, either make changes to the current gradient fill or start from scratch.

- By default, the gradient fill's beginning (left), midway (middle), and ending (right) colors are mapped to the image's shadows, mid-tones, and highlights, respectively.
- **Choose one or both of the gradient options or none at all:**
  - In order to lessen banding issues and smooth the appearance of the gradient fill, dither adds random noise.
  - Reverse flips the gradient map by changing the gradient fill's orientation.
- Press **OK.**

Apply the Invert filter

An image's colors can be reversed with the Invert filter. Use this command to create a positive from a scanned black-and-white negative or to create a positive from a black-and-white picture negative, for example. Note: The Invert command cannot create accurate positive images from scanned color negatives because the color print film has an orange mask in its base. When scanning film with a slide scanner, make sure you are using the correct settings for color negatives. Each pixel's brightness value is translated into its inverse value on a 256-step color-values scale when an image is inverted. For instance, a pixel with a value of 255 in a positive image is converted to 0.

- Choose **an image, layer, or area.**
- Pick **Filter > Adjustment > Invert.**

Apply the Posterize filter

You can designate how many brightness values, or tonal levels, each channel in a picture has by using the Posterize filter. Pixels are then mapped to the nearest level that matches. In an RGB image, for instance, selecting two tonal levels yields six colors: two for red, two for green, and two for blue. This command is helpful for producing unusual effects in photos, including wide, flat regions. When you decrease the number of gray levels in a grayscale image, its effects become more noticeable. However, it also results in intriguing effects for color photographs.

Note: You can convert an image to grayscale and choose the desired number of levels if you want a certain amount of colors in it. After that, change the image's color mode back to its original setting and add your desired colors to the various gray tones.

- Choose an image, layer, or area.

- **Get any of the following done;**
  - Pick **Filter > Adjustments > Posterize.**

  - Create a new Posterize adjustment layer or open an existing one using the Layers panel or Layer menu.
- To achieve the desired effect, move the slider or enter the desired number of tone levels, then click **OK.**

Apply the Photo filter

The process of placing a colored filter in front of the camera lens is replicated by the Photo Filter command. By adjusting the color temperature and balance of the light that passes through the lens and exposing the film, a colored filter can be used. To apply a hue change to an image, you may also select a color preset using the Photo Filter command. You can use the Adobe Color Picker to provide color when using the Photo Filter command to make a custom color adjustment.

- Get any of the following done;
  - Select the **Photo Filter under Filter > Adjustments.**

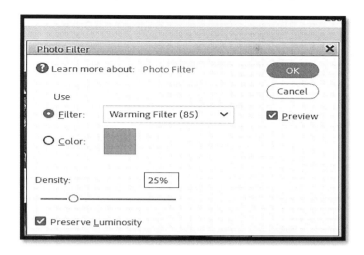

- ○ Select **Photo Filter under Layer > New Adjustment Layer. In the New Layer dialog box, click OK.**

- • **Do any of the following in the dialog box of Photo Filter to pick the filter color;**

  - ○ **Warming Filter (85) and Cooling Filter (80)**   These are color conversion filters that adjust an image's white balance. When an image is taken at a lower light color temperature (yellowish), the Cooling Filter (80) adjusts the image's color to a bluer tone to make up for the lower light color temperature. On the other hand, if the picture was shot at a higher color temperature (bluish), the Warming Filter (85) warms the image's colors to make up for the higher ambient light color temperature.

  - ○ **Warming Filter (81) and Cooling Filter (82)**   these are light balancing filters that are used to make small color corrections to images. The image is made warmer (yellower) by the Warming Filter (81) and cooler (bluer) by the Cooling Filter (82).

  - ○ **Individual Colors**   Use a hue modification on the picture based on the color preset that you select. The Photo Filter command determines the color you can choose. You can use a complementary color to counteract any color cast in your shot. Additionally, colors can be applied to create unique color effects or upgrades. For instance, the underwater color mimics the color cast that results from taking underwater photos, which is greenish-blue.

- • Pick a preset from the **Filter menu after selecting the Filter option.**

- To define the color of a custom color filter, select the Color option, click the color square, and utilize the **Adobe Color Picker.**
- Verify that **Preview** is chosen in order to see the effects of applying a color filter.
- Make sure the **Preserve Luminosity option** is chosen if you want to avoid having the color filter dull the image.
- Use the Density slider or type a percentage in the Density text box to change the image's color saturation. A greater color correction is applied with a higher density.
- Press **OK.**

The Styles panel

You may easily add effects to a whole layer using layer styles. You can examine a number of predefined layer styles in the Effects panel and apply a style with a single mouse click. When you make changes to that layer, the effect's borders are updated automatically. For instance, when you edit the content on a text layer that has a drop shadow style applied, the shadow updates instantly. Since layer styles are cumulative, you can apply numerous styles to a layer to get a complicated effect. For every layer, you can apply a single style from each style library. A layer's style settings can also be altered to modify the outcome. A style symbol shows up in the Layers panel to the right of the layer name when you apply a style to it. The contents of a layer are related to its style. The effects are adjusted in tandem with any moves or changes made to the layer's contents. You can modify a layer's style settings or apply other style settings or attributes from the dialog box by selecting **Layer > Layer Style > Style Settings.**

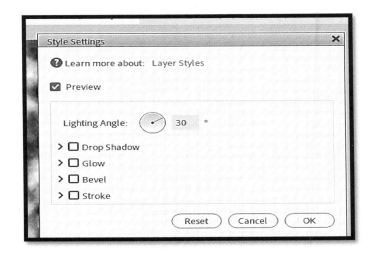

Angle of Lighting indicates the illumination angle at which the layer will receive the effect.

- ○ **Shadow Drop** defines the separation between a drop shadow and the content of the layer. The sliders allow you to adjust the size and opacity as well.
- ○ **Glow (Exterior)** describes the size of a light that comes from the layer's content's outer edges. The slider can also be used to adjust the opacity.
- ○ **Glow (Within)** describes the size of a light that comes from the layer's content's inner edges. The slider can also be used to adjust the opacity. Size of the Bevels describes the amount of beveling that runs along the inner margins of the content of the layer.

Work with layer styles

A layer can have special effects applied to it, its styles hidden or shown, and even its scale changed (for example, by adjusting the size of a glow effect). Transferring a style from one layer to another is simple.

Apply a layer style

- Choose **a layer in the Layers panel.**
- Pick Layer Styles from the category menu in the effects panel.
- **Get any of the following done;**
  - ○ Choose **your preferred style and choose Apply.**
  - ○ Click **twice on a style.**
  - ○ Move **a style onto a layer**

In case you're not happy with the outcome, you may undo the style by selecting **Edit > Undo or by pressing Ctrl+Z (Command + Z on Mac OS).**

Hide or show all layers styles in an image

- **Select from the following options:**
  - **Layer > Style of Layer > Conceal All Effects.**
  - **Layer > Style of Layer > Display All Effects.**

Edit a layer's style settings

To change the effect, alter the style parameters of a layer. Additionally, you can delete a style from a layer and copy style settings between layers.

- Select **Style Settings under Layer > Layer Style.**
- Click **Preview** to see how your image has changed.
- Click **OK** after making any necessary adjustments or adding new layer style options.

Copy style settings between layers

- Choose the layer that has the style settings you wish to duplicate from the Layers panel.
- Select **Layer > Style > Copy Layer Style from the menu.**
- In the Layers panel, select the destination layer, then select **Layer > Layer Style > Paste Layer Style.**

Remove a layer style

- To remove a style, select **the layer that contains it in the Layers panel.**
- Select **Layer > Style > Delete Layer Style.**

Graphics Panel

The Graphics panel gives you a single area to add text styles, theme embellishments, and artwork to your photos.

- Select **Window > Graphics to bring up the Graphics panel.**

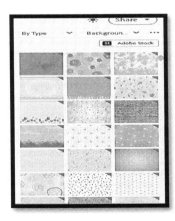

The following parts of the Graphics panel offer a variety of stuff to improve your photographs. For instance, a range of frames, backgrounds, graphics, forms, and text are available for selection. A drop-down menu located beneath every tab facilitates the selection of appropriate frames, backgrounds, pictures, shapes, or text to duplicate. Thumbnail representations of the artwork or effects that you can apply or add to an image are always displayed in each section. A menu of category options and related subcategories is provided in the majority of sections.

Add stylized shapes or graphics to a picture

Anytime that shapes and graphics are added as additional layers to images; they don't alter the source image in any way when you add them.

- Select **a category (like By Event or By Activity) and a subcategory (like Baby or Cooking) from the Graphics panel's menu.**
- Select **any color of your choice for the shape from the toolbox.**
- **Take one of these actions:**
  - Click **a thumbnail twice.**
  - Drag **the image to the thumbnail.**
- Make use of the Move tool to have the shape or graphic relocated or resized.

Add an artistic background to a picture

An image's original background layer is replaced when you apply an artistic backdrop. For instance, you could use the selection tools to make a layer that isolates your family from the background of the kitchen, and then swap out the background of the kitchen for one of nature.

- Pick the background layer of your image and pick **Layer > Duplicate Layer.**

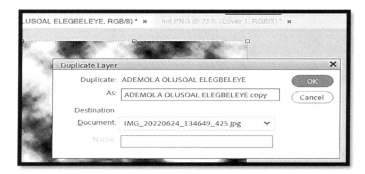

- **After naming the layer, click OK.**
- In the Layers panel, choose the **Background layer.**
- From the drop-down menu in the Graphics panel, choose **Backgrounds.**
- **Take one of these actions:**
  - Click **a thumbnail twice.**
  - Drag **the image to the thumbnail.**

Add a frame or theme to a picture

A blank (gray) space for the image appears in frames when you add a theme or frame to a photo project. Drag and drop an image to the empty space from the Photo Bin.

- Select **Frames from the drop-down menu in the Graphics panel.**
- Take one of these actions:
  - Choose **an image > Click Apply.**
  - Click **a thumbnail twice.**
  - Move **the thumbnail to the background that is empty.**
- Drag **the preferred picture to the frame from the Photo Bin.**
- To apply the modification, use the slider to resize the image within the frame or theme border. Alternatively, choose the **Cancel icon to undo the changes.**
- After centering the image with the Move tool, choose the **Commit or Cancel icons to make the change effective.**

Activity

1. Briefly describe the effects panel.
2. Make use of the adjustment filters to enhance your picture.
3. With the use of the styles panel, add styles to your picture.

CHAPTER 12

PHOTOSHOP ELEMENTS TRICKS

Swap out a face

Using Photoshop's Object Selection tool, you may select any desired element from an image. It can be used to grasp an individual feature, such as an eye, nose, or the entirety of a face or head. You can select the face you want to replace in an image by cutting it out using the Object Selection tool. Once you have, save it as a separate layer. Working with a face that is larger than the one you are trying to replace is a smart idea. A huge face fits over a small one more easily. You can produce a higher-quality face by increasing resolution, which will prevent you from having to cope with pixelation deformities brought on by resizing. Then, you can progressively resize and align the features. Drag the face from the new image and position it over the face in the primary photo. To show the original characteristics beneath the face you're using, reduce the opacity of the face layer. Align the lips, nose, and eyes, then layer the new face on top of the old one gradually. Once you've positioned it how you like, return the opacity to 100%. The new face should be positioned over the old one as naturally as possible.

Swap out a background

You can quickly erase a background and replace it with another photo, color, or preset option.

This can be done with almost no difficulty at all when you make use of the Replace Background Guided Edit.

- The first step is to make a choice of your picture. Open your preferred photo to be used in Guided mode and then choose Special Edits and choose the Replace Background feature.
- Once you have done the above, the very next thing is for you to make a choice of your subject. This can be done when you choose the Select Subject button so you can instantly choose your preferred subject.
- **In this step, you are to choose an entirely new background.**
  - To include a picture as the new background, select **Import a photo.**
  - For the inclusion of the background presets, choose **Presets.**

- o To ensure the background is made transparent, choose **None.**
- o To also include a preferred color as the background, choose **a Color.**
- In this fourth step, you are to get your selection refined. If need be, you can click the Refine Edge choice to have your selection refined.

Remove warts and blemishes

Face-aware technology is used by the Adjust Facial Features workflow to recognize and modify a person's facial features in a picture. Simple sliders can be used to raise or decrease the influence of facial characteristics like the jaw, nose, lips, and eyes in a portrait photo.

- Launch **a picture in Photoshop Elements.**
- Choose **Enhance then click on Adjust Facial Features.**
- The person's face is highlighted in a circle in the Adjust Facial Features dialog box, signifying that the face-aware feature has identified a face in the image.
- Double-click the slider to return adjustments to a specific attribute. Changes made to that attribute are undone.
- **Take one of these actions:**
  - o Click **Reset** to remove the changes you have made to your facial characteristics.
  - o Click **OK t**o apply the changes made to the face features.

Remove big things from your photos

When you drag the Healing Brush over significant regions of imperfection, it fixes them. Items on a grassy field, for example, can be taken out of a background that is uniform.

- Choose the **Healing Brush tool.**
- Make a choice of the size of a brush from the Tool Options bar and configure healing brush choices;

  - o **Mode** determines how the pattern or source integrates with the current pixel structure. The original pixels are covered over by new ones in normal mode. The Replace mode maintains the texture and grain of the film at the brush stroke's edges.

- Source specifies the source to be used in pixel correction. Pixels from the current image are sampled. Pixels from the pattern you specify in the Pattern panel are used by Pattern.
- **Aligned** retains the current sample point while constantly collecting pixels, even when the mouse button is released. Every time you stop and start painting again, deselect Aligned to keep utilizing the sampled pixels from the first sampling point.
- **Sample Every Layer**   To sample data from the current layer and below, all visible layers, or the current layer itself, select Sample All Layers.

- To view sample data, place the pointer in any open image and hit **Alt (or Option on Mac OS)**.   Unless one of the photos is in grayscale mode, the two pictures must be in identical color mode when you are applying a sample from one to another.
- To combine sampling data and existing data, drag the image over the defect. Every time you let go of the mouse button, the sampled pixels blend in with the surrounding pixels. Make a selection before using the Healing Brush tool if the edges of the region you wish to heal have a lot of contrast. Enlarge the selection to encompass the desired healing region while adhering strictly to the border of pixel contrast.

Activity

1. Swap out a face.
2. Swap out a background.
3. Remove things from your picture.

CHAPTER 13

ADVANCED PHOTO EDITING TOOLS

Scan your photos

You can obtain scanned images of your slides, negatives, and photos by connecting Elements Organizer to your scanner. Scanners can provide images in two different ways:

- Utilize the plug-in scanner driver module that was included with your scanner. This program can be used to scan and open photos directly in Elements Organizer using the TWAIN interface, or it can be used to work with Windows' 32-bit Elements Organizer.

Note: Only Windows is supported for the TWAIN manager.

To scan and save your photographs, use the stand-alone scanning software that was included with your scanner.

After that, you have the following options for importing the photographs into Elements Organizer:

- Choose **Import.** Choose **from Scanner.**
- Click on **File > Get Photos and Videos > From Scanner.**

Get photos from scanners

Make sure you've installed all of the software that came with your scanner before attempting to scan and then launching your photos in Elements Organizer. Examine any documentation that accompanied your scanner carefully to ensure that it is connected to your computer correctly.

- Verify that your scanner is turned on and connected.
- **Perform one of the following actions in Elements Organizer:**
  - Press **Import. Choose Using Scanner.**
  - Choose **File > Use Scanner to Get Photos and Videos.**
- Select **the scanner name from the Scanner option in the Get Photos From Scanner dialog box.**
- To choose a location for storing the pictures, click **Browse.**

- The **Save As option allows** you to select a file format. The default format, JPEG, is typically the best option. If JPEG is selected, you can adjust the scan quality by using the Quality slider. The file size increases with increasing quality.
- Press **OK**. Elements Organizer starts the driver that came with your scanner if it is a TWAIN-compatible scanner. To scan your photo, refer to the driver software's instructions. Usually, you may also pick a region to scan or fix any color problems you may notice.

The Getting Photos dialog box displays a preview of the scan after the photo has been scanned. The photographs are assigned the import date by the Elements Organizer.

Scan photos using a TWAIN driver

A software driver called TWAIN is used by some digital cameras, frame grabbers, and scanners to acquire images. Elements Organizer needs a source manager and TWAIN data source from the manufacturer in order for your TWAIN device to function. Install the TWAIN device and accompanying software, restart your computer, and use the scanner to import images into Elements Organizer. (For installation details, consult the documentation provided by the maker of your device.)

- You can choose **File > Get Photos and Videos > From Scanner or Import > From Scanner in Elements Organizer.**

The image is displayed in the Elements Organizer once it has been scanned. Please take note that on certain scanners (like the Canon MP960), the scanning progress bar will open at the back of Photoshop Elements when you push the button for the first time. To advance the progress bar, shrink the Photoshop Elements window.

Download photos from your digital camera

Some digital cameras use Windows Image Acquisition (WIA) functionality to import photos. Photoshop Elements allows you to import photographs straight into the program when you utilize WIA. Photoshop Elements is compatible with Windows and any digital camera or scanner software.

- Select **WIA Support under File > Import.**
- Select **a location on your computer** where you want to save your picture files.

- Verify that **Photoshop's Open Acquired Image(s) option is selected.** Deselect this option if you wish to alter the images later or if you are importing a lot of images.
- Choose **Create Unique Subfolder Using Date Today** if you want to save the imported images straight into a folder with the current date as its name.
- Select **"Start."**
- Choose **which digital camera to import your photos from.**
- Select **the image or images to be imported:**
  - To import the image, click **on it from the thumbnail list.**
  - If you want to import numerous photographs at once, **hold down Shift while clicking each one.**
  - To import every image that is accessible, click **Select All.**
- To import the picture, click **Get Picture.**

Camera RAW installation

Comparing Photoshop Elements to Adobe Camera Raw, Photoshop offers more editing options.

You must follow these steps in order to install the Adobe Camera Raw plugin:

- In Elements Organizer or Photoshop Elements, select **Help > Install Camera Raw.**
- Open Photoshop Elements and choose **File > Open in Camera Raw.**

Edit in Camera RAW

An image file is created when a digital camera's image sensor takes a picture. Usually, a picture file is compressed and processed before being saved to the memory card of your camera. Cameras may, however, also keep an image as a raw file, meaning they don't need to process or compress it. Consider raw camera files to be negatives for photos. Instead of depending on the camera to process the information, you may open a raw file in Photoshop Elements, make changes, and save it. You can adjust the white balance, tonal range, contrast, color saturation, and sharpness while working with camera raw files. Make sure your camera is set to save files in the raw file format before using raw files. The files include filename extensions like NEF, CR2, CRW, or other raw formats when you download them straight from the camera. Only cameras that Photoshop Elements is compatible with may open raw files.

Your edits that were made with the use of Photoshop Elements are usually not saved to the original raw file (non-destructive editing). You have the option to open a treated raw file in Photoshop Elements after utilizing the functionality of the Camera Raw dialog box to process the raw image file. After editing the file, you can save it in a format that is compatible with Photoshop Elements. Nothing has changed from the original raw file. One way to interpret the raw file format is with a Process Version. Process Version 2012 is the version that is utilized by default. You can work with the newest and enhanced features in the raw file format by using this method of understanding the format. Three Process Versions (one current and two old) are included in Photoshop Elements.

The whole list of variants is as follows:

- Process Version 2012 (Adobe Photoshop Elements 11 default) which is used to date
- Adobe Photoshop Elements 10 uses Process Version 2010.
- Process Version 2003, or older, as utilized in Adobe Photoshop Elements

The default Process Version 2012 is utilized when you open a raw file that hasn't been opened in any previous version of Photoshop Elements. But an older Process Version is used when you open a raw file that was opened in a previous version of Photoshop Elements.

- Click the **Camera Calibration tab** in the Camera Raw 9.1 dialog box to verify the Process Version applied to your raw image. The Process Version that is currently in use is shown in the Process field.

You are able to deal with the most recent improvements in the raw format using Process Version 2012. Nonetheless, you can decide to apply an older Process Version to your more recent raw photographs if you have a large number of raw images that were opened using earlier versions of Photoshop Elements (and so utilizing older Process Versions). This preserves your previous workflow and aids in maintaining consistency while processing photographs from the past and present.

Opening and processing camera raw files

- Click on **File > Open in the Edit workspace.**
- Click **Open after browsing to choose one or a couple of camera raw files.** The tone range of the picture at the current settings is displayed via the histogram in

the Camera Raw dialog box. The histogram automatically updates as you make changes to the settings.

- Alter the view of the image with the use of the controls like Zoom tool, and options like Shadows and Highlights which show clipping in the preview area.

Please note that when you select Preview, an image preview with your adjusted parameters is shown. When Preview is deselected, the camera raw image is displayed with the hidden tab's settings in addition to the current tab's original settings.

- Choose the **Rotate Image icons** to flip the image 90 degrees clockwise or counterclockwise.
- Select **a choice from the Settings pane (Settings menu > Previous Conversion)** to execute the settings used in the previous camera raw image or the camera's preset settings. For example, processing photographs with identical lighting circumstances rapidly is made possible by using the same settings.
- Configure options to modify the white balance this is optional.

It is important to note that as you make adjustments to the pixels in your image using the Camera Raw dialog box, you can keep an eye on their RGB values. To see the RGB values just below the pointer, place the Zoom, Hand, White Balance, or Crop tools over the preview image.

- Use the Exposure, Brightness, Contrast, and Saturation sliders to change the tone. Choose **Auto** if you want to make the changes automatically and undo the manual ones. Press **Alt (Option in Mac OS) and select Reset** to return all options to their original settings.
- **Get any of the following done;**
  - Click **Open Image** to open a copy of the camera raw image file in Photoshop Elements with the camera raw settings applied. The image can be altered, and it can be saved in a format compatible with Photoshop Elements. There are no changes made to the original camera raw file.
  - Click **Cancel** to exit the dialog box and undo the changes.
  - Click **Save Image** to save the edits to a DNG file.

Adobe suggests using the Digital Negative (DNG) format as the industry standard for camera raw files. Because DNG files include both the raw camera sensor data and the image specification, they are helpful for archiving camera raw photographs. Rather than being kept in sidecar XMP files or the camera raw database, camera raw picture settings can also be saved in DNG files.

Adjust sharpness in camera raw files

You may get the desired edge definition by adjusting the sharpness of the image using the Sharpness slider. An adaptation of the Adobe Photoshop Unsharp Mask filter is the Sharpness adjustment. This adjustment enhances the contrast of the pixels by the amount you provide and finds pixels that differ from surrounding pixels based on the threshold you specify. The Camera Raw plug-in determines the threshold to be used when opening a camera raw file by taking into account the exposure compensation, ISO, and camera model. You have the option to apply sharpening to previews only or to every image.

- Zoom **the preview picture to about 100%.**
- Choose **the Detail tab.**
- To raise or reduce sharpening, drag the **Sharpness slider to the right or left. Sharpening is turned off at zero.** For crisper photos, generally move the Sharpness slider to a lower number.

Use the camera raw Sharpness slider in Photoshop Elements if you don't intend to make many edits to the image. Toggle off camera raw sharpening if you do intend to make significant edits to the image using Photoshop Elements. After you've finished all the other editing and resizing, use Photoshop Elements' sharpening filters as the final step.

Reducing noise in camera raw images

The Camera Raw dialog box's Detail tab has options for minimizing image noise or the glaringly unnecessary visual artifacts that deteriorate image quality. Image noise consists of two types: chroma (color) noise, which appears as colorful artifacts in the image, and luminance (grayscale) noise, which gives an image a grainy appearance. Photographs captured with less advanced digital cameras or at high ISO settings may have observable noise. Grayscale noise can be reduced by sliding the Luminance Smoothing slider to the right, and chroma noise can be reduced by moving the Color Noise Reduction slider to the right. For a better look, preview photographs at 100% when adjusting Luminance Smoothing or the noise of the color Reduction.

Save changes to camera raw images

Modifications you make to a camera raw file can be saved. The camera raw picture with your modifications is saved as a.dng file by the Camera Raw dialog box. Photoshop Elements does not open a file that has been saved automatically. (The Open command may be used to open a camera raw file. The file can then be edited and saved just like any other picture.)

- Make edits to a few camera raw photos using the Camera Raw dialog box.
- Press the **Save Image icon.**
- If you are saving more than one camera raw file, you will be prompted to choose where to save the file and how to name it in the Save Options dialog box.

Supplementary choices

- **Embed Fast Load Data**: increases the pace at which the raw image is reviewed by embedding a substantially smaller duplicate of the raw image within the DNG file.
- **Use Lossy Compression**: causes a loss of quality and shrinks the size of your DNG file. Suggested exclusively for unprocessed photos to be archived and never be printed or utilized for other reasons (such as production).
- **Embed Original Raw File**: this choice saves all of the main camera raw picture data in the DNG file.
- Choose **Save.**

Open a camera raw image in the Edit workspace

You can open and edit a camera raw image in the Edit workspace after processing it in the Camera Raw dialog box.

- Make edits to one or a few Camera Raw photos using the **Camera Raw dialog box.**
- Select **Open Image** from the menu. The image appears in the Edit workspace and the Camera Raw dialog box closes.

Important controls for Camera Raw

- **Zoom tool**   When you click anywhere within the preview image, the preview zoom is set to the following preset zoom value. To zoom out, use **Alt-click (Option-click in Mac OS X)**. To zoom in on a specific location, drag the Zoom tool within the preview image. To bring the Zoom tool back to 100%, **double-click on it.**

- **Hand tool**   if the preview image has a zoom level set higher than 100%, this function moves the image within the preview window. When using another tool, you can access the Hand tool by holding down the spacebar. To customize the preview picture in the window, **double-click the Hand tool.**
- **The White Balance tool Adjusts** the color of the whole image and eliminates color casts by setting the clicked region to a neutral gray tone. The color adjustment is reflected in the Temperature and Tint parameters.
- **The crop tool** erases a portion of a picture. To pick the area you wish to keep, drag **the tool inside the preview image** and hit **Enter.**
- **Straighten tool The** Straighten tool can be used to realign a picture either horizontally or vertically. In order to allow for the straightening of the image, this tool also crops or resizes the canvas.
- **Red Eye removal** helps to take off the red eye in flash pictures of people as well as green or white eyes in pets.
- **Rotate buttons** this button rotates the pictures either in a clockwise or anti-clockwise manner.

Custom camera settings

Photoshop Elements uses information from the file to determine the type of camera used to create a camera raw file, which it then uses to apply the proper camera configurations to the picture. You can alter your camera's default settings if you consistently make the same modifications. Additionally, you can alter the settings for every camera type you own, but not for several of the same models.

- Click the **options button** and select **Save New Camera Raw Default** to save the current settings for the camera that produced the image as the default.
- Click the **menu button** and select **Reset Camera Raw Default to utilize Photoshop Elements' default camera settings.**
- Click the **options button** and select **"Clear Imported Settings" to remove the previous settings.**

Photoshop Elements Preferences and Presets

Preferences

You can set up Photoshop Elements' Preferences to suit your needs and specifications for the best possible performance. You can customize the UI mode, enable soft notifications, control zoom with the scroll wheel, reset preferences, control warning dialogs, and more in the General category of the Preferences dialog box.

Switching to Light and Dark mode

The application's UI color mode can be adjusted to either light or dark from the options.

To change to either Light or Dark mode, take these steps:

You can use one of the following techniques to open the Preferences dialog box:

- On Windows, choose **Edit > Preferences > General; on Mac OS, choose Photoshop Elements > Preferences > General.**
- Choose either **the Moon or Light icon.** To customize the application, pick the Preferences button to bring up the Preferences dialog box.
- The Preferences dialog box will become apparent on the display. From the drop-down menu, choose the preferred UI Mode. Click **OK.**
- There will be a notification on the screen telling you to restart the application. Click **OK.**
- For the modification to take effect, **relaunch the application.**

Restore default preferences

Photoshop Elements Editor's preference settings govern various aspects such as file saving, using plug-ins and scratch disks, displaying images, cursors, and transparencies, among other things. The preferences file might be harmed if the application behaves strangely. All preferences can be returned to their original settings. It should be noted that deleting the preferences file is an irreversible action.

- **Take one of these actions:**
    - As soon as Photoshop Elements launches, press and **hold Alt+Control+Shift (Mac: Option+Command+Shift)**. To remove the Adobe Photoshop Elements settings file, select Yes.

- To reset preferences on the next launch button, go to **Edit > Preferences (Mac: Photoshop Elements > Preferences > General)**, **select it,** and then click **OK.** All preferences are returned to their initial values when you restart Adobe Photoshop Elements.

Photoshop Elements Editor creates a new preferences file the next time you launch it. Look up the name of the preference in Help to find more details about a particular preference option.

Redisplay disabled warning messages

There are times when alerts or prompts appear in the form of messages. To stop these messages from showing up, click the Don't Show Again button within the message. The messages you've disabled can also be reset at a later date.

- To access General, go to **Edit > Preferences in Windows. Select Preferences > General under Photoshop Elements on a Mac**.
- After selecting Reset All Warning Dialogs, click **OK.**

About Presets

Pop-up panels that open in the Tool Options bar when in advanced mode provide you access to pre-made libraries of brushes, color swatches, gradients, patterns, layer styles, and custom shapes. Presets are the objects that are found in each library. Pop-up panels provide a thumbnail image of the preset that is currently selected when they are closed. A pop-up panel's display can be altered to show presets by name, as thumbnail icons, or with both names and icons. To load alternative preset libraries, utilize the Presets Manager. The Photoshop Elements program folder's Presets subdirectory contains distinct library files containing presets.

Use preset tool options

- Choose **the tool that you wish to use.**
- Click **the pop-up panel** in the Tool Options bar. (Pop-up panels are exclusive to certain tools.)
- **Take one of the following actions:**
  ○ Choose the panel menu icon to view and choose the preset libraries that are presently loaded.

- o Click **on a library item to choose a preset.**
- o To store a brush, open the menu on the pop-up panel, select the **Save Brush command**, type a name into the given dialog box, and click **OK.**
- o To save a gradient or pattern, select the **New Gradient or New Pattern command from the panel menu**, type a name into the given dialog box, and click **OK.**
- o Open the pop-up panel menu, select the **Rename command**, type a new name, and click **OK** to rename a brush, gradient, or pattern in the panel.
- o Click an object, open the pop-up panel menu, and then click the **Delete command** to remove a brush, gradient, or pattern from the panel. In Mac OS, you can also click a brush or gradient while **holding down the Alt (Option) key.**
- o Open the pop-up panel menu in order to save a library of brushes, gradients, or patterns. Select **the command to save brushes**, gradients, or patterns from the menu, name the library file, and click **Save.**
- o Open the menu on the pop-up panel, select the **Load command**, then choose the library file you wish to add and click **Load** to load a library of brushes, gradients, or patterns.

Remember that the Load command expands your collection of brushes by adding the brush library. Selecting **a preset library of brushes** causes your existing collection of brushes to be replaced.

- • Click **Append** to add resources from a library to an already existing library. Click **Append** after selecting the library file you wish to include.
- • Select a library file from the menu's bottom section, open the pop-up panel menu, and click **OK** to replace the panel's current set of gradients. Alternatively, you can click Load after selecting a library file via browsing.
- • Select a library from the Brushes menu to replace the current collection of brushes or patterns in a panel.

Note however that you can also select **Preset Manager** from the menu in the pop-up window and load another library of brushes, gradients, or patterns using the **Preset Manager** to replace the existing set.

- • To bring up the preset palette of brushes, gradients, or patterns, select the **Reset command from the pop-up panel menu.**

Change the display of items in a pop-up panel menu

- **Take one of these actions:**
    - Click **the menu icon located in the top-right corner** of the pop-up panel to access the menu and adjust the display of a single panel.
    - Click the **More button after selecting Edit > Preset Manager** to access the **Preset Manager** and adjust the display for every panel.
- **Choose a view option;**

    - **Text only** shows the name of each item.
    - **Small Thumbnail or Large Thumbnail** shows a thumbnail of each item.
    - **Small List or Large List** shows the name and thumbnail of each item.
    - **The stroke Thumbnail** shows a sample brush stroke and brushes thumbnail. Note that this choice is available just for brushes alone.

Use the Preset Manager

The Photoshop Elements preset brush, color swatch, gradient, style, effect, and pattern libraries can be managed in the Advanced mode by using the Preset Manager (Edit > Preset Manager). You can make a collection of your preferred brushes or go back to the original defaults, for instance. Every kind of library is a file that has a default folder and a file extension of its own. Preset files have been put on your computer in the Photoshop Elements software folder's Presets folder. In the Preset Manager, you can remove a preset by choosing it and then selecting **Delete**. To return a library's default elements, you can perpetually use the **Reset command.**

Load a library

- Select **Brushes, Swatches, Gradients, Styles, Patterns, or Effects from the Preset Type menu in the Preset Manager.**
- **Take one of these actions:**
    - After choosing a library from the list by clicking **Add, click Load.** To load a library from another folder, navigate to there, and choose the library from there. Preset files are set up on your computer by default in the Photoshop Elements software folder's Presets folder.
    - Select **a library** from the menu's bottom part by clicking the **More button.**
- Choose the **Done button** when you are through.

Save a subset of a library

- To pick multiple contiguous presets in the **Preset Manager,** use **Shift-click**; to select **multiple noncontiguous presets**, use **Ctrl-click (Command-click in Mac OS).** The new library contains only the presets that have been chosen.
- After selecting **Save Set**, give the library a name. Move to the novel folder prior to saving if you wish to store the library in a different location than the normal one.

Rename a preset

- Choose from the following options in the **Preset Manager:**
  - From the list, pick a preset, and then select **Rename.**
  - In the list, **double-click a preset.**
- Put in a different preset name. You are asked to provide several names if you choose more than one preset.

Activity

1. Scan your pictures.
2. Download pictures from your camera.
3. Edit pictures in camera raw.
4. What are presets?

CHAPTER 14
LEARN ABOUT YOUR PHOTOSHOP ELEMENTS FILE

The Info panel

When in Advanced mode, the Info panel shows the color value underneath the pointer and provides file information about the image. Other helpful information can also be found in the Info panel, based on the tool being used.

- To view the Info panel, select **Window > Info (F8).**

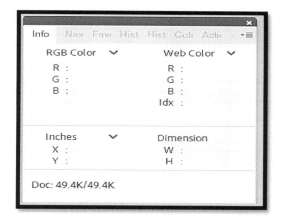

- Choose **a tool.**
- **To use the tool, drag the pointer inside the image or move it into it. Depending on the tool you're using, the following data might show up:**
  - The colors beneath the pointer's numerical values
  - Where the pointer's x and y coordinates are.
  - The dimensions of an active selection, or the width (W) and height (H) of a marquee or shape as you drag.
  - When you click **on the image**, the x and y coordinates of your starting point will appear.
  - As you shift a selection, layer, or shape, its location changes along the x and y coordinates.

o The angle of rotation during a transformation, the angle (A) of a line or gradient, or the angle that changes when you move a selection, layer, or object. The distance (D) that changes when you move a layer, shape, or selection.

o The proportion of width (W) and height (H) changes when a selection, layer, or form is scaled.

o The skew angle of a selection, layer, or shape, is expressed as either a horizontal (H) or vertical (V) angle.

Set color modes and units of measurement in the info panel

- **Take one of these actions:**
  - **Select a color mode from the pop-up menu to alter the way color values are displayed. Additionally, you can select Panel Options from the Info panel's More menu, after which you can select a color mode for the First** Color Readout or the Second Color Readout:

    o **Grayscale** shows the grayscale values under the cursor.
    o **RGB Color** shows the RGB (red, green, blue) values under the cursor.
    o **Web Color** shows the hexadecimal code for the RGB values under the pointer.
    o **HSB Color** shows the HSB (hue, saturation, brightness) values under the cursor.

  - Click **the pop-up menu** and select a different unit of measurement to replace the one that is now shown. Additionally, the Info panel's More menu offers Panel Options. Select a measurement unit from the Mouse Coordinates menu, then press the **OK button.**

Display file information in the info panel or status bar

The data shown in the status bar and info panel can be modified. (The current magnification is shown in the leftmost area of the status bar at the bottom of the document window. Information about the currently open file is shown in the area adjacent to the leftmost one.)

- Choose **Panel Options from the More menu.**

- **Choose a view option;**

  - **Document Sizes** provide details about the quantity of data present in the picture. The image's printing size is indicated by the number on the left, which is roughly equivalent to the size of the flattened, saved PSD file. The estimated size of the file, including layers, is shown by the number on the right.

  - **Document Profile** shows the name of the color profile being used by the picture.

  - **Document Dimensions** shows the size of the picture in the units in use currently.

  - **Scratch Sizes** shows the RAM and scratch disk space used for the picture processing. The RAM that Photoshop Elements is now using to display all open images is indicated by the number on the left. The RAM that Photoshop Elements may use to process photos is shown by the number on the right.

  - **Efficiency** shows the portion of time that is truly spent carrying out a task as opposed to reading from or writing to the scratch disk. Photoshop Elements uses the scratch disk and runs more slowly if the value is less than 100%.

Save or delete metadata templates

You can store the metadata entries in metadata templates if you frequently enter the same metadata. You can enter data into the templates and avoid having to repeatedly type metadata in the File Info dialog box. You can find files and photographs by searching for information in the Photo Browser.

- Select one of the following actions when the File Info dialog box appears (**File > File Info**):
    - Click **the drop-down menu** in the File Info dialog box's button row, then choose **Export** to save metadata as a template. After naming the template, click **Save.**
    - You can select the **Show Templates Folder** to remove a metadata template. Choose **the template** you wish to remove by browsing through them, and then hit **Delete.**

File Info

Each image file created by your digital camera captures details about the shot, including the shutter speed, aperture, date and time of the shot, camera model, and more. This data is referred to as metadata, and it may be viewed and expanded upon in the Photoshop Elements File Info dialog box and the Properties panel of the Elements Organizer. s you edit and arrange your collection, you can add file metadata to assist in identifying your photographs, such as a title, keyword tags, and descriptions. Photoshop Elements automatically logs your modification history and adds it to the file's metadata as you work on your images. Additionally, a Digimarc watermark check is immediately performed on opened photos. Photoshop Elements indicates the presence of a watermark in the image window title bar and adds information about it to the Copyright Status, Copyright Notice, and Copyright Info URL sections of the File Info dialog box. To identify photos as your own creations, you can apply visual watermarks to them. File metadata does not track visual watermarks.

View or add file information

The camera data, caption, and additional authorship and copyright information for the file are shown in the File Info dialog box. You can edit or add data to Photoshop Elements files by using this dialog box. You add data, and XMP (Extensible Metadata Platform) embeds it into the file. A single XML architecture known as XMP is made available to Adobe products and workflow partners, facilitating the standardization of document metadata creation, processing, and exchange across publication processes. You can speed up the process of adding information to files by using metadata templates if you have metadata that you frequently enter for various files. The data that is shown for the Camera Data metadata category cannot be changed. Keywords are displayed in the File Info dialog box when tags are added to a file using the Photo Browser. Certain file formats, like BMP and PDF, do not allow tags to be used as keywords.

- When a picture is open, select **File > File Info.** In the Photo Bin, you can also select **File Info by doing a right-click on a thumbnail.**
- For detailed information to appear, select **the Description tab** at the top of the dialog box. You can add or change the document title, author details, keywords, and copyright information in the description. To incorporate the data, enter the text into the corresponding fields and select OK. Select the desired copyright status by selecting an option from the drop-down menu.

Activity

1. Add information to your file.
2. What is the use of the info panel?

CHAPTER 15

MANAGE YOUR FILES WITH THE ORGANIZER

Auto Curate

Selecting your greatest pictures by hand from an album or catalog can be challenging and time-consuming. Elements Organizer intelligently scans your photos with Auto Curate, selecting the best ones with a single click. Once your photographs have been automatically selected by Elements Organizer, you can start working on fascinating photo projects right away, like calendars and slideshows. In addition, you may browse through them to revisit your favorite moments, add them to albums, and share them on social media.

- Choose **Auto Curate** from the menu in the top-right corner of the Media view.

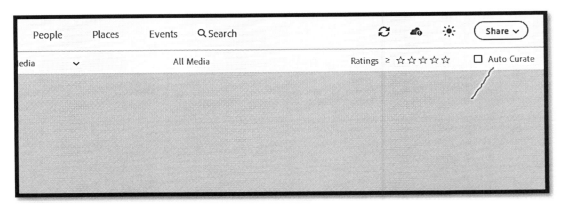

- The **Auto Curate slider** allows you to select how many photos you desire. As an alternative, you can type the desired number of photographs in the text field.
- Elements Organizer shows your best photographs in the grid based on the number of photos you've specified.

After auto-curating, you can get to do the following;

Instantly edit photos

- Choose the **instant edit icon** located in the window's bottom panel to swiftly modify your photos.

- Click **the edit icon** in the lower panel of the screen to open the editor workspace and begin making more in-depth modifications to your photos.

Create or add photos to an album

- On the window's left side, click **the add icon next to My Albums.**
- Located **on the widow's right side** is the New Album section. Drag and drop all of the carefully chosen photos from the grid onto the New Album panel.
  Drag and drop an image to the bin icon located in the lower-left corner of the New Album screen to remove it.

The Media Browser area

Elements Organizer offers four views. You can arrange and view your media using the Views tab by grouping your images according to the people in them, the locations where they were taken, and the events that are connected to them. The files are initially shown in the Media view when you import media. After that, you can annotate faces in the images, pinpoint the location where the picture was shot, and construct event stacks in the aforementioned views:

- **Media:** This screen shows the different media files. You may browse the files in this view; use the Instant repair option to fix images, the Tags/info option to view information about individual files, and other activities. For further details about the Media view, see the remainder of this page.
- **People** It is possible to mark the persons that appear in your images. You can organize stacks according to the persons identified in the photographs by using a person's View.
- **Places** Pictures have a unique connection to the locations where they were taken. In the Places pane, you may add location tags to your pictures.
- **Events** Stacks of events with images from the event can be made. For instance, you might make an event for Dan's birthday and tag pictures from it.

By default, the Media view opens with all of the media when you launch Elements Organizer. Thumbnails of the media files in the Elements Organizer's core region, or grid, are displayed in the Media view. You are able to see media (pictures, audio files, and video files) that are stored in your catalogs, folders, and albums. In the Media view, you can choose to select objects to edit, add to projects, and tag them.

Configure viewing preferences for the Media view

- To access the **Media view**, select the **Media tab.**
- Take one of these actions:
  - Select **Edit > Preferences > General on Windows.**

  - Select Adobe **Elements Organizer > Preferences > General on Mac OS**.

- **Indicate the display options as needed like the following;**

  - **Print Size** indicates the print size of the media (Windows).
  - **Date (Newest First) Select Show Newest First within Each Day** to arrange photos within a day such that the most recent photos are seen first. To see older photos first, select **Show Oldest First within Every Day.**
  - **Date Format** Choose the date format in which you would want the timestamp for pictures to appear. It is not available in some languages.

290

- **Allow Photos to Resize** Choose **Allow Photos To Resize** if you want to resize photos beyond 100% of their original size and up to the largest possible space. To see small photographs at their true size even when there is more space for them to be displayed, deselect this option.
- **Use System Font** (Only Windows) Choose Use System Font if you want to use the operating system's typefaces to display text in the Elements Organizer user interface. **Adjust Date and Time By Clicking On Thumbnail Dates**
- Click to **choose the photo**, then choose **Adjust Date And Time By Clicking On Thumbnail Dates** to change the details of the date and time.

Sort files in Media View

You can choose to sort your media files in any of the following ways;

- **Newest** The latest media files that have been imported or taken are shown first. (Unless otherwise noted in the Preferences dialog box, the media files are displayed within a given day in the chronological sequence in which they were taken, oldest first.) When you add tags to the imported media files, it's helpful to view the files in the newest order.
- **Oldest** Media files are shown according to their date stamp order, with the oldest imported files being shown first.
- **Name** Sorts media files by name alphabetically.
- **Import Batch** This option reveals the media files together with the batches in which they were imported.

Hide and show media files in the Media view

Without erasing them from your hard drive, you can mark media files to conceal them from visibility in the Media view. As an alternative, you can unmark hidden files to make them always visible or make them temporarily resurface.

Hide media files by marking them

- Choose which media files to conceal. To pick every media file in a set of related files, **Shift+click on the first and last file**. Click **non-adjacent files** using **Ctrl+click (Windows) or Command+click (Mac OS) to pick them.**

- **Select the media files to be hidden by going to Edit > Visibility > Mark As Hidden.** Each media file that is selected has a Hidden icon appear in the lower-left corner.

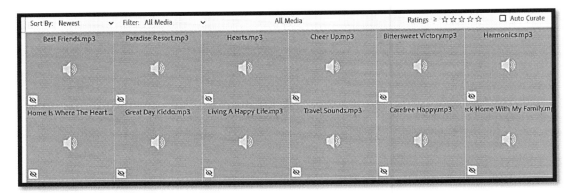

- Select **Edit > Visibility > Hide > Hidden Files** in the Elements Organizer to conceal the selected media files.

Remove the Hidden icon from the media files

- To display the media files that have been marked as hidden in the Media view, select **View > Hidden Files > Show All Files.**
- Choose the media files that you wish to have the Hidden icon removed from.
- To pick all of the photographs in a group of adjacent photos, shift-click the first and last image in the group. Click **on non-adjacent photos** with **Ctrl+click (Windows) or Command+click (Mac OS) to choose them.**
- **Select Mark as Visible under Edit > Visibility.**

View and manage files by folders

The My Folders panel, which opens in the left pane beneath Albums, shows folders from which media can be further arranged into Albums. You can control folders, add documents to your catalog, and add or remove folders from the Watch Folders status from this panel. The folder structure is shown in two views.

- **Tree view** You can alternate between the Tree and List views in the Folders panel. The media contained in the folder can be located physically with the aid of the Tree view. In the tree view, the default does not display a folder's subfolders. To view a folder's subfolders, pick it, then **right-click (Windows) or Control+click (Mac OS) and choose Show All SubFolders.**

- **List view The** Folders panel opens in this view by default. You can click on any folder in this display, which is a simple organizational structure, to see the media that is included within.

The folder panel shows all of the hard drive folders that Elements Organizer has imported material from by default. An icon for a managed folder can be found in folders holding managed files. Managed files are those that are automatically or manually imported into a catalog. There is a symbol for watched folders. Elements Organizer imports appropriate files from watched directories automatically. A monitored and controlled folder symbol appears for folders that are both monitored and controlled. Using the choices in the My Folders panel, you can view files within a folder and carry out various tasks.

- Under the **My Folders tab,** the Folder hierarchy is displayed on the left side of the organizer, and the grid displays the thumbnails of the images.
- Choose **a folder** to see the media files inside. The Media view grid displays thumbnails for the files within that folder.
- Choose **the folder** you want to add files from, then drag & drop the media files from the grid into the album.
- Choose one of the following actions from **My Folders to handle files and folders:**
  - Choose **the folder from which you wish to transfer a file to an alternative location.**
  - Drag the file's thumbnail from the Media view to the destination folder in the folder panel to reposition it in a different folder.
  - In order to open the folder in Explorer, select **Reveal in Finder (Mac OS) or Reveal in Explorer (Windows) by performing a right- or control-click in the folder hierarchy panel.**
  - Right-click in the left panel and select **Add To Watched Folders or Remove From Watched Folders** to add or remove the folder from the watched-folder status.
  - To rename the folder, select **Rename Folder by performing a right-click (Windows) or Control+click (Mac OS) on the folder. Next, enter a new name.**
  - In the folder hierarchy panel, **right-click (Windows) or Control+click (Mac OS) to delete the folder**, then select **Delete Folder.**
  - Instant album creation is possible from the folder panel. The quick album now includes every photo in the chosen folder. Choose **the folder, perform**

a right-click (Windows) or control-click (Mac OS), and choose "Create Instant Album" to instantly create an album by the folder name.

Select files in the Media view

To work with a media file, choose it in the Media view. The outline of a chosen thumbnail is dark blue.

Take one of these actions:

- Click **the thumbnail of an item to choose just that one.**
- Holding d**own Shift while clicking the first and last objects you wish to pick will select numerous nearby items.**
- Holding **down Ctrl while clicking (Windows) or Command while clicking (Mac OS) the desired objects will select multiple non-adjacent items.**
- Select **Edit > Select All or Edit > Deselect to select or deselect every item in the Media window.**

The Organizer Catalog

Elements Organizer stores information about imported media in files called catalogs. Basic information in the file, such as the filename and location, is updated when you import media. The file in Elements Organizer is updated as you continue to work on it to reflect your modifications. All of that information is kept even if you move your media files and catalog to a different computer or to a different version of Elements Organizer.

The following information can be found in the catalog file;

- The media file path and name.
- The location and name of the related audio file.
- The original, full-resolution file's path, filename, and volume name (if the original is kept offline on a CD or DVD).
- If the file has been edited, the path and filename of the original, unmodified version.
- The brand name of any scanner or camera connected to the collection of imported media files.
- Captions with a media file you have added.
- Notes that you've included in a media file.

- The time and date the media file was created, as well as whether or not its creation date is known for sure.
- The media file has been assigned keyword tags.
- Albums that contain the media file.
- The media file's history includes printing on a nearby printer, exporting, sharing via email or the internet, and sending it to an online photo finishing service. The history also reveals the batch (with import date and time) and whether the media file was downloaded from an internet source.
- Modifications made to the media file (rotation, cropping, red eye correction, etc.).
- The pixel count of all images and video files.
- Project settings (kind of project, display of captions, displaying page numbers, and so on).
- Metadata such as file format details, copyright, EXIF, pixel measurements, and IPTC data.

Creating a catalog

Photoshop Elements adds material to a default category when you import it. You can stop here if you want to utilize this default catalog file for all of your media. Sometimes, though, you'll want to make more than one catalog. For instance, you should make different catalogs for pictures of your family and pictures of your place of employment.

- **Get any of the following done;**

    o   Choose **File > Manage Catalogs.**

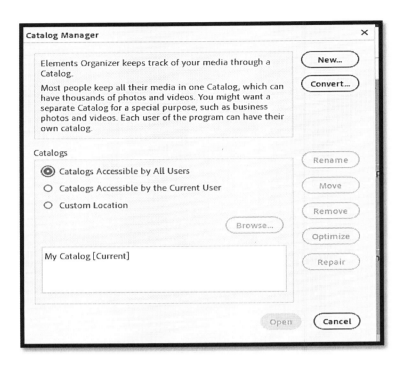

○ Tap **Ctrl + Shift + C (Windows) or Command + Shift + C (Mac OS).**
- **Take one of these actions:**
  - ○ Select **Catalogs Accessible by the Current User or Catalogs Accessible By All Users (Windows only) to specify a predetermined location for the catalog.**

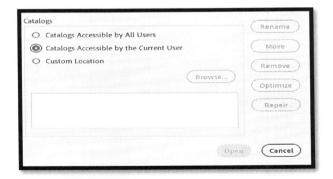

It should be noted that Photoshop Elements' Windows Application Store version does not have the Catalog Accessible by All Users or Catalog Accessible by the Current User settings. Default Catalog Location and Custom Location are the only two options available in the Windows Application Store edition.

- Click **Browse** after selecting **Custom Place** to pick a custom place. Navigate **to the catalog file's location on your PC.**
- Choose **New.**
- In the Enter a name for the New Catalog dialog box, insert a name for the catalog.
- Select **OK.**

Open a catalog

- **Get any of the following done;**
    - Choose **File > Manage Catalogs.**
    - Choose **Ctrl + Shift + C (Windows) or Command + Shift + C (Mac OS)**
- Choose the **catalog from the list that is in the dialog box of Catalog Manager.**
- Choose **Open.**

Moving or modifying media files

Elements Organizer contains file references; do not move or alter them outside of the program. You get a prompt to reconnect to the file if you transfer it or make changes to it outside of Elements Organizer. The following instructions can be used to relocate or edit files related to a catalog.

Moving files

Use the Move command to move the files within your catalog.

- In the Media view, pick **media files.**
- Take one of these actions:
    - Choose **Move under File.**

- In Windows, press **Ctrl+Shift+V; in Mac OS, press Command+Shift+V.**
- To change the location of the media files, click **Browse.**
- Press **OK.**

Renaming files

Use the Rename command to change the file names in your catalog. This command allows you to rename several pictures using the same base name.

- In the Media view, pick **media files.**
- **Take one of these actions:**
  - Click on **File > Rename.**

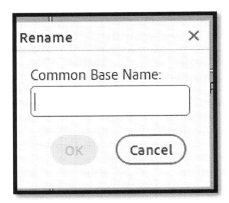

- In Windows, press **Ctrl+Shift+N; in Mac OS, press Command+Shift+N.**
- **Take one of these actions:**
  - If only one media file has been chosen, click **OK after giving the media file a new name.**
  - If you have more than one media file selected, click **OK after giving each media file a common base name**. You can rename the photographs as Birthday-1, Birthday-2, Birthday-3, and so on if you have five photos selected and Birthday is the common base name.

Deleting

Use Delete from Catalog to always remove the media files from the catalog. Even after being removed from your computer, media files can still be seen in the Media view but without an icon. A media file can be deleted from your catalog by selecting it, clicking **Edit**

> Delete from Catalog, or by using the Delete button. You have the option to delete the media file from the hard drive in addition to the catalog.

Editing files

To edit your media files, open Adobe Premiere Elements or Photoshop Elements from Elements Organizer. Use the command **Edit > Edit with [Application name]** to edit the media file. Use Photoshop Elements Editor to edit, for instance. It's also possible to modify the filename and file type (from BMP to JPEG, for instance) with this command without getting a missing file error. Once you've completed editing, update the thumbnails if required.

- **Take one of the subsequent actions:**
  - (Windows) Choose **Edit > Preferences > Editing.**
  - (Mac OS) Choose **Elements Organizer > Preferences > Editing.**
- **Choose the subsequent options that are available;**
  - **Use a Supplementary Editing Application**: make this choice in order to select any other application for editing.
  - **Show Photoshop Elements Editor Options only**: make this your preferred choice so you can choose Photoshop Elements as an editing application.
  - **Show Premiere Elements Editor options only:** To select Premiere Elements as your editing program, select this option.
  - **Show options for both Editors**: To select Photoshop Elements and Premiere Elements as your editing software, select this option.
- Choose **OK.**

Delete a catalog

Only when many catalogs are linked to Elements Organizer are you able to remove a catalog. Ensure you make a new catalog before deleting the existing one if you already have one and wish to remove it.

- Shut down Adobe Premiere Elements and Photoshop Elements Editor.
- **Choose from the following actions in the Elements organizer:**
  - Choose **Manage Catalogs under File.**
  - In Windows, press **Ctrl+Shift+C; in Mac OS, press Command+Shift+C.**

- Make sure the **Catalog Manager dialog box** has more than one catalog listed. Make a catalog if required.
- Choose the catalog you wish to delete from the Catalog Manager dialog box.
- After selecting Remove, select **Yes.**

Switch between Album and Folder Views

A folder is the same as your hard drive's storage folders. The folder tree that you see in your operating system (Windows File Explorer or its Macintosh equivalent, Finder?) is the same as what you see in the folder view. You can use an album as an organizing tool to arrange your media any way you choose—under any name, in any sequence, according to any standard you choose. Similar to keyword tags, they allow you to drag the album label to the media or vice versa after creating the album, making the media a part of the album. You can modify the "sort by" order to Album Order once you've created and selected an album. Once the media is in the grid, you may **click and drag it into the desired viewing sequence.**

Sync your media to the Cloud

You can choose whether or not to have local files synchronized to the cloud when Elements Organizer is started for the first time following the conversion of an older version catalog, or whenever a new catalog is generated.

- Check the box labeled **"Do not sync media to the Adobe Cloud"** if you want to avoid syncing your local media with Adobe Cloud.
- In the background, the **Auto-Sync procedure** carries out your selected preferences.

Auto Sync Preferences

- Choose **Edit > Preferences > Auto Sync.**
- Make a choice of the catalog media type you would like to instantly upload.
  - To download full-resolution cloud media, click **the option labeled "Automatically download full-resolution cloud media."**
  - To specify the path where you want to download the media, select **Browse.**

Auto Sync details

You can with ease have a view of the status of the synced files by following the provided steps;

- Choose **the Cloud icon.**
- By choosing the **Sync Now icon**, you can proceed to sync your files on-demand.

Cloud files can be easily filtered with the use of the provided dropdown choices;

- **Local Media Only**: this choice will display files that can only be found in the Elements Organizer catalog and that have not been synced to the cloud.
- **Synced Media:** this choice will display files that have been synced to the Cloud or that can be found on the cloud alone.
- **All Media**: this choice displays both Local and Synced media.

Sync selective media

- On-demand, you can sync a certain file selectively with the cloud.
- Sync Selected Media can be selected by right-clicking on the media file.
- If the file is just a thumbnail, the cloud's full-resolution media will be downloaded.
- Local modifications to the file would be synchronized with the cloud.
- The local file would be updated in sync with any changes made to the file in the cloud.

Auto Analyze your media

Elements Organizer creates categories for your images and videos automatically by analyzing them. We refer to these tags as "smart tags." Elements Organizer, for instance, creates Smart Tags with the following examples: Family, Kids, Park, Beach, Smiling, Ocean, Flowers, Sunset, Garden, and Soccer. You can easily search using the content of your photographs and videos by using Smart Tags. Once your images and videos are imported, Elements Organizer scans your files and automatically adds tags (called Smart Tags) that are pertinent to your media. These Smart Tags then make it simple to filter and locate images and videos. Find related images and videos by searching for a tag in the search bar or by filtering using the Smart Tags in the search window. Click on the **Search button** located in the upper-right corner of the main window to open the Search window or bar. The Search window's Smart Tag panel shows your images and videos. These are arranged according to the persons, locations, activities, objects, and other elements found in your media. Enter a Smart Tag's name in the Search window to find it. For instance, enter "house" into the Search field to find images and videos of houses.

Manage your files with Keyword Tags

You can add customized keywords, such as "Dad" or "Florida," to PDFs, projects, video files, audio recordings, and images in the Media view. You can quickly arrange and locate the labeled files thanks to keyword tags. You can avoid manually organizing your media assets into subject-specific directories or renaming files with content-specific names when you utilize keyword tags. You can just add one or more keyword tags to every media file as an alternative. Selecting one or more keyword tags in the Keyword Tags window will then allow you to retrieve the desired media files. When you enter a term into the Search textbox, you can also locate media files that have particular keyword tags. You could, for instance, make a keyword tag named "Anna" and include it with any media file that includes your sister Anna. Next, choose the tag "Anna" in the Keyword Tags tab to quickly identify every media file that belongs to Anna that is saved on your computer.

Any keywords you choose can be used to create keyword tags. You can choose a combination of keyword tags to locate a specific individual at a certain location or event when media files contain several keyword tags. For instance, to get all images of Anna with her daughter Marie, you can search for all keyword tags that include "Anna" and all keyword tags that include "Marie." You can also look for all keyword tags that include "Anna" and "Cabo" to locate every photo that shows Anna taking a vacation in Cabo San Lucas.

Using the Keyword Tags panel

The Organize tab's Keyword Tags panel is where you create and manipulate keyword tags. Travel is the default category that Elements Organizer has included in the Keyword Tags panel. Furthermore, media files with pre-attached tags show up under the Imported Keyword Tags category when you import them. In addition to making your own categories and subcategories, you may arrange tags under these categories.

In the Keyword Tags panel, you can do the following:

- See every keyword tag, category, and subcategory that exists. To expand or collapse the keyword tags underneath a category or subcategory, click **the triangle next to it.**
- Generate, modify, and remove keyword labels.
- Sort the keyword tags into groups and subgroups.
- Navigate **up and down the keyword tag list.**

Create a keyword tag

To arrange media files you've just uploaded to your catalog, you can make new keyword tags under any category or subcategory. The indicator for new keyword tags is a question mark.

- In the Keyword Tags panel, click the **New button and select New Keyword Tag.**
- Select **a category or subcategory to put the tag in using the Category menu in the Create Keyword Tag dialog box.**
- Enter **the name of the keyword tag in the Name box.**
- Enter any information you would like to add about the tag in the Note box. (You may state that the tag symbolizes pictures from vacations, for instance.)
- Press **OK.**
- The keyword tag is displayed beneath the category or subcategory you have chosen in the Keyword Tags panel.

Attach keyword tags to media files

You can attach a keyword tag to media files that are related to it once you've made one. A media file can have more than one keyword tag attached to it. When a tag is attached to a media file for the first time, the picture becomes the tag's icon. The first media file you choose becomes the tag's icon when you drag numerous media files to a keyword tag.

- Choose the media files in the Media view you wish to apply the tag to. (Ctrl-click/Cmd-click the media files to choose multiple photos.)
- **One of the following actions will connect a single media file to a single tag:**
  - Select **the media files and drag the tag from the Keyword Tags window onto them.**
  - Drag a**nd drop the media files onto the Keyword Tags panel tag.**

- **To add keyword labels to several media files, take one of the subsequent actions:**
  - Drag the **tag onto a chosen media file from the Keyword Tags tab.**
  - Drag **one or more keyword tags onto a chosen media file after selecting them.**
  - Drag **the images onto any selected keyword tag in the Keyword Tags panel after selecting one or more tags.**

Note that you need to tap the album in the Albums tab in order to apply a tag to all of the media files within it. In the Media view, choose every media file. From the Keyword Tags panel, choose the appropriate keyword tag and affix it to them.

Find media files by their keyword tags

- Enter the tag's name in the box's Search bar to see a list of tags that correspond to the letters you input. When you write D, for instance, all tags that start with that letter are shown. You are able to pick the necessary tag. Any media files that include any of those keyword tags are detected by the application. All photographs in the hierarchy are displayed by the application if you choose a keyword tag category or subcategory that has nested subcategories of its own. Consider the following scenario: You have a subcategory called "Wedding" with the keyword tags "Bride" and "Groom." Elements Organizer shows all media files labeled as "bride" or "groom" when you choose the "Wedding" subcategory.
- Additionally, you can click on the tag to look for related media. The advanced search menu appears once you click **on the tag.** You can change the searches and choose different keyword tags to look for related media.

Create and apply tags quickly

Easily create and apply tags with the Elements Organizer interface Keyword Tags textbox. Depending on the letter you choose, this textbox shows a portion of the list of available tags. For instance, the textbox will fill with a list of tags that start with the letter S if you type the letter S. Part of this list is available for viewing. You can either create a new tag and apply it, or choose an existing tag from this list and apply it to the chosen group of assets.

Create tags quickly

- Choose a media file.
- Insert the name of the tag in the Image Tags field.
- Choose **Add.**

Apply tags quickly

- **After choosing the assets you wish to tag, take one of the following actions:**
  - In the Keyword Tags textbox, type **the tag's name.**
  - To see a list of tags that start with the letter A, type any letter, like A. Choose **the desired tag to utilize**.
- Press **Add.** The chosen assets are given the tags.

Create new keyboard tag category or subcategory

- Click the New button and select New Category or New Sub-Category from the Keyword Tags panel on the Organize menu.
- **Take one of these actions:**
  - Enter the name of the new category in the Category Name field. To choose the color you wish to use for the keyword tags in that category, click **Choose Color**. Next, **click on the Category Icon list to choose an icon.**
  - Enter the name of the new subcategory in the Sub-Category Name field. Next, select **a category to put the subcategory in using the Parent Category or Subcategory menu.**
- Once you click **OK**, the Keyword Tags window will update with the new category or subcategory.

Write keyword Tag Information into your files

Upon exporting tagged JPEG, TIFF, or PSD files from Elements Organizer, the tag information is automatically added as an IPTC (International Press Telecommunications Council) keyword in the output files. This ensures that the tags are attached in the recipient's version of Elements Organizer upon media file import and prompting the import of associated tags. You can manually enter the tag information into the IPTC Keyword area of the file header if you choose to share or email a media file instead of utilizing the Elements Organizer export or e-mail functions.

Import and export keyword tags

You can exchange media files with people who share your interests by importing and exporting keyword tags. Assume, for instance, that you have developed a list of keyword tags for media assets associated with your pastime. Your friends who have the same interest can apply your saved tag set to their own media files by importing the tags into their Keyword Tags panel. Alternatively, you can apply your friends' keyword tags to your own media assets by importing them. After that, you and your buddies could look for media files associated with your shared pastime using keywords you both share. You can share your current set of keyword tags with another person by saving it, together with the whole hierarchy of categories and subcategories in your Keyword Tags panel and the tag symbols. Extensible Markup Language (XML) files are created from the exported tags file.

- Choose **the New button in the Keyword Tags panel** and select **Save Keywords Tags to File.**
- Select one of the following and choose **OK;**
  - ○ **Export All Keyword Tags** designs a file that has all of the keyword tags and tag hierarchy.
  - ○ **Export Specified Keyword Tags** generates a file with all of the keyword tags and the category or subcategory tag hierarchy that you choose from the list.
- Select the location and give the file a name in the Save Keyword Tags To File dialog box that displays. Next, select **Save.**

Import keyword tags from the file

You can import an existing set of keyword tags, including the complete hierarchy of categories and subcategories as well as the icons (stored as an XML file using Save Keyword Tags to File). It is also possible to import keyword tags by importing photos that already include other tags. Keyword tags are appended, for instance, when media files are emailed, exported, altered, or have tags added.

- Click the **New button and select Import Keyword Tags From File from the Keyword Tags panel.**

- In the Import Keyword Tags From the File dialog box, which displays the keyword tags, categories, and subcategories, choose the XML (Extensible Markup Language) file and click **Open.**

Find People in Your Files

By classifying the images, you can further enhance your ability to recognize faces in pictures. A group shows photo stacks with individuals tagged in them. You could, for instance, make a group called Work and tag images of individuals who are in your professional network.

- In the lower right corner of the screen, click **the Groups symbol.**
- Add and arrange groups in the Groups pane. To add a new people group, **click the plus sign (+). Colleagues, Family, and Friends are the three groups that are available by default.**
- Type in the group's name.
- Choose **a group** to add this group to as a child or subgroup by selecting it from the drop-down list Group. When creating a new group, don't choose anything from the Group list. Type in the group's name.
- Select **OK.**

Add People to Groups

A group can have faces added to it in any of the following methods:

- Drag one or more stacks to the group name in the right pane after selecting them.
- Drag the group name over a stack after selecting one or more of the stacks.

Manage your photos by Place

You can annotate your images with location information in the Places view. This makes it simple to locate pictures from a vacation you'd like to reminisce about or from a place you'd desire to visit again. With Elements Organizer's interface with Mapbox, you can easily find and organize your images and videos by linking them to the locations where they were taken. Elements Organizer preserves location data and automatically arranges imported photographs in the correct spot on the map if the photos you import have GPS information. If the imported photographs lack GPS data, you may still link the photos to locations on the map by either searching for the locations or just dragging and dropping the photos onto them. You can also use drag-and-drop or a place search to link movies to locations on the map. To see and arrange media files according to the geographic data, use the **Places view.**

Pinned and Unpinned tabs

In the Places view, Elements Organizer shows the media files in the UnPinned tab that lack location information. The Pinned tab shows media assets that have location information associated with them (such as images that you have manually tagged in the Places view or that were taken with a GPS-enabled device).

Viewing media files before adding location information

Once your media files have been loaded, select the **UnPinned tab**. This is where all the media files without location data are shown. By default, the **Group by Time option is chosen**. With the help of this feature, you can more easily add geographical information to media files made within a time period and categorize your photos according to date and time. For instance, you can label every photo you take on your birthday with the location of Hawaii, which makes it simpler for you to arrange pictures that may have been taken on the day you celebrated your birthday in Hawaii. The Number of Groups slider allows you to adjust how many tracks are shown. Across the period these files were made, more media files are grouped together when the slider is moved to the left (in the direction of Min). Consequently, when you move the slider to the left, less music is presented. Likewise, if you shift the slider to the right (toward Max), more tracks appear on the screen.

Adding location information to your media files

You may add location information to your media files (link media files to locations on a map) in a number of simple ways with Elements Organizer:

- Locate and mark **a place (in the Places view UnPinned tab).**
- Use the **Add Location button (available in the Media or Places views' UnPinned tabs).**
- **Drag and drop media files onto the map (located in the Places view's UnPinned tab).**

The media files you wish to link to locations on the map can be chosen in the UnPinned tab of the Places area. Next, look up the desired location for the selected media files using the search box located above the map. Verify if the Group by Time option is chosen and that you are in the UnPinned view. To get to the desired track, move the Number of Groups slider. Next, select the **track and choose the Add Location button to map all the photos within that track.** A location can be appended to a collection of chosen media files. These files may come from various tracks or from the same track. After choosing the photos in the UnPinned tab, click the **Add Location option in the Action panel.**

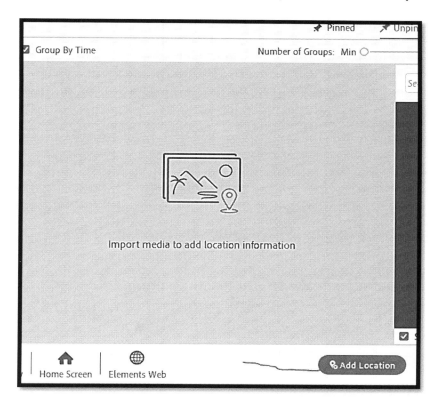

To view your media files with location data included in the Places view, select the Pinned tab (you can examine the media files that you manually associated with places on the map or those that have GPS data imported). The preceding image illustrates how the photos are arranged in a stack in the Pinned view. The number of photos in the stack is visible in the pin's upper-right corner. Hover your cursor over the stack of photos to see a bigger version.

Manage your media files by Date or Event

Even if your media files are not categorized, Elements Organizer automatically arranges them all in the Media View Timeline. The Timeline is broken up into years and months; by clicking on a month, you can see photos from that year or month. Use the End point markers to view photographs for a specific month or year. A green bounding box surrounds the first image in each bar that appears when you click on it in the timeline. Each image represents a month. Each bar's height in the timeline corresponds, either by date or batch, to the total number of files in each month. Additionally, the Timeline allows you to choose a time range to view media files that were taken or scanned inside that window. The month that corresponds to a bar in the Timeline is displayed in a tooltip that displays when you hover your cursor over it. The range (month and year matching to the end point marker's current location) is displayed in the tooltip when the mouse is hovered over either of the markers. The timeline displays all of the bars when a search is applied, but only the bars that match the media displayed in the grid are active. Every other bar is not active.

- To see the Timeline, select **View > Timeline.** As an alternative, press **Command + L (Mac OS) or Ctrl + L (Windows).** Only the media view has access to the timeline. The option to View >Timeline is hidden and the timeline will not be seen in any other view.

To narrow down searches, you can use the Timeline with keyword tags, albums, or folders. For instance, use the Courtney keyword tag in your search to get images of Courtney taken over time.

- Select **a month from the Timeline that includes Courtney's media files, then drag the endpoint markers to view the media that was captured or scanned during the allotted time.**

It is shown by a half-blank bar in the Timeline if you have media files that are not showing up in the search results right now. The timeline displays all bars when you perform any type of search, including album, tag, folder, advanced, or full-text searches. However, only the bars that match the media that is displayed in the grid are active. The disabled condition will be displayed for all other bars.

View and find media files using the Timeline

- Verify that you can see the Timeline. Click **View > Timeline if required.**
- **Execute one of these actions:**
  - To find the area of the Timeline you want to search, use the arrows at either end of the timeline.
  - To view the first media file associated with a bar in the Timeline, click **on it or drag the date marker to it.**
  - Drag the markers at the Timeline's endpoints to see a range.
  - Select **View > Adjust Date Range.** Click **OK** after entering the start and end dates to define the range you wish to see. Select **View > Clear Date Range to go back to the previous range.**
  - Within the specified range, media files are displayed by Elements Organizer. Refine your range by dragging the end-point marks.

Instant Fix a photo

With the tools in the Instant Fix editor included in the Elements Organizer's task pane, you may rapidly fix the majority of frequent photo issues. You can quickly edit or apply eye-catching effects to multiple photographs at once with these tools.

You can, for instance:

- Crop a photo
- Remove red eye
- Apply various effects
- Adjust light and color
- Improve clarity

After making the necessary changes to the copies of the chosen images, the Instant Fix editor saves the copies to the version sets of the original photos. It is important to remember that Elements Organizer's Instant Fix editor is designed to allow for quick adjustments and effect applications. Clicking the **Editor Button** will open the full-featured Photoshop Elements Editor where you may modify your photographs.

Editing photos using Instant Fix

- In the Media view, choose **one or more images.** (To pick multiple photos, use the **Ctrl or Cmd keys**.)
- Choose the **Instant Fix icon in the Action panel.**

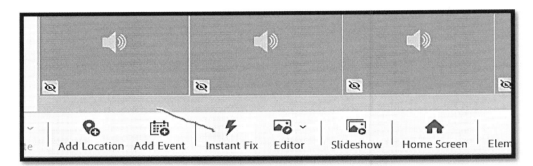

- The images are opened in Elements Organizer's integrated Instant Fix editor. Either the **Single-image Edit view or the Multi-image Edit view is shown,** depending on how many photos are selected. If the Edit screen is unable to display all of the photos, you can use **the < or > buttons** to go through the images. Try utilizing the various edit capabilities and other view-specific functionalities while you're in the Edit view. The following sections provide explanations for some of these adjustments.

Applying edits and effects

All of the photographs or just one can have different edits and effects applied at the same time. You can choose from the following edits and effects. Try out the many edit settings that the Instant Fix editor offers. One of the effects options in Effects is the Antique Light effect, as seen in the sample below. When you click the Instant Fix button in the Action panel, any modifications you make are applied to all the photos you selected. The only ones not included in this list are the Crop, Red-eye, and Flip functions, which are exclusive to the Single-image view.

If you want to use an effect on just one picture, you can either:

- Double-click **the image in the Multi-image view, or**
- Click **that photo and then select the Single-image view icon.**

312

The Single-image view is where the picture is shown. You can now edit this picture however you like. The Bueno effect on a single shot is seen in the following image.

Applying or undoing changes

- Click the **Save button to apply an effect while still in the Instant Fix editor.**
- Select the **Done butto**n to implement the modification and return to the Media view.
- Choose the **Undo button to reverse a modification.** The Undo option allows you to go back and undo each modification individually. If you made five adjustments to an image, for instance, you could use the Undo button to go back and undo each of the five effects individually (by selecting the button five times).
- Press the **Redo button** to undo a modification.
- Use the **Reset button** to erase all of your adjustments from a photo.

Back up your Organizer catalog

It is advised to regularly backup your catalog in case your system breaks, you need to upgrade your operating system, or you need to transfer your data to a different computer. You may back up not just the catalog's organizational structure but also all of your images and videos using the Elements Organizer. The terms "keywords, tags, people, places, events, albums, ratings, etc." describe the structure of a catalog.

Auto Backup and Restore Catalog Structure

The Catalog Organization Structure alone—that is, the keywords, tags, persons, places, events, albums, ratings, and so on—can now be scheduled to automatically back up on a regular basis when you close the program. Your photographs and videos are not included in this backup. When the Elements Organizer launches, you will have the option to restore the most recent backup of your organization structure in case something goes wrong with the catalog or organization structure. Older backups will be automatically deleted by the software and replaced with the most recent ones.

Manually Backup and Restore

By selecting an option from the **File > Backup Catalog menu**, you can manually start a backup of the catalog at any moment.

- **Backup Catalog Structure**: Create a backup of the keywords, tags, persons, places, events, albums, and other organizational components of your current catalog, omitting your images and videos.
- **Complete Backup**: Create a full backup of all the images and videos in the collection, including the organizational structure.
- **Backup your catalog incrementally**, including any newly added or edited images and videos since the last complete backup.
- If you have more than one catalog, select **the one you wish to backup.**
- If the "reconnect missing files" dialog appears when you select **File > Backup Catalog**, please finish the process to reconnect files to prevent problems when you restore the catalog. You need to reconnect files in order for them to show up in the catalog after you restore the backed-up Catalog Structure.

Manually backing up a catalog

- In the first step of the Backup wizard, choose **Next** after you have chosen one of the choices for backup.
- **In the 2nd step of the Backup wizard, configure the choices below;**
  - Choose **the hard disk or removable media destination (where you wish to save the backup) from the Select Destination disk list.**
  - Click on the **Backup Path option in the Options section.**
  - To ascertain what has changed since the last backup when doing an incremental backup, consult the previous backup file. To choose the prior backup file, click **Browse.**
- Choose Save Backup after the Elements Organizer has calculated the size and also made an estimate of the time that the backup needs.

Manually restoring a catalog

Your computer recreates the contents of the backup catalog when you restore one that has been backed up.

- **You can use a hard drive or CD/DVD to restore the backup:**
  - Put any removable media, like a CD/DVD or memory card, that you have backed up into your computer. It should be noted that macOS does not support CD or DVD restores.
  - Verify that the external hard drive you used for your backup is linked to your computer.

- Choose File under Restore Catalog.
- **Indicate just where the backup files can be found in Restore From;**
  - If your backup file happens to be on either a CD or DVD choose CD/DVD.
  - If your computer's hard drive or another portable media contains your backup files, choose Hard Drive/Other Volume. Find the backup file by **clicking Browse.**
- Choose **Restore.**

Restore a catalog from one computer to another

Follow these steps to transfer a catalog from one computer to another:

- Make sure the first PC has a complete backup.
- Put the backup file on a detachable disk.
- Attach the detachable drive to the other PC.
- Restore the file backup.

Activity

1. Highlight what album and folder views mean.
2. With the use of auto curate, adjust your pictures.
3. What is metadata?
4. Modify your pictures with the use of keyword tags.
5. Manage your picture by place.
6. Instant fix a picture.

CHAPTER 16
CREATE FUN PIECES

Create an Organizer Slideshow

A great approach to exchanging media assets is with slideshows. You can quickly make slideshows with Elements Organizer and include text, images, music, themes, and more. Once a slideshow is assembled, you have the option to share it or store it as an MP4 file. Users of Mac and Windows can create slideshows with Elements on both supported systems. You are prompted to update slideshows made in older versions of Elements when you access them in Elements.

Quickly create a slideshow

- Choose **the files** you would like to make use of in the slideshow in the Media view.
- Choose **Create > Slideshow.**

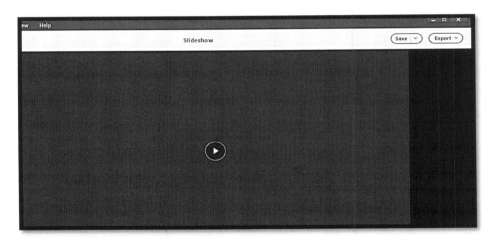

- Choose **your preferred theme** in the Slide show dialog. For instance, Memories or Array then choose **Next.**

Elements give you a brief preview of the slideshow with effects and background music based on the theme you chose. While some themes only show one image on each slide, others could show two or three photos.

316

- To store the slideshow or have it exported, you can make use of the preview controls.

  - **Export** choose Export to Local Disk or Facebook
  - Export to Local Disk indicates the name of a file and location and chooses a preset quality for the slideshow. Choose OK. The slideshow will then be stored locally as an MP4 file.

Facebook   Get any of the following done;

- Give Elements permission to share the slideshow on your Facebook profile. Elements ask you to enter your Facebook credentials if needed.
  To facilitate media sharing, you can also decide to download your Facebook friend list locally.
- Click **Complete Authorization in Elements Organizer.**
- Give the slideshow a title and a description.
- To upload, click **on it.** After checking the upload progress, click **Done.**

Save As Save the slideshow project.

- Insert a preferred name for the slideshow.
- Choose **Save.** The slideshow project will then be stored in the media browser with the date currently in use.
- You have the option to alter the slideshow's settings and add, remove, or reorder media. In the preview controls, select **Edit** to personalize the slideshow. The Slideshow Builder dialog box is displayed to you by Elements.

Customize the slideshow

Through the Slideshow Builder dialog, you can alter the slideshow. When you click Edit in the preview controls or exit the preview, Elements launches the Slideshow Builder. To rapidly see the effects of the current options while you're still editing the slideshow, click **Preview in the Slideshow Builder dialog box.**

Add media from the catalog to the slideshow

- Click **Add Media and choose Pictures and Videos** From Elements Organizer from the Slideshow Editor dialog box.

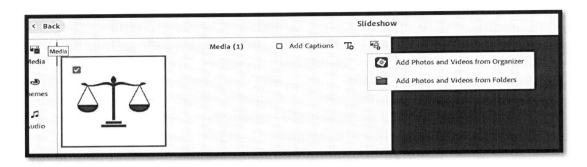

- To see a collection of media files, select **one or more of the following choices from the Add Media dialog box:**

  o All Media shows every media file that is presently visible in the Media view.

  o **Grid-Sourced Media** shows every media file in your catalog that is presently visible in the Media view grid.

  o **Show Media with Star Ratings** Presents media files to them along with a star rating.

  o **Display Media Hidden** makes hidden media files visible.

  o **Enhanced** To view material based on the following selections, click Advanced to expand the options:

  o **Album** Choose the album or albums that you wish to include media with.

  o **Keyword Tags** Decide which keyword or keywords you wish to have media added for.

  o **Persons Choose** the individuals from the drop-down menu to add material that is associated with their names and displayed beneath a stack of persons. For instance, John Doe appears in every picture tagged under the "people" stack.

  o **Places** Choose the locations from the drop-down menu to add the tagged and identified media to the locations stacks.

  o **Events** To add the media to a certain event stack, choose the events from the drop-down list.

- Decide which slideshow objects to add to your presentation. To select every item on the screen, use Ctrl+A (or the Select All button). To deselect every item, press Shift-Ctrl+A (or the Deselect All button).

- **Select one of the subsequent options:**

- ○ **Add a Few Media Items** Leave the Add Photos dialog box open for additional selections, add the objects to your project, and reset the checkboxes.
- ○ **Done** closes the dialog box, adds the chosen media files to your project, and then opens the Slide Show dialog box again.

Making an album with all the media assets you plan to utilize for your presentation is a good place to start when working with a new slideshow. You may quickly reorganize media files and change captions when your album is visible in the Media view. After that, you may include the album in your project by using the Add Media button.

Add media from a folder to the slideshow

- Choose **Media > Add > Pictures and Videos From Folder.**
- Choose the media you wish to add by navigating to it, and then click **Open.** Elements Organizer imports the media.

Add captions to the slideshow

- Make sure the Slideshow Builder's Captions On option is turned on.
- In the Slideshow Builder, click **the area beneath a media item.**
- Add **a caption.**

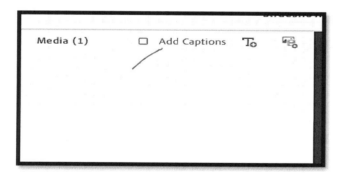

Add text slides to the slideshow

- Click **Add Text Slide in Slideshow Builder.** A text slide that is blank is added by Elements to the Slideshow Builder's media section.
- Select **the empty slide and type some words.**
- Slides should be rearranged if needed to place the text slide in the proper location within the slide sequence.

Add music to a slideshow

Your slideshow experience is enhanced with music. You can import audio files from any location on your computer or from the catalog in Elements Organizer.

- Choose **Audio in the Slideshow Builder**.

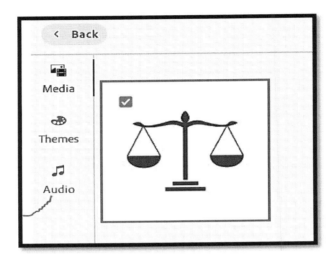

- **Take one of these actions:**
  - Select **a song from your Elements catalog that is listed.**
  - To choose a different song, click **Browse.**

Save changes to the slideshow

After you've finished personalizing the slideshow, take these actions:

- Click **Save in the Slideshow Builder dialog box.**
- Give **the slideshow a name.**
- Press **Save.** Elements attest to the slideshow's successful saving.

Create a Photo Collage

Although there are various ways to make a collage or montage with Photoshop Elements, the simplest one is as follows. You add each new image as a distinct layer to the collage image by following the instructions below. You can work on each image separately with this technique. Once all of your photographs have been combined into the final image, you can move or resize the layers, which are the additional images.

- Select **Window > Layers** if the Layers panel is not visible.

Create a collage

- To start with a fresh, blank image, select **File > New**. Choose an image size that corresponds to the size of the print you want (e.g., 8 × 10 inches at 150 pixels per inch on a white background).

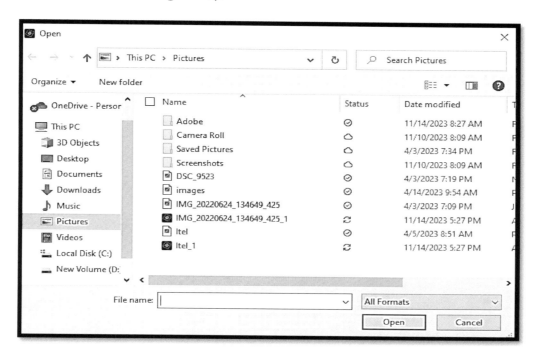

Note: Your photographs may appear at a surprising size in the collage image if their resolution or pixels per inch differs. To adjust the image sizes, follow the instructions on layer transformations below. For additional details regarding resolution, view the online help.

- To add the first image (Image 1) to the collage image, select **File > Open.** Both the collage picture and the original image (picture 1) are now shown simultaneously for you.
- Click on **the Move tool.** To move an image from the Image 1 window to the composite image window, click anywhere within Image 1 and then let go of the mouse button. The collage image window shows Image 1. Layer 1 is a new layer that contains Image 1.

- To track your layers, double-click **"Layer1"** in the Layers panel and give it a new name.
- Just the composite image should be shown after you close the Image 1 window. Both the newly renamed layer and the Background layer are now visible in your Layers panel.

Resize, reposition, and rotate the images or layers in the collage

- To target a layer in the Layers panel, click **once on the layer you wish to change.**
- Select **Image > Transform > Free Transform**

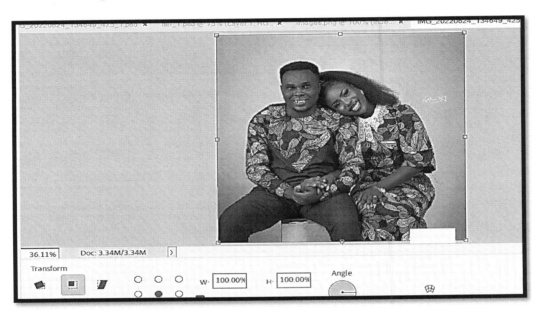

Note: Verify that the right layer is selected in the Layers window before transforming your layer.

- Observe the bounding box encircling the layer's edges as well as the eight anchor points total on each of the four corners and sides.
  - Drag **the anchor points to resize the layer.**
  - To reposition the layer, click **and drag inside the enclosing box.**

If a layer appears larger than the collage image, move it in either direction until a corner of the image is visible. Next, you can use the anchor point in the viewable corner to change the image.

- To rotate the layer, move your pointer just outside of the bounding box, click, **and drag.** When your cursor switches to a double-headed, curving arrow, you can rotate the layer.
- To approve or commit the transformation, select **the check box located in the top option bar of the screen**. Alternatively, click **the circle with the cut through it to undo the change.**

Create a Photo Reel

Favorite shots with their own text, effects, and graphics are sped through in reels. To make sharing easier, save them as GIFs or MP4s.

- To open the desired photographs for producing a photo reel, select **File > Open.**
- Choose **Create > Photo Reel.**
- Each of the chosen images will be arranged into frames that appear in the timeline. To rearrange the photos, drag and drop.
- Select **a photo layout in the Layout section** that complies with the standards of your favorite social media network. There are standard settings available in the Layout section for Instagram, Facebook, YouTube, TikTok, Snapchat, Twitter, and Threads.
- By tapping over the time shown on the photo thumbnail, you can adjust the display time unique to each picture frame that appears in the Photo Reel. For a uniform application across all of your photographs, check **the Apply to All checkbox.**
- To modify other attributes linked to each picture frame, click **the three-dot icon** that is present over the thumbnails.
- Utilizing **the Type tool**, add your preferred text to your images. Based on your needs, you can also change the text's font, size, style, color, leading, tracking, alignment, and other attributes.
- **Add the preferred effects to your picture by going after either of the provided workflows;**
  - Pick the preferred Effects thumbnail and add the effect along to the chosen image.

o Add the desired effect to all of your pictures by choosing **Apply** to all photos for a much more consistent look.

If you would like to go back to the added effect, choose No Effect.

- Click **any thumbnail** to select the required graphics from the Graphics section.
- To save the Photo Reel in MP4 or GIF format for convenient sharing, select **Export > Save.**

Create a Quote Graphic

Using pre-set templates, a ton of modification choices, and fun animation features, you can add inspiring quotations or personalized phrases to your photos to create shareable artwork that is perfect for social media and print.

Enter the workspace

A new option has been added to the Create drop-down menu located in the application's upper-right corner: Quote Graphic.

- Choose **Create > Quote Graphic.**

- Choose **a blank canvas, a photo, or a template.**
- Choose **your preferred size.**

Take note:

- To create a canvas with custom sizes, select **Start from Scratch > Custom.**

- To open the chosen photo from the Photo Bin and apply the default text style, click the **"Start with a photo" option.**
- To adjust the size, select **Preferences > Units & Rulers > Photo Project Units.**

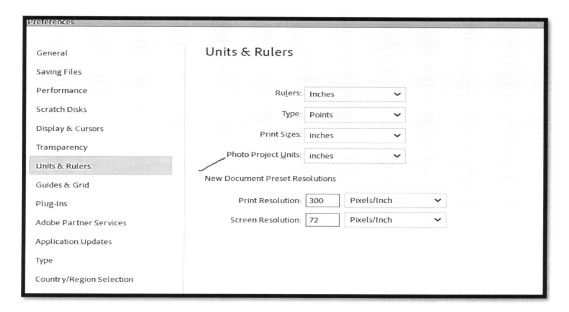

Change Background

To alter the background of your project or to import a picture to use as a background, utilize the Background panel.

Backgrounds and Effects are the two tabs in the Background panel.

- **Backgrounds**: to alter the background or change it totally, make use of the Backgrounds tab to import one.

Importing a picture from your computer, photo bin, or organizer catalog album should be your first step.

Or

To create a solid color or gradient background, use the color picker or gradient option.

Or

Choose from the collection of background presets that are provided.

- **Effects**: To add an effect over the background, make use of the Effects tab.

Add text

For the addition or modification of text, make use of the Text panel.

- To edit the text, double-click on it or select **Edit Text.**
- To add text, either vertically or horizontally, select the **Add Text or Add Vertical Text option.**

Customize the Quote Graphic

To alter the text style, create a shape to surround text, add graphics, etc., click the **Text panel.**

Three tabs are available in the Text panel: Style, Shape, and Graphics.

- **Style:** To modify text styles, including shape and other associated attributes, utilize the Style tab (**Text > Style**).
- **Shape:** To modify the shape enclosing the text, employ the Shape tab (**Text > Shape**).
- **Graphics:** To add a graphic to your composition, employ the Graphics tab (**Text > Graphics**).

Save and Print

You can have your image saved as a picture or as an animated GIF or MP4 file.

Save

- Click **Save from the Taskbar.** Your created Quote Graphic can be saved in a number of different file types, including MP4, GIF, PSD, BMP, JPEG, PNG, and more.
- Click **Save in the animate panel** to save the animation as a GIF after it has been applied.

Print

Choose **Print** in the Taskbar to have the Quote Graphic printed.

Create Photo Prints

With the use of your home or office printer, you can print your pictures.

- Choose the pictures you wish to print from the Organizer workspace.
- Choose **Create > Print Photos.**
- Choose **"Local Printer"**

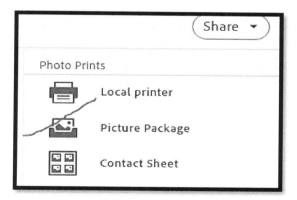

Note: Elements Organizer (Mac OS) prints using Photo Editor. Before continuing, make sure Photoshop Elements is installed on your computer.

- Choose **Print** after you have indicated your printing options.

Print photos at home

- Choose **the pictures** you wish to print. Only the first frame of a video clip that you attempt to print will print.
- Go to **File > Print menu.**

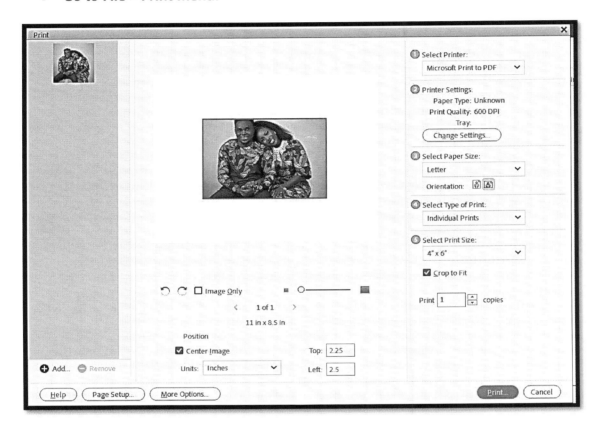

- Use the navigation buttons to flip back and forth between the pages if you are printing multiple photo pages. Use the rotate icons to adjust the orientation of the images.
- **Get any of the following done in order to alter page layout and printer configurations;**
  - To configure the settings for printing the pictures on a page, click **Page Setup.** Set the paper source, size, orientation, and margins in the Page Setup dialog box.

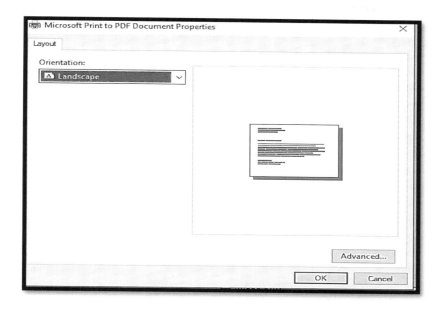

- From the **Choose Printer menu,** pick a printer. Make sure that Adobe Acrobat is installed on your computer before printing to a PDF file.
- Click **Change Settings** to adjust the Printer settings. Indicate the selections for paper size, paper tray, print quality, and kind of paper.
- From the Select Paper Size menu, choose **the paper's size.**

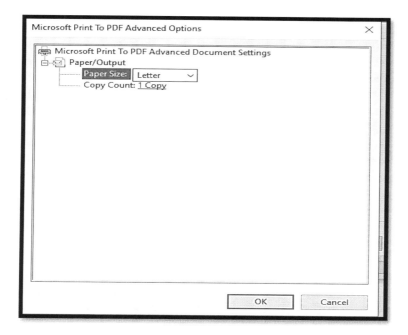

- Choose an option from the **Select Type of Print menu** to define the print type. Set up extra settings for every choice as needed.

  - **Individual Prints** print separate copies of each chosen image. Click **More Alternatives to see further alternatives**.
  - **Contact Sheet** prints the chosen photo selections as thumbnails. Do the following with regard to contact sheets:

    - Choose h**ow many columns the layout will have under Columns.**
    - To view more print options, choose **Show Print Options.**
    - Click **Date** to print the date that corresponds to the picture.
    - Click **on Caption** to print the caption for the picture.
    - Choose **File Name** to print the filename linked to the image.
    - Click on **Page Numbers** to print page numbers for several contact sheets.

  Picture Package gives you the option to arrange several copies of a single shot on a page, just like traditional portrait studios. For image packages, take the following actions:

  - Choose **a layout that allows for the inclusion of several copies of the image.**
  - Choose **the image's border from the Choose a Frame menu.**
  - Choose **Fill Page With Initial Picture.**
  - From the **Choose Print Size menu,** pick **a print size.** Choose a smaller photo size if you want more images on the same page.

- Choose Crop to fit to adjust each individual image to the designated print layout. To ensure that the image matches the print layout's aspect ratio, it is cropped and resized as needed. If you wish to avoid having your images cropped, deselect this option.
- Put a number in Print Copies if you want numerous copies.
- Press **Print.**

Select multiple media files

- Go to **File > Print menu.**
- Click **Add** in the Prints dialog box.
- **Choose one of the following options from the Add Media dialog box:**

- Click **All Media** to choose every media in the open catalog.
- Choose **Media from the Grid** to select every piece of media that is open in the Media view right now.

- **Depending on your needs, choose the following options from the Advanced section:**
    - Click **Show Media with Star Ratings** to view the media that you have rated.
    - Click **Show Hidden Media** to choose Hidden Media.

Printing choices

- Go to **File > Print menu.**
- Tap **More Choices.**
- **Perform the following actions in Photo Details:**
    - Choose **Show Date** to print the date that corresponds to the picture.
    - Choose **Show Caption** to print the caption that goes with the picture.
    - Choose **Show File Name** to print the filename linked to the picture.
- **Indicate the following in Layout:**
    - Choose **One Photo per Page** if you want a page to have just one picture on it.
    - Specify **a value in Use Each Photo (n) Times** if you want different versions of the same photo on different pages.
- Choose **Flip Image** if you want to print the image on a material, such as a t-shirt.

Custom print size

To alter the printed image's dimensions utilize the More Options dialog options.

- To view more options, click the **Print dialog box.**
- To resize the photo to fit the size of a printed page or other medium, select **Scale to Fit Media.**
- Enter the **required values for the Height and Width of the printed picture to select a custom size.**
- Choose the units for the given dimensions from the Unit menu.
- The printed image's resolution should be specified. Go to your printer's user manual to find out the appropriate resolution.

Create a Photo Book

With the aid of photo projects, you can quickly produce professional-looking picture books, greeting cards, calendars, collages, [CD/DVD labels (relevant for 2022 and previous versions)], and CD/DVD cases. The picture projects that are available in Photoshop Elements are listed by clicking the Create button, which is located in the top-right corner of the program window. The Photo Projects Format (.pse) format is used to store photo projects. The photo projects can be shared via email, saved to your hard drive, or printed using your home printer. Photo books make wonderful mementos of your experiences. Creating photo albums is made simple with Photoshop Elements' multiple size and theme options.

- Choose **Create > Photo Book.**

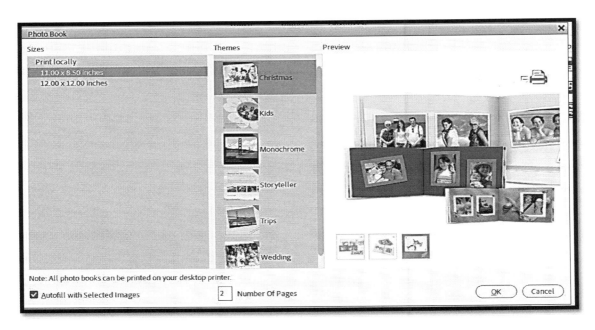

- **In the Photo Book dialog box, choose OK after you have done any of the following;**
    - o Decide on the photo book's size.
    - o Decide on a theme.
    - o To use the photographs you have selected in the Photo Bin, select Autofill with selected images.
    - o Indicate how many pages the picture book will have (between 2 and 78).

332

- **The following options along with the project will be opened in the lower-right corner;**
  - ○ **Pages**: this displays to you the pages of the photo book.
  - ○ **Layout**: this reveals the layout of the photo book.
  - ○ **Graphics**: enables you to alter the background frames, and graphics in the photo book.

Do the following;
  - Get your photo book and include pictures in it.
  - Include the background.
  - If there is a need for you to include more pictures on a single page, add frames.
  - If need be, include graphics.
- To select the manner in which you wish to see and edit the photographs you want to work with, click either **Advanced Manner or Basic Mode.**

  You can move text or graphics and add text in the Basic mode.

  You have access to the entire toolkit and layer options in the Advanced mode. The choices allow you to alter layers and perform image retouching.
- **To save the photo book, get any of the following done;**
  - ○ Click **Save from the Taskbar.**
  - ○ Select **Save from File**. Projects can be saved to a different location, but by default, they are saved in your My Pictures folder.
  - ○ In Windows, press **Ctrl+S; in Mac OS, press Command+S.**
- **To get the photo book printed, get any of the following done;**
  - ○ Choose **File > Print.**
  - ○ Choose **Ctrl + P for Windows and Command + P for Mac OS.**

You cannot print the picture book if one of the photos in it has been relocated from its original position on your computer. The project can still be saved, though.

Create a Greeting Card

Get greeting cards created in very easy steps.

- Choose **Create > Greeting Card.**

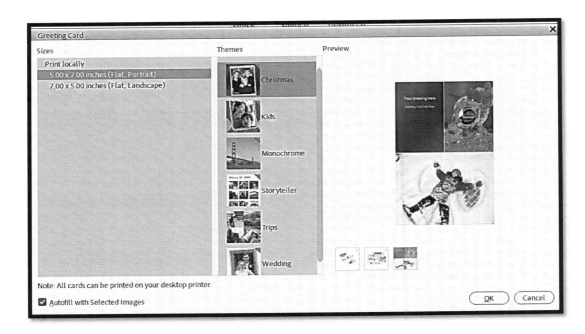

- **In the greeting card dialog box, do any of the following and choose OK;**
  - Choose **the greeting card's size.**
  - Decide **on a theme.**
  - To use the photographs you have selected in the Photo Bin, select **Autofill with selected images.**
- **The project will then open with the options below in the lower-right corner;**
  - **Pages:** this choice shows you the pages of the greeting card.
  - **Layout:** displays the layout of the greeting card.
  - **Graphics:** enables the altering of the background, frames, and graphics in the greeting card.

Do any of the following;
- Enhance your greeting card with images.
- Include the backdrop.
- If you would want more photographs on one page, add frames.
- Incorporate graphics if needed.
- To select the manner in which you wish to see and edit the photographs you want to work with, click either **Advanced Mode or Basic Mode.**
  You can move text or graphics and add text in the Basic mode.
  You have access to the entire toolkit and layer options in the advanced mode. The choices allow you to alter layers and perform image retouching.

- **To store the greeting card, use one of the following actions:**
  - Click **Save from the Taskbar.**
  - Selec**t Save from File**. Projects can be saved to a different location, but by default, they are saved in your My Pictures folder.
  - In Windows, press **Ctrl+S; in Mac OS, press Command+S.**
- **The greeting card can be printed by doing one of the following:**
  - Click **OK** after choosing **File > Print.**
  - Click **OK** after pressing **Ctrl+P (Windows) or Command+P (Mac OS).**

Create a Photo Calendar

Display your pictures by designing photo calendars with the use of Photoshop Elements.

- Choose **Create > Photo Calendar.**

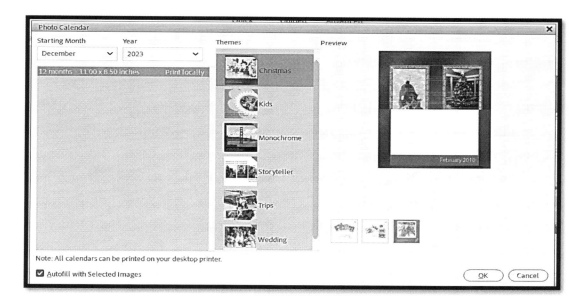

- In the **Photo Calendar** dialog box, do any of the following and choose **OK;**
  - Choose **Starting month and year.**
  - Choose a size for the calendar.
  - Decide **on a theme.**
  - To use the photographs you have selected in the Photo Bin, select **Autofill with selected images.**
- The project will then open with the options below in the lower-right corner;

- o **Pages**: this choice shows you the pages of the photo calendar.
- o **Layout:** displays the layout of the photo calendar.
- o **Graphics**: enables the altering of the background, frames, and graphics in the greeting card.

Do any of the following;
- Enhance your photo calendar with images.
- Include the backdrop.
- If you would want more photographs on one page, add frames.
- Incorporate graphics if needed.
- To select the manner in which you wish to see and edit the photographs you want to work with, click either **Advanced Mode or Basic Mode.**
  You can move text or graphics and add text in the Basic mode.
  You have access to the entire toolkit and layer options in the advanced mode. The choices allow you to alter layers and perform image retouching.
- **To store the greeting card, use one of the following actions:**
  - o Click **Save from the Taskbar.**
  - o Select **Save from File**. Projects can be saved to a different location, but by default, they are saved in your My Pictures folder.
  - o In Windows, press **Ctrl+S; in Mac OS, press Command+S.**
- **The greeting card can be printed by doing one of the following:**
  - o Click **OK** after choosing **File > Print.**
  - o Click **OK** after pressing **Ctrl+P (Windows) or Command+P (Mac OS).**

Create Prints and Gifts

- Choose **your pictures**. There is really no need to spend so much time choosing another service as they are already in your organizer.
- Click to create. With just a snap you will get there within Photoshop Elements.
- Create any you really love. Choose your products, sizes, and styles.

Create a Video Story

You may make a powerful narrative about a life event using your images and videos. Using a methodical, step-by-step methodology, the Video Story option within the Create menu enables you to showcase your images and videos from an occasion (like a wedding) in a narrative style. You follow a step-by-step process to arrange your materials into chapters and incorporate music, narration, captions, and other components. With features like the ability to choose from pre-made mood selections (such as Classic and Sentimental), you can enchantfully turn your video tale into a remarkable encounter.

Create a video story

To make a video story, take these actions:

- Click **Video Story under Create**.
  Or
  In Premiere Elements, click **Create your Video Story from the start screen.**
- A video story creation guide is displayed by Adobe Premiere Elements. To view the tips, use the left and right arrows.
  - Click **Skip** to begin constructing the video tale after viewing the tips.
  - To exit the Video Story workflow and go back to the program workspace, click **Exit.**
- To begin constructing the video tale, select a category. To start the video tale with a generic theme, click generic. You will see an Online Content Download that shows content being downloaded for that theme if the theme is not installed on the computer.
- To view the different available themes, use the **left and right arrows**. The chosen theme is previewed in the image that is presented.
  To view images and videos from your timeline, select **Use media from my timeline,** and then click **Get Started.**
  All of the images and videos from your timeline are visible in the story asset view of the Video Story process when you select the **Use Media from my timeline option.**
- To import story assets for your tale, click on one of the media sources from the list of available import options. Below is a list of the media sources that you can import images, videos, and audio files from. To import media from any of the following sources, click your preferred media source:
  - Videos and images can be imported from Elements Organizer.
    Flip or videos.
  - **Cameras**: You may import videos from memory/disk devices, FLIP, and AVCHD cameras.
  - **Images from Cameras or Devices**: Bring in images from phones, external disks, or digital cameras.

- o **Files & Folders**: Import audio, video, and picture files from your computer's hard disk.
- To get a preview of the video clip, click **on any of the videos**. To remove a file from the story assets, click the file you want to select and then **hit Delete.** To remove all of the clips from the chosen story asset, press **Ctrl + A and then Delete**. The file remains in the spot where it was saved.
- Select **Next**. While creating the Story Overview, all of the files found under Story Assets are accessible and included.
- You can now arrange the images and videos in chapters for a more ordered arrangement. There are several chapters in the story. Arrange the images and videos into chapters to manage and arrange your video tale. Drag and drop tale elements to the relevant chapter from the left pane. Drag and drop, for instance, the behind-the-scenes film footage of the pre-party to the Party Preparations feature chapter. **You can also do the following tasks in the Story Overview view:**

  - o **Add Media**: To add new images and videos to the Story Assets window, click the Add Media button.
  - o **Story Title and Credits**: The first chapter is a video titled "Story Title." This video is where your video story begins. In a similar vein, the video story's final video is the Story Credits video. While you can add as many video clips as you like to the other chapters, the Story Title and Story Credits chapters can only have one video.

- **In the Story Overview window, you have control over the chapters. To make the flow of your story more organized, add, hide, or delete:**

  To conceal the Story Title and Story Credits chapters, use the "Hide" option. Some chapters cannot be hidden.

  - o **Add chapter**: To add a new chapter, click **Add Chapter in the Story Overview panel** or click Add Chapter on the Action bar. To alter the way the tale flows, you can rearrange the chapters as well as the clips within them.
  - o **Preview of videos**: To view a preview of a video clip that has been added to a chapter, click **the play button.**
  - o **Undo and Redo**: To go back and redo an action, select **Undo or Redo** from the Action bar.

- In Detail View, the chapters are shown in a linear fashion. With the aid of Detail View, you may alter the chapters by previewing the movies, rendering them, annotating the chapters, marking favorite scenes, and more.

  - To quickly adjust and observe the arrangement of clips in different chapters, select Overview from the top pane. You can also hide and delete clips.
  - **Chapter Preview**: To view a preview of a chapter, click **play in the Story Chapters tab**.
  - Premiere Elements employs Pan and Zoom for picture assets by default if your video story contains image elements. You have the option to turn off Pan and Zoom for any or all of the pictures in your video narrative.

- **The following tasks are available in Detail View:**

  - Modify the title of your video narrative. There is an editable title for each chapter.
  - **Story Chapters**: The sequence in which the chapters appear can be altered. In the Story Chapters pane, drag and drop a chapter to reorder it.
  - **Story Assets**: Select a chapter to upload media to.
  - Hover your mouse cursor over a video clip to mark your favorite moments. For a shortcut to favorite moments, click the star. Your greatest moments can be preserved in a video clip.

- **In Overview View, you can do a number of operations on chapters, including**

  - **Hide chapter**: To conceal a chapter in the movie, click on it. Only the first and end chapters (Story Title and Story Credits) are hidden.
  - **Edit chapter**: Click **to make changes to the chapter.**
  - **Delete Chapter**: To remove a chapter from the video story, **click on it.**
  - Modify the narrative heading for your video tale. There is an editable title for each chapter.
  - **Delete pictures and videos:** To remove a picture or a video from the chapter, click the **delete icon.**
  - **Add Chapter**: To add a new chapter to the video tale, click the **Add Chapter button on the Action bar.**

- Choose **Preview Mode** in order to preview the video story you have just created.

- Choose **Publish Movie** in order to publish the video story. Choose from the choice of **Public + Share.**

Add captions and narration to the workflow

To give your video story more depth and perspective, you may add narration and captions to each chapter.

To add a caption or narration to a chapter, take the following actions:

- Choose a chapter in Detail View.
- From the Action bar, select **Add Narration or Add Caption.**
- To add or modify a caption, move the **CTI to the frame in the video clip that needs it. Choose Add/Edit to include or modify the captions.**
- As an alternative, choose Add Narration if you would like to include narration in the previous step.

Create a Highlight Reel

AI and automation swiftly transform your movies into attention-grabbing videos by emphasizing action, close-ups, and high-quality photography. Thanks to Adobe Sensei.

To make the Highlight Reel, take these actions:

- To construct the Highlight Reel, select **Add Media** to access compatible media files, such as pictures and videos.
- Choose **Highlight Reel under Create.**
- Drag and drop the media into the Highlight Reel view in the sequence that you want it to appear.
- You can select the layout in the Layouts area that best fits the requirements of the social media network of your choice. The Layouts area offers a variety of settings for Instagram, Facebook, YouTube, Pinterest, LinkedIn, and Snapchat.
- Optionally, choose **the preferred audio track** from the workspace's Audio Tracks area. By using the Upload audio from computer button found on the Your Tracks tab, you can even upload audio files from your system.
- Automation and artificial intelligence (AI) swiftly transform your recordings into captivating videos by emphasizing action, close-ups, and your best material. By

using the **Change the Look button**, you may even alter the generated reel in addition to previewing it.

- Using the Audio Tracks choices found on the left panel, you can **optionally switch the audio track.**
- To save the Highlight Reel for simple sharing, choose **Export to Social.**

Activity

1. Create a photo collage.
2. Create a photo reel.
3. Create a greeting card.
4. Create prints and gifts.
5. Create a video story.
6. Create a highlight reel.

CHAPTER 17

SHARE YOUR PHOTOS AND VIDEOS

It's now easier and simpler than ever to share your movies. Everything you require to save and distribute your completed project is included in the Export & Share section. Your project can be saved for viewing on a computer, DVD player, smartphone, online, and other platforms. All of the export formats that are available are shown in a single panel under the Export & Share option. The different media options that you can select are represented by individual tabs on the Export & Share panel.

- After selecting **Export & Share**, select **the appropriate media type tab.** Select from Social Media, Audio, Image, Disc (Windows), Devices, and Quick Export. The media category selection options and settings are shown.
- Choose **an output format for the given media type.** The alternatives that are available are shown below:

  o **Quick Export**: multi-device, web-based Devices: PC, TV, smartphone, Windows Custom Disc: DVD
  o **Social media**: Facebook, Instagram, Vimeo, YouTube, and Vimeo
  o **Audio**: Track, Frame, GIF, or Custom Image

- If necessary, adjust the recommended settings. To fit your needs, you can select to modify the parameters. You can choose a resolution and then the formats for that resolution based on the output you want. Along with other parameters, you can set the Frame Rate and Quality for a few of the formats. To generate customized export settings, click **Custom>Advanced Settings;** alternatively, use the **Presets drop-down box to choose an existing custom preset.**
- Before exporting your video, view a preview of it. Watch a trailer for your film to make sure the audio quality, clip length, and other aspects are what you want.
- Input the file name and choose **an output location. Press Save.** The output is created by Premiere Elements and saved to the directory you choose.

Device

You cannot access the edited video in the Advanced or Quick View timelines as a stand-alone file until you export or share it in a video format. Once exported, you can transfer it to different computers, play it back on yours, and use it with other media players or editing software. You may export movies to be played again on a variety of devices, including your PC, TV, phone, and tablet. The H.264 compression standard is used to compress all mobile files. Choose **the particular media format under the Devices heading. You can choose from Computer, TV, Mobile, and Custom.** Premiere Elements also has specialized device options, so you can easily export your movie in formats compatible with particular mobile devices. H.264 compression is used for all mobile file compression. To get the best results, use the suggested settings. You can adjust the parameters by clicking on **advanced parameters** if your project calls for them.

Prior to burning to a DVD or a Blu-ray disc;

- Make that your burner and the player are compatible with the disc you have chosen.
- Check the disk's available space. The compressed data and any scratch disk files generated during export must fit on adequate free hard drive space.
- In the event that Adobe Premiere Elements is incompatible with your DVD burner, you can burn an ISO image on a DVD using the burner's included software. Select the desired selection from the Type drop-down menu.

If a single drive partition isn't large enough for your scratch disk files, you can use the **Edit > Preferences > Scratch Disks / Adobe Premiere Elements > Preferences > Scratch Disks command to pick a new partition.**

Social Media

You can export your movie from Premiere Elements in file formats that can be shared online. The Export & Share tab allows you to upload your video straight to the internet. Within the Social Media category, choose an online sharing site. You have Facebook, Instagram, Vimeo, YouTube, and Facebook. The fastest way to export your video is to use the suggested parameters. Additionally, you can alter the settings to fit a certain circumstance. But don't forget to check that your movie's data rate is suitable for the desired viewing device.

- Click **Begin Share** to start the authorization process for sharing to **Vimeo and YouTube**. Once that's done, you can proceed with the chosen platform's sharing method.

Keep the video in a personal folder, then upload it to the chosen platform to share it on Facebook and Instagram.

Audio

To begin the authorization procedure for sharing to Vimeo and YouTube, click **Begin Share.** After that's finished, you can continue using the sharing technique on the selected platform. Store the video in a private folder and post it on Facebook and Instagram by uploading it to the desired site.

Image

Any frame or still-image clip can be exported as a still-image file. The Advanced view timeline or the Monitor panel's current time position is where the frame is exported from. The frame shows up in the Project Assets section after the export. It's also possible to make animated GIFs from brief video clips. To make an animated GIF, select GIF and select a resolution. A GIF should not last longer than ten seconds. A video or clip can alternatively be exported as a series of still photos, with each frame saved as a different still photo file. Go to **Advanced Settings** and choose the option to **Export As Sequence**. The following situations can benefit from exporting as a sequence:

- When an animation that needs a still image sequence or does not support video formats needs to use a clip.
- When you wish to use a clip in a 3D program that needs a still image sequence or does not support video formats. Premiere Elements automatically assigns file numbers when you export a clip.

Share your photos via email

With Elements Organizer, you may send and receive files over email on any of the three supported platforms: Macintosh, Windows 32-bit, and 64-bit. You can transfer files using any email account, including Gmail, Yahoo!, AOL, Microsoft, and others. For pre-configured email providers like Gmail, Yahoo!, AOL, or Microsoft, Elements Organizer offers a simple email profile setup. You can specify the technical information required by other service providers in order to configure the email profile.

Setting up the profile for a preset service provider

- Choose **Preferences > Email** from within Elements Organizer.

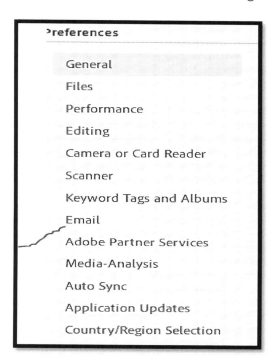

- Select **New.**

- Give your profile a name. Select any name that will aid in identifying your profile in the future.
- Choose a provider of services from the pre-arranged list.
- Enter **the email address, password, and your name on the Email Settings screen.**

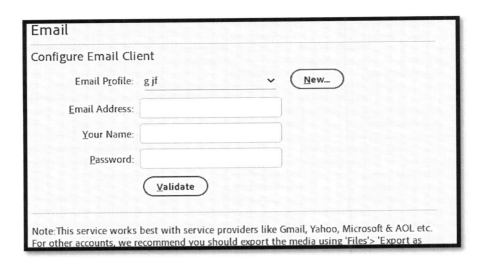

- Tap **"Validate."** Elements show a confirmation message after validation is successful.

Note: In order for validation to be successful if your computer is protected by a firewall, the firewall needs to permit connectivity on ports 465 and 587. If you receive an error message indicating that these ports are banned, get in touch with your system administrator.

- Choose **OK.**

Set up the profile for other service providers

It is advised to use **Files > Export as New Files** to export the media for use with other service providers. You can then share the exported files by logging into your email account through a browser.

- Choose **Preferences > Email from within Elements Organizer.**
- Select **New.**
- Give **your profile a name**. Select **any name** that will aid in identifying your profile in the future.
- Choose **other from the list of service providers.**
- Enter **the following information on the Email Settings screen:**
  - o Your electronic mail address
  - o Your name

- o Your email address's password
- o Your email service provider's SMTP server address
- o The SMTP port number used by your email service provider.
- o Your email service provider's connection security protocol (SSL/TLS, STARTTLS, or None).

- Choose **Validate.** Elements will then show a confirmation message once the validation has gone through successfully.

If your machine is protected by a firewall, the firewall must allow communication on ports 465 and 587 for validation to succeed. If you notice an error message about this problem, contact your system administrator.

- Finally, select **OK.**

Share files by email

- From the grid of the Elements Organizer, pick **out some media.**
- Click **Share > Email in the right window.**
- You have the option to convert non-JPEG photographs before emailing them if your selection contains any of them. To convert photos to JPEG, select it.
- Decide on the largest file size that you wish to send the media. If you would want to email the media at its original size, select Use **Original Size.**
- Choose **the photo quality** you wish to email at on a scale from 0 (Low) to 12 (Maximum).
- The **Next button** should be clicked.
- Using the Elements Contact Book, choose **one or more recipients.**

Note: For the time being, you can leave the Select Recipients field empty if you're utilizing Microsoft Outlook on Windows or Mail/Microsoft Outlook/Entourage on a Mac. You have to designate at least a single recipient if you're using a different email client.

- Give **the email a subject line.**
- Change **the default message if needed.**
- Select **Next.** Elements launch the email client with a prewritten message whether you're using Apple Mail/Microsoft Outlook/Entourage (Mac) or Microsoft Outlook (Windows).
- After making the required adjustments, send **the message.**

Share a PDF slideshow by email

Much like you may share individual photographs, you can also share a PDF slideshow including images.

- Choose **a few pictures** from the grid of the Elements Organizer.
- Choose **Share > PDF** Slideshow from the right pane.

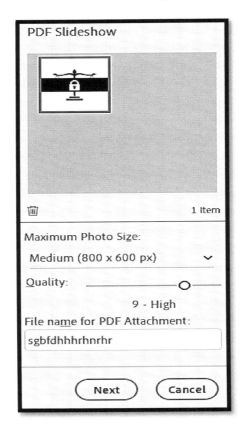

- Decide on the largest size you wish to send the media via email. To email the media in its original size, select **Use Original Size.**
- Choose **the quality** at which you wish to email the pictures, ranging from 0 (Low) to 12 (Maximum).
- Give **the PDF file a name.**
- Select **Next.**
- Choose **one or more receivers from the contact book for Elements.**
- Give **the email a subject line.**

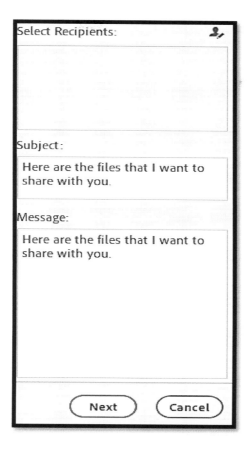

- Change the default message if needed.
- Select **Next.** Elements launch the email client with a prewritten message whether you're using Apple Mail/Microsoft Outlook/Entourage (Mac) or Microsoft Outlook (Windows).
- After making the required adjustments, **send the message.**

Share your photos on Flickr

Photoshop Elements allows you to share photographs directly with websites like Flickr. Photoshop Elements has a Share menu that allows you to view the photo-sharing services that are available to you.

- Click the **Share option in Editor and pick Flickr**. You will be requested to automatically save files if the photos that are open at the moment have not yet been saved. Click **OK to continue.**

- (First Use) Photoshop Elements needs your permission to work with Flickr if you haven't shared with them previously. To allow Photoshop Elements to upload images to your Flickr account, follow the on-screen prompts.
- Choose t**he following options for the image or collection of images you're uploading on the Flickr dialog**:

  o **Add / Remove photos**: To upload or remove photographs to Flickr, choose the plus (+) or minus (-) icon over the Items preview area.
  o **Sets**: A set is a collection of images that you can post. This works better for Flickr slideshows. After checking the Upload as a Set box, change the Set parameters. You can make a new set or select an already existing one. Give the Set a name and a description.
  o **Audience**: To restrict or manage the Set's visibility to outside users, utilize the Who can see these photos? Area.
  o **Tags:** offers a set of keywords to get the album tagged with.

- **The Flickr dialog box shows two buttons once the photographs have been uploaded:**

  o **See Flickr.** To open and see the uploaded photographs in your web browser, use this button. The web browser allows you to copy the URL to your Flickr photos.

  o **Done**. To exit the dialog box, select **Done.**

Share your video on Vimeo

Take these actions to share videos on Vimeo:

- Choose **Export & Share from the Video Editor workspace.**
- After choosing the **Social Media menu, choose Vimeo.**
- Adjust the suggested values as necessary.
- Click on **Begin Share**.
- Give Adobe Premiere Elements permission to access your YouTube account if this is your first attempt to access YouTube from within the program.
- Add the movie's description, title, and tags. Choose **a category, then Public or Private based on your privacy settings.**
- Click on **Upload.**

Share your video on YouTube

Take these actions to share videos on YouTube:

- Choose **Export & Share from the Video Editor workspace.**
- After choosing the Social Media menu, choose **YouTube.**
- Adjust the suggested values as necessary.
- Click on **Begin Share.**
- Give Adobe Premiere Elements permission to access your YouTube account if this is your first attempt to access YouTube from within the program.
- Add the movie's description, title, and tags. Choose **a category, then Public or Private based on your privacy settings.**
- Click on **Upload.**

Create an Elements Organizer Contact Book

Using the contact book makes it easier for you to keep track of the email addresses you frequently use. Elements Organizer's contact book configuration enables you to distribute images to an individual or group of individuals quickly.

Add an entry to the contact book

- Choose **Edit > Book Contacts.**
- Select **"New Contact" from the menu.**
- After **entering the contact's name, email address, and any other desired information, click OK.**

Import addresses into the contact book (Windows only)

Addresses can be imported from Outlook or Outlook Express to save typing them in. Additionally, addresses from vCard files can be imported. An automated email signature with the sender's contact details is called a vCard (VCF) file.

- Choose **Edit > Book Contacts.**

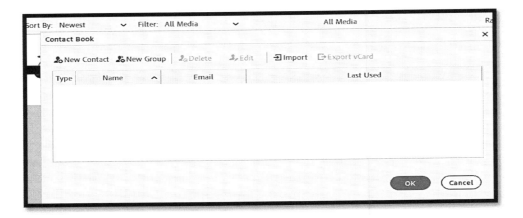

- Press **Import.**
- Choose the option you wish to import contacts from in the **Choose Contact Source dialog box.** Choose the **VCF file from your computer under vCard Files.**

Delete or modify an entry in the contact book

- Choose **Edit > Book Contacts.**
- Click **Delete** after selecting one or more entries from the list, and then click **OK.**

Edit an entry in the contact book

- Click **Edit and then Contact Book.**
- After making your selection, double-click the entry or select **the Edit button.** After editing the entry, click **OK.**

Create a group in the contact book

- Click **Edit and then Contact Book.**
- Press the **"New Group" icon.**

- Fill up the G**roup Name text box with the group's name.**
- To include someone in the group, choose **an entry from the Contacts list, then click** the **Add button** to add it to the Members list. To add a neighboring contact, shift-click; to add a non-neighboring contact, use **Ctrl-click.**
- Select one or more entries from the Members list, then click the **Remove button to remove the selected contacts from the group.**
- To exit the dialog box for the New Group, click **OK.** Your contact book now includes the group.
- Select **OK.**

Export contact information to vCard files (Windows only)

- Click **Edit and then Contact Book.**
- Click **the contact you want to choose**. Use the **Ctrl-click keyboard shortcut to select several contacts.**
- To Export vCard, click on it. After deciding on a place for the vCard file on your computer, click **OK.**

Activity

1. Share your picture via email.
2. Share your pictures on Flickr.
3. Create an elements organizer contact book.

Conclusion

The 2024 version of Adobe Photoshop Elements, a basic photo-editing program, was published. The revised version, which is powered by AI, has a better user interface and several additional capabilities that make editing photographs simpler. Likewise, the business unveiled Premium Elements 2024, a basic video editing application. Photoshop Elements 2024 has a totally redesigned user interface, replete with a unique dark mode and easily accessible functionality. One of the standout features of the 2024 edition is the new match color tool, which lets users adjust a picture's color with a single click using either a custom or one of the presets that are already included. With just a few images, Photoshop Elements 2024 can now produce short reels (vertical films), to which users may also add graphics, text, and other effects. The upgrade also makes it simple to embellish images with a variety of artistic graphics. The Photoshop Elements 2024 license additionally provides free access to Adobe Stock images. You can download the Photoshop Element 2024 app on both Mac and Windows platforms. In a similar vein, cell phones running the iOS and Android operating systems also have companion apps. The Elements edition costs $99.99 for a one-time license and does not require a subscription, in contrast to full-fledged Photoshop. Keep in mind that Adobe also provides a discount on the most recent license purchase if you already own a license for Photoshop Elements 2023.

INDEX

3

33 million pixels, 27

4

4K video resolution, 27, 28

A

A larger value sharpens a wider band of pixels, 153
A million pixels, 28
A pixel's color, 28
A pixel's description of a specific color, 28
A selection of a layer's contents, 193
A smaller pixel value, 88
A software driver, 271
A7 III camera, 28
About Blending Modes, 126
About color, 34
About Histograms, 209
About monitor resolution, 196
About Presets, 279
about the filter gallery, 26
accentuate the effect, 88
Access licensed images, 68
Access licensed images from the Adobe Stock
    website, 68
achieve distinctive styles, 19
acquire knowledge, 18
action bars, 19
activate the popup slider, 53
Add a frame or theme to a picture, 266
Add an artistic background to a picture, 265
Add an entry to the contact book, 351
Add captions and narration to the workflow, 340
Add captions to the slideshow, 319
Add custom presets, 221
Add effects, 76, 254

Add effects, textures, and frames to your pictures., 76
Add foreground and background to your photo., 183
add graphics, 326, 353
Add information to your file., 287
Add media from a folder to the slideshow, 319
Add media from the catalog to the slideshow, 317
Add music to a slideshow, 320
Add People to Groups, 307
ADD PHOTO EFFECTS, 247
Add Photo Effects and Filters, 26
ADD PHOTO EFFECTS AND FILTERS, 247
Add quick frames to your picture., 76
Add quick textures to your photo., 76
add straight-edge segments, 136
Add stylized shapes or graphics to a picture, 265
Add text, 169, 319, 326
Add Text guided Edit, 77
Add Text Guided Edit, 20
add text overlay, 109
Add to and subtract from a selection, 134
Add To Selection, 134, 137, 145
Adding a new brush to the brush library, 157
Adding location information to your media files, 308
adding people to groups, 26
additional channel, 33
adjust facial features, 25
Adjust Facial Features, 225, 268
Adjust light and color, 311
Adjust Lighting, 216, 217, 218
Adjust panels, 68
Adjust panels in the panel bin., 68
Adjust sharpness in camera raw files, 275
adjust the brightness, 20, 217
Adjust the color curves in your picture., 231
adjust the degree, 91, 150
adjust the effect by using the available choices, 93
adjust the glow's intensity, 92
Adjust the highlights and shadows, 209
adjust the layer mask, 74
adjust the output's parameters, 20
adjusting color, 25

355

adjusting color curves, 25

adjusting color for skin tone, 25

adjusting lighting, 25, 205

adjusting sharpness, 25

adjusting the contrast, 128

Adjustment Filters, 257

adjustment for Fuzziness, 94

Adjustment layers, 32, 232

Adjustments, 69, 74, 257, 258, 260

adjustments to photographs, 32

Adobe Acrobat's primary format, 42

Adobe Illustrator, 30

Adobe Photoshop (Elements), 18

Adobe products like Illustrator and Premiere Pro., 38

Adobe Sensei's advanced capabilities, 18

Adobe Stock from the Backgrounds panel, 68

Adobe Stock photos, 64

Adobe Systems Incorporated, 37

advanced mode, 49, 50, 73, 74, 86, 87, 176, 177, 179, 181, 205, 208, 216, 253, 256, 279, 334, 336

Advanced Photo Editing Tools, 26

ADVANCED PHOTO EDITING TOOLS, 270

advertising mediums, 30

aged paper appearance, 74, 75

AI Edits, 75

Align your pictures for photo merging., 117

Aligned, 143, 147, 149, 269

Allow Photos to Resize, 291

alpha channel, 33

alpha channel operates, 33

Alpha Channels, 33

Alter the size of your picture, 97

alter the text's font, 97, 99

alternative overlay option, 190

Always Ask, 63

Amount, 139, 150, 152, 153, 188, 201

An image, 29, 91, 151, 169, 181, 195, 198, 200, 212, 235, 239, 259, 265, 272

Angle, 102, 153, 156, 163, 226, 229, 263

Anti-aliased, 43, 135, 136, 171, 184

append file extensions, 63

append file extensions with lowercase characters, 63

applications and web browsers, 60

application's UI color mode, 19, 278

applies settings, 44

Apply a filter, 248

Apply a gradient, 163, 164

Apply a layer style, 263

apply a technique, 71

apply a text style, 110

apply adjustments, 144

Apply filters one after the other to create effects, 248

apply several copies, 147

Apply style to text, 245

Apply tags quickly, 305

apply the color match effect in quick mode, 72

Apply the Invert filter, 259

Apply the Photo filter, 260

Applying color, 118

Applying edits and effects, 312

Applying or undoing changes, 313

Arrange menu, 132

Artistic Effect settings, 19

artwork, 19, 43, 44, 69, 74, 252, 264, 265, 324

as the global leader in image editing., 37

Ask If Original, 63

Attention to detail, 29

Audio, 320, 340, 341, 342, 344

Auto Analyze your media, 301

Auto Backup and Restore Catalog Structure, 313

Auto Curate, 288

Auto Fixes, 203

Auto Hide, 147

Auto Panorama, 116

Auto Select Layer, 132

Auto Selection tool, 50, 83

Auto Smart Fix, 21, 216

Auto Smart Tone, 203, 204

Auto Sync details, 301

Auto1, 70

Auto2, 70

Auto3, 70

Auto4, 70

Auto5, 70

auto-generated content, 18

Automatic cropping suggestions, 175

Automatic Erasure, 173

Automatic modifications, 18

automatically adjust tone, 22

Automatically convert to black and white, 220
Automatically Fix Red Eyes, 138
Auto-Smart Styles, 70
Autumn, 71

B

B&W, 93, 94, 95
Background, 21, 22, 40, 75, 95, 126, 159, 160, 186, 187, 201, 232, 234, 236, 237, 238, 266, 322, 325, 326
background color, 118, 121, 123, 124, 126, 159, 160, 173, 182, 190, 201, 237, 256, 257
Background Contents, 40
Background Eraser tool icon, 159
background layer., 68
Background layer., 40, 126, 234, 236, 237, 266
Backup Catalog Structure, 314
Backup your catalog incrementally, 314
Baseline (Standard), 60
Baseline Optimized, 60
basic features of color, 34
basic photo fixes, 69
basic photo-editing, 69, 353
basic photo-editing program, 353
basic photo-fixing tools, 69
BASIC THINGS YOU OUGHT TO KNOW, 27
basic video editing application, 353
Basics, 20, 77, 82, 84, 87
beautiful panoramic effects., 116
beautiful two-color creation, 75
begin a new selection, 137
Behind, 127
Bicubic, 199
Bicubic Sharper, 199
Bicubic Smoother, 199
big selection, 150
Bilinear, 199
birthdays, 19
bite-sized business cards, 30
bitmap, 34, 40, 42, 120, 126, 164, 166, 248
bitmapped, 43
Black & White, 71, 91
black and white edits, 24
Black and White Guided Edit, 91, 94

Black and White menu, 95
black-and-white, 18, 23, 72, 75, 89, 91, 94, 117, 151, 210, 213, 221, 259
black-and-white image, 72, 89, 94, 210
black-and-white picture, 75, 91, 117, 259
black-and-white pictures, 23
blend color, 127, 128
Blend Images, 116
Blue Tone, 72
Blue Wash, 71
Blues, 70
blur color, 151
Blur feature, 153
Blur filters, 149, 150
Blur the edges of a selection, 185
Blur the edges of a selection by feathering, 185
Blur tool, 50, 149
Blur, Smudge, and Sharpen, 149
border of contrasting pixels, 143
bracket keys, 188
bright red jumper, 89
Brighten Eyes, 111
Brightness, 34, 121, 128, 214, 216, 217, 228, 256, 274
brightness (HSB), 34, 120
Brush and Pencil tools, 118
Brush Settings, 156, 157, 160
Brush Settings and options, 156
Brushes pop-up menu, 146
brush's size, 83, 84, 94, 189
Burn tools, 154
Burnt Edges, 72
business unveiled Premium Elements, 353
buttons, 19, 54, 95, 99, 104, 169, 183, 207, 244, 250, 277, 312, 328, 350
Byte Order, 61

C

Camera Raw, 205, 209, 272, 273, 274, 275, 276, 277
camera raw images, 276
Camera RAW installation, 272
camera's light-tight chamber, 72
Cancel current action button,, 82
Canvas Resizing, 201
catchy animations, 19

cell phones running the iOS, 354

cell phones running the iOS and Android operating systems, 354

central position, 116

certain pictures, 64, 66, 67, 68, 138

certain regions of a picture, 222

Change color, 89, 210

Change print dimensions, 197

Change print dimensions and resolution, 197

Change text color, 245

change the border's size, 109

change the color background, 75

change the color component's range, 90

Change the color of an object, 91

change the contrast, 220

change the degree of color fall-off, 90

Change the display of items in a pop-up panel menu, 281

Change the guide and grid settings, 48

Change the opacity, 33

Change the rulers' zero origin, 47

Change the rulers' zero origin and settings, 47

Change the stacking order, 238

Change your picture to black and white., 117

character frame, 99, 100

Characteristics, 226

Charcoal, 71, 248

Check the scan quality and tonal range, 208

choice from the menu of the Image Quality, 60

choice of source picture, 140

choose a background or sky with a single click, 19, 22

Choose **a color for the remaining portion of the canvas**, 102

Choose a **Computer**, 139

Choose a font family and style, 244

Choose a font size, 244

Choose **a gradient**, 164

Choose a layer to edit., 242

Choose **a soft-edged brush**, 185

Choose a tool, 51, 134, 243, 283

Choose **advanced mode**, 67

Choose characters, 243

Choose Clone Overlay, 147

Choose **Constrain Proportions**, 45, 198, 199

Choose License for free button to download, 68

Choose **Multi-Photo Text**, 98

Choose **Paint Brush**, 102

Choose **Refine Edge**, 137, 144

Choose **Slim Down**, 111

Choose the **Add Text guided edit** card, 20

Choose **the Brush tool**, 155, 157

choose the Brush tool symbol, 155

Choose the **Gradient tool from the Toolbox's Draw section.**, 164

choose **the Lasso tool**, 135

Choose the **Preview menu**, 153

Choose the **Sponge tool.**, 154

choosing the **appropriate Style**, 78

chroma, 34, 121, 275

chrome feel, 74, 75

Classic effect, 70, 252, 253

Clear the Colors, 188

clear view of the landscape, 112

clever algorithm, 203

Click **on an eye's crimson region**, 139

clicking the **Text Style button**, 110

clone stamp tool, 25

Clone Stamp tool, 50, 146, 147, 148

Clone Stamp Tool, 84, 146

Close a file, 46

Closed Eyes window's box, 111

clothes, 19

Cloud, 37, 256, 300, 301

cohesive image., 32

Collage, 116, 320

collages, 18, 21, 23, 332

color and texture, 32, 50, 136

color correction, 75, 205, 208, 216, 262

color field, 119

Color Match, 19, 69, 72, 73, 74, 252, 255

color options, 126

color pop, 89

color profile, 63, 285

Color Swatches window, 123, 124, 126

Colored Pencil, 71

colorful patterns, 23

color-guided edits, 24

colorize black-and-white photographs, 18

Colorize Photo, 221, 222

colorizing photo, 25

colorizing photo haze removal, 25

combination of RGB, 28

Combine photos, 115

combine sampling data, 143, 269

Combine the best-lit elements from two photos, 112

combining two photos, 100

Command-drag in Mac OS, 90

Commit current action, 80, 81, 82

Commit current action button, 80, 81, 82

common display resolutions, 27

common editing jobs, 69

common photo-fixing features, 69

company logos, 30

comparable image material, 117

compatible file format, 205

Complete Backup, 314

complete library, 124

composite picture, 63

composition in the Editor workspace, 69

compression method, 60

computer monitors, 34, 120, 167

computer screen, 27, 122

Conclusion, 353

configure marquee tool options, 135

Configure options, 149, 274

configure parameters, 58

configure the subsequent choices, 147

Configure the subsequent choices, 114

Configure the subsequent Type tool, 171

Configure viewing preferences for the Media view, 290

considerable section, 35

Construct backgrounds, 248

Content-Aware, 117, 142

Content-Aware Fill Transparent, 117

Content-Aware Fill Transparent Areas, 117

Contiguous fills, 162

Continuous, 161

Contrast, 188, 214, 216, 217, 218, 228, 274

control panel size and group special, 123

control the amount of colors, 34

Conversion difficulties, 30

Convert to Black and White, 219

Convert To Black and White, 219

Copper, 70

Copy a selection using commands, 191

Copy a selection with the use of commands, 134

Copy style settings, 264

copying and pasting, 133, 191

correct an image's exposure, 69

Correct color in Quick Mode, 205

Correct Skin Tone Guided Edit, 84

Correcting color, 208

correctly exposed picture, 112

cracked paint texture, 74, 75

create 3D effects, 18

create a boundary, 136

create a boundary for a freehand selection, 136

Create a collage, 321

Create a custom brush shape from a picture, 158

Create a Greeting Card, 333

Create a greeting card., 341

Create a group in the contact book, 352

Create a Highlight Reel, 340

Create a highlight reel., 341

Create a keyword tag, 303

Create a new blank file, 39

Create a new layer from part of another layer, 236

Create a Photo Book, 332

Create a Photo Calendar, 335

Create a photo collage., 341

Create a Picture Stack, 104

Create a Puzzle Effect, 105

Create a Video Story, 336

create an element organizer contact book, 26

Create an elements organizer contact book., 353

create an inspirational Quote Graphic, 21

Create and apply tags quickly, 304

create and edit text, 25

Create and Edit Text, 25

CREATE AND EDIT TEXT, 243

Create Clipping Mask, 228

Create Fun Pieces, 26

CREATE FUN PIECES, 316

Create Meme Template., 96

Create or add photos to an album, 289

Create Panorama, 117

Create Photo Prints, 327

Create Prints and Gifts, 336

Create prints and gifts., 341

Create quote graphics, 18
Create tags quickly, 305
Create Texture, 141
create transparent sections, 33
Create warped text icon, 78
Creating a catalog, 295
creating a photo collage, 26
Creative, 37, 75
creative overlays in the Elements Web companion
   app, 19
creative potential, 21
Crop a photo, 311
Crop Photo Guided Edit, 84
Crop to a selection boundary, 175
Cross Process, 71
current background color, 40
Current File., 61
Custom camera settings, 277
Custom Method, 108
Custom Pattern, 163
Custom print size, 331
Custom Workspace, 54, 55, 234
Customize the slideshow, 317
customized preset, 20
customized shape, 78
customizing templates, 18
Cut and paste a selection into another photo, 191
Cut and paste a selection into another picture., 194
cutting and pasting a selection, 25

D

Darker burn, 127
Date Format, 290
decent exposure, 112
Deep Blue, 71
default layer translucent, 40
default meme template, 96
default placements, 55
Define a feathered edge for a selection tool, 185
Define a feathered edge for an existing selection, 186
Define a gradient, 164
Defringe a selection, 190
dehaze, 21, 75
dehaze or colorize a photo, 21

Delete a brush, 157
Delete a catalog, 299
Delete a layer, 234
Delete or modify an entry in the contact book, 352
Deleting, 298
Depth of Field effect, 106
describe screen resolutions, 28
deselect **Resize Windows to Fit**, 130
design a web graphic, 39
designate the new selection area, 137
Designer patterns, 144
destination photographs, 133, 191
Device, 342
dialog box of Adobe Stock, 64, 66
dialog box of the Photoshop Elements Print, 36
dialog boxes, 19, 53, 209
Diamond gradient, 163
Difference Clouds, 248, 256
different backgrounds, 19, 21
different colors, 28
different file format, 58
Diffuse Glow option, 92, 95
Diffused Colors, 72
digital camera, 44, 45, 63, 195, 209, 271, 272, 286
Digital design, 37
digital display, 27
digital image, 23, 27, 28, 37, 195
dimensions and resolution, 197, 198
discontiguous, 160
discount on the most recent license purchase, 354
Display a picture at 100%, 129
display Filenames, 36
display the image, 91, 206
Display the image size of an open file, 196
dissimilar pixels to blur, 150, 151
Dissolve, 127
Distribute menu Spaces, 132
Dodge, 154
dogs, 19
double exposures or color pops., 18
Download photos, 271
download pictures from your camera, 26
Download pictures from your camera., 282
download the Photoshop Element 2024 app, 354
downsample, 198

DPI, 28, 31

drag **the Brush tool within**, 155

Drag **the desired region into selection**, 135

drag **the Fuzziness slider**, 91

dragging **over the region that encompasses the color spectrum**, 137

dragging the adjustment slider, 89, 211

Drawing a rectangle, 167

Drawing a rectangle, square, or rounded rectangle, 167

drawing tools, 118

drop shadow, 99, 262, 263

duplicating an image, 35, 55

dynamic file format, 42

E

---

easily accessible functionality, 353

edges of color transitions, 151

Edit a layer's style settings, 264

Edit an adjustment or fill layer, 230

Edit an entry in the contact book, 352

Edit in Camera RAW, 272

Edit pictures, 68, 282

Edit the layer masks, 230

Edit tool preferences, 52

Edit workspace, 39, 58, 63, 131, 133, 134, 153, 167, 184, 185, 186, 191, 246, 273, 276

editable documents, 37

editable files with PSD sizes, 37

Editing files, 299

editing photographs, 353

Editing photos using Instant Fix, 312

editor workspace, 24, 68, 289

Editor.app/Contents/Required/bwconvert.txt, 221

Effect and add an effect, 102

Effects, Adjustments, Textures and Frames, 69

either the vertical or horizontal flip button, 97

Elements contains all the capabilities, 18

Elements Web, 19, 23

Elements Web and import images, 23

eliminate backgrounds, 22

eliminate blemishes, 140

Eliminate Color, 220

eliminating jargon, 23

Ellipse Tool, 167

Ellipse Tool,, 167

Elliptical Marquee tool only, 135

embellish images with a variety of artistic graphics, 353

Employ Photo Ratio, 174

employ Photoshop, 37

Employ the Text and Border, 109

employ the Text on Path tool, 81

employ the Text on Selection tool, 80

Employ the vignette effect, 87

Employing the Auto or Quick selection tools, 101

Encapsulated PostScript, 30

English-only beta, 19, 22

English-only beta Elements, 19

English-only beta Elements Mobile companion app, 19

Enhance, 23, 25, 49, 50, 88, 89, 90, 110, 139, 146, 148, 149, 151, 152, 153, 200, 203, 209, 210, 212, 214, 215, 216, 217, 218, 219, 220, 221, 222, 223, 224, 225, 227, 268, 334, 336

Enhance your photographs, 23

enhancing an image's shadows, 128

Enhancing your picture, 25

Enter **a Feather value**, 135, 136

Enter the new text by typing, 110

Enter the workspace, 324

enthusiasts, 18

Equalize filter, 257

Erase a part of your picture with the use of the erase tool., 183

Eraser Tool, 106, 159

Eraser tool parameters, 159, 160

Every guided edit has a corresponding image, 91, 95, 106

Examine the figures in the Pixel Dimensions box, 200

Examine the Quick and Advanced versions, 72, 255

EXIF, 63, 295

exit the dialog box, 274, 350, 353

expanded using saved swatches, 124

Experience editing in a modern, 19

experiment with a new background, 64

Explore a variety of categories, 64, 66, 68

Explore various categories, 67

exploring the redesigned web companion app, 23

Export contact information, 353
Export contact information to vCard files, 353
Export contact information to vCard files (Windows only), 353
Export vCard, 353
Exposure, 100, 112, 113, 114, 154, 274
Eye tool, 50, 139, 207
Eye Tools, 138
eyedropper's sample size, 122
eye-pleasing fonts,, 19
Eyes, 110, 111, 139, 226

F

Face Shape, 110, 226
Face Tilt, 110, 226
Face-aware technology, 225, 268
Facebook, 26, 317, 323, 340, 342, 343, 344
facial features in your picture, 231
Fade, 156
Faded Vintage, 72
fast modifications or enhancements, 18
Fast photo correction, 19
Faux bold, 171, 246
Faux Italic, 171
Favorite shots are sped through in reels, 20
Feather, 88, 135, 136, 185, 186, 188
Feathering, 184, 185, 248
Feature, 226
fifty-five classic effects, 70
File Extension, 63
File format, 58
file in a new layer, 43
File Info, 36, 56, 286, 287
file information, 26, 35, 55, 283, 284, 286
File menu, 21, 58, 64
File Name, 58, 330, 331
File Size, 85
file-by-file basis., 63
Files of Type menu, 40, 43
Fill a layer, 162, 192
Fill a layer with a color or pattern, 162, 192
Fill or stroke a selection, 192, 194
filling or stroking a selection, 25
films and photographs, 19

Filter Gallery, 247, 249, 250, 251
Filter menu, 247, 249, 251, 261
Find People in Your Files, 307
Finger Painting, 152
first digital cameras, 23
Fit a picture to the screen, 129
FIX AND ENHANCE, 203
FIX AND ENHANCE YOUR PHOTOS, 203
Fix and Enhance Your Picture, 25
Fix Photos, 207
fix the problem to your satisfaction., 141
Fixed Ratio, 135
Fixed Size, 135, 167, 168
Flatten a Layer, 237
Flatten an image, 241
flattened file size of your image, 241
Flickr, 80, 84, 86, 88, 93, 94, 101, 103, 105, 106, 108, 111, 349, 350
Flow pop-up slider, 154
Follow the guided edit steps., 21
Font Family, 171, 244
Font Style, 171
foreground color boxes, 118
Forehead height, 226
four Photoshop workflows, 21
Frames, 69, 74, 75, 99, 266
free access to Adobe Stock images, 354
Free Adobe Stock Photos, 21
Free Adobe Stock photos and Imagery, 64
From Center, 167
frontmost picture, 56
full high definition, 27
full ultra-high definition TVs, 27
full-fledged Photoshop., 354
fun edits, 24
Fun Edits, 95, 96, 98, 100, 101, 102, 104
functionality, 18, 54, 228, 271, 273
fundamental color-programming, 27

G

gadget cases, 19
Gaussian Blur, 150
generate visual writing with an additional photo, 97
generated font, 244

Geometric Distortion Correction, 116

Get Faces Clean Up with the Perfect Portrait Guided Edit, 110

Get free images from Adobe Stock, 21

Get photos from scanners, 270

get rid of anything unwanted, 142

get the best of pictures, 25

GET TO KNOW PHOTOSHOP ELEMENTS 2024, 39

Get to Know the Photoshop Elements Toolbox, 25

GET TO KNOW THE PHOTOSHOP ELEMENTS TOOLBOX, 118

get your knowledge tested, 24

get your preferred results, 101

getting the horizon straightened, 18

Gifts service in Photoshop Elements, 19

Give specific dimensions for the width and height, 85

give the impression of depth, 23

gives the picture a retro feel, 72

Going a little in-depth, 26

Golden, 70

GoPros, 28

Gradient Map filter, 258

gradients or patterns, 79

graphics editor designed for photographers, 18

Graphics Panel, 264

grayscale, 34, 40, 120, 143, 154, 158, 219, 221, 248, 257, 258, 259, 269, 275, 284

Grayscale noise, 275

great occasions, 18

Green, 33, 70, 71, 72, 93

green checkmark, 97, 99

Grey Tone, 72

Guided Edit, 39, 88, 101, 102, 103, 104, 105, 106, 110, 205, 267

guided edit option, 84

guided edit tool, 20

Guided Edits, 24, 39, 77, 88, 95, 102, 111

GUIDED EDITS, 77

guided fixes, 25

Guided mode, 54, 77, 82, 87, 91, 92, 93, 94, 95, 106, 108, 178, 267

guided modifications, 18, 77

Guides & Grid, 48

Guides and Rulers, 47

H

Hand tool, 49, 51, 128, 129, 131, 192, 197, 277

handle scenarios in photographs, 112

Hard Light, 127, 191

Hard-edged freehand lines, 173

Hardness, 156

Haze Removal, 223

hazy look, 150

healing brush, 25, 142, 268

healing brush options, 142

Healing Brush tool, 50, 142, 143, 268, 269

Heavy Vintage, 72

Hide and show media files in the Media view, 291

Hide media files by marking them, 291

High Definition, 27

High Key guided edit, 95

high tolerance, 160, 161

highest resolution, 28

Highlight Skin Tones, 180

Highlight the filter's edges, 248

Highlight what album and folder views mean., 315

Highlights, 154, 178, 179, 180, 214, 216, 217, 218, 274

high-quality visuals, 30

high-resolution image, 29

high-resolution published results, 153

Holga, 71

Horizontal Distortion, 78, 246

horizontal manner, 29

Horizontal Type Tool, 78

hours of pixel-by-pixel retouching, 18

HSB color models, 118

HSB model, 34, 120, 121

Hue, 34, 89, 90, 91, 120, 156, 206, 210, 211, 212, 213, 220, 221, 228, 256

huge amount of picture data, 37

I

Ignore Camera Data, 63

Image, 31, 45, 60, 61, 63, 91, 133, 166, 175, 179, 182, 183, 191, 195, 197, 198, 199, 200, 201, 213, 241,

254, 258, 271, 272, 274, 275, 276, 305, 321, 322, 331, 342, 344

image a Black & White, 71

image after adjusting, 149, 173

Image Compression, 61

image editors, 18

image elements, 142, 339

Image previews, 63

Image Resizing, 195

Image Size, 31, 45, 133, 183, 191, 195, 197, 198, 199, 200

image size and canvas size, 24, 25, 38

Image Size vs. Canvas Size, 31

image-correcting control, 206

image's brighter, 95

image's layers, 58

images with Photoshop Elements, 18

Import keyword, 306

important benefits, 30

important characteristics, 142

impressionist, 155

Impressionist Brush tool, 155

Impressionists, 149

Improve clarity, 311

improve images, 18

Improve performance with filters and effects, 251

Improve uninteresting backdrops., 144

In Advanced Mode, 67

In Guided Mode, 65

In Swift / In Skill, 103

include a photo in the text, 99

Include All Subfolders, 45

Include floral designs, 144

Include the style of a text, 79

Increase Contrast, 92, 110

Indent Sides By, 168

indexed color., 34

Indicate picture compression, 60

Individual Colors, 261

individual pixels, 29, 30, 31, 126

Infinite resolution, 30

initial text style, 110

initiation of the workflow., 20

innovative concepts, 18

Insert text into your image., 246

Insta360, 28

Instagram, 323, 340, 342, 343, 344

instant access, 19

Instant Fix a photo, 311

Instant fix a picture., 315

instant-fixing a picture, 26

instantly blur or eliminate a background, 21

Instantly edit photos, 288

Instructions, 154

INTRODUCTION, 18

J

JPEG Artifacts, 21, 75

JPEG Artifacts Removal, 21

K

keyword tags, 26, 286, 295, 300, 302, 303, 304, 305, 306, 307, 310, 315

kinds of adjustments, 204

kittens, 19

L

Larger file sizes, 30

larger variety of files and directories, 23

lasso selection tool, 25

Launch a picture in Photoshop, 96, 100, 101, 109, 221, 223, 224, 225, 268

launch and import pictures, 40

Launch the **Graphics panel**, 67

launch the preferred picture, 65, 67

Layer data in TIFF files, 62

layer data., 62

Leading the menu, 171

learn about auto-curate, 26

learn about auto-fixes, 25

learn about edge detection, 25

learn about how to resize an image, 25

learn about search-guided edits, 24

learn about the info panel, 26

learn about the new features, 24

Learn about Your Photoshop Elements File, 26

LEARN ABOUT YOUR PHOTOSHOP ELEMENTS FILE, 283

Learn as you are working, 18

learn to shape and resize your text., 25

Left-Right, 226

Lens Blur, 150

Lens Flare, 257

Less useful for complex pictures, 30

lesser and simpler alternatives, 18

Levels, 209, 216, 218, 219, 228

License for free button, 68

License for Free button, 64, 66, 67

license for Photoshop Elements 2023., 377

License History, 68

light and dark mode settings, 19

Light Leaks, 72

light or dark from the options, 19, 278

light or dark interface, 24

LIGHTEN AND DARKEN, 84

Lighten and Darken Guided Edit, 84

lighten or darken an image, 84

Lighter file sizes, 30

Lighter pixels, 153, 224

Limited Edition, 18

Limited resolution, 30

Linear gradient, 163

Lips, 110, 226

list of formats, 59, 60, 61

Load a library, 281

Load Swatches option, 125

locate decent books, 23

Location, 165, 166, 194, 296, 308, 309

Lock or unlock a layer, 234

Lomo Blue, 71

Lomo Contrast, 71

Long Edge, 85

Low Key guided edit, 95

low-resolution, 29, 59, 61

M

Magic Wand tools, 184

Magnetic Lasso, 50, 184, 185

Magnetic Lasso tool, 50

Maintain Canvas Size, 183

maintaining the original, 236

make a choice of source pictures, 140

Make a copy of an existing layer., 235

Make adjustments that are impactful in a swift manner, 18

Make amazing designs, 18

Make amazing designs and share them with ease, 18

Make changes to the effect, 74

make learning Elements easier, 23

Make other special color adjustments, 209

make small-scale edits, 83

make the picker float, 146

Make use of a shape tool or the Type tool., 235

making a specific image, 35, 55

making a specific image the frontmost image, 35, 55

making frowns into grins, 18

making use of a raster file, 29

making use of Photo Elements, 18

Manage your files with Keyword Tags, 302

Manage Your Files with the Organizer, 26

MANAGE YOUR FILES WITH THE ORGANIZER, 288

Manage your media files by Date or Event, 310

Manage your photos by Place, 307

Manage your picture by place., 315

managing your files, 26

Manually backing up a catalog, 314

Manually Backup and Restore, 313

Manually restoring a catalog, 314

Manually straighten a picture, 181, 183

Mask filter's effects, 153, 224

Match the color and tone, 19

Maximum image size limit, 200

Maximum image size limit in the Editor, 200

Maximum image size limits, 200

maximum resolution, 28

megapixel, 28

Megapixel, 28

megapixels, 201

Merge one layer into another., 242

merge particular layers., 32

millions of pixels, 27

minor grid lines, 48

mixed-up ideas, 28

mobile device, 22

Modernized workspaces, 19

modification of the vignette's intensity, 88

modifies an image's overall hue,, 89

Modify, 49, 90, 91, 111, 130, 132, 145, 152, 172, 176, 177, 207, 212, 220, 231, 251, 315, 339

modify color, 34, 120, 232

modify the Color Swatches panel's thumbnail presentation, 123

modifying photos, 53

monitoring, 53

most well-liked one-click modifications, 21

Motion Blur, 152, 153

Move a selection, 131

move and scale object-guided edit, 24

Move and scale objects in guided edits., 117

Move the content in a layer, 238

Move **the title bar** of the panel, 55

move the white triangles across the slider, 119

move the **Zoom slider**, 97

Move tool, 49, 53, 131, 132, 133, 166, 191, 192, 238, 243, 265, 266, 321

Moving files, 297

Moving or modifying media files, 297

mugs, 19

multipage projects, 35, 55

Multi-Photo writing guided edit, 97

multiple degrees of editing, 69

Multiply, 127

multiply the horizontal and vertical pixel measurements, 27

N

Navigate to **Guided mode**, 20

Navigator panel, 128, 130, 131

Nearest Neighbor, 199

New Adjustment Layer, 89, 90, 210, 212, 217, 218, 221, 228, 261

New Artistic Effect, 21

New Blank File, 39

new edition of Photoshop Elements, 24

New light and dark modes, 19

new match color tool, 353

new photograph, 204

New Selection, 137, 145

new tools, 18

No Restrictions, 174

Normal, 59, 126, 135, 151, 178, 235

number of character frames, 99

number of pixels, 27, 29, 122, 152, 190, 195, 198, 209

O

object edges and shadows., 142

Object Removal Guided Edit, 82

Obtainable variants, 70, 71, 72

Old School, 71

omitting details, 149

One at a time, make tiny brushstrokes., 142

one megapixel, 28

one-click repairs, 19

One-click selection, 22

one-time license, 354

On-screen, 153, 224

opacifying the surrounding environment, 106

Opacity, 53, 92, 94, 115, 147, 149, 155, 159, 160, 161, 164, 165, 173, 175, 193, 194, 253

Opacity option, 53, 159

Open a camera raw image, 276

Open a catalog, 297

Open a file, 40

Open Closed Eyes, 111, 139

Open in the Quick or Advanced workspace., 186

Open photos, 35, 55

Open Recently Edited File, 41, 64

Open the **Tools panel**, 22

opened your preferred picture., 20

opening and closing photographs, 35, 55

Opening and processing camera raw files, 273

opening closed eyes, 18

option configured to Use Lowercase, 63

Option in Mac OS, 90, 91, 134, 136, 143, 198, 211, 212, 214, 240, 256, 274

Optional, 99, 100, 101, 111, 122, 124, 136, 145, 146, 164, 206, 246

options bar, 132, 137, 139, 144, 145, 146, 149, 152, 154, 170, 171, 172, 174, 185, 243, 244, 245, 246

Orange Wash, 71

order prints, 19, 87

Organizer, 23, 36, 57, 58, 69, 140, 200, 201, 270, 271, 288, 290, 293, 294, 297, 301, 305, 307, 313, 316, 327, 344

organizer catalog, 26, 326

Other transform options, 246

over the border, 80

Over the border, 109

Over the eye region, make a selection., 139

over the path's boundary, 82

overlapping material, 115, 116

overlapping portions, 115

Overlay guided edit, 109

oversharpened, 152

oversharpening, 152

Overview of This Book, 23

P

Paint / Pattern, 161

paint over sections, 102

Panel Bin, 33, 53, 54, 55

panel is adjacent to Effects., 21

Panel menus, 53

Panels assist you in managing, 53

Panels in the advanced mode, 54

panel's More menu, 125, 284

Paste between photos with Photomerge Compose, 111

Paste one selection into another, 191

pattern stamp tool, 25

Pattern Stamp tool, 50, 148, 149

Pattern Stamp tool icon, 148

Pattern Stamp tool settings, 149

PC gaming monitors, 27

PDF, 30, 42, 43, 44, 60, 61, 287, 329, 348

pencil drawing, 71

Pencil Sketch, 71

perceive color, 120

Perfect Portrait, 110

perform fast alterations, 18

permanent alterations, 232

personalize the blur, 108

Perspective, 52, 116, 176, 177

Perspective Crop tool, 52, 176, 177

photo and video highlights, 18

photo and video highlights and slideshows, 18

photo and video library's entire contents, 19

photo bin, 24, 99, 178, 179, 326

Photo Bin taskbar icon, 36

photo book, 26, 332, 333

Photo Browser, 35, 56, 58, 138, 286, 287

photo calendar, 26, 336

photo editing, 18, 175

photo effects, 69, 143, 254

photo merge-guided edits, 24

photo online, 80, 88, 93, 94, 101, 105, 108, 111

photo prints, 26

photo reel, 26, 323, 341

Photo Reel, 20, 323, 324

photography, 23, 27, 28, 153, 223, 340

Photography manipulation, 37

Photomerge, 111, 112, 113, 114, 115, 116, 117

Photomerge Compose tool, 111

Photomerge Panorama, 115

Photoshop creations, 37

Photoshop Documents, 36

Photoshop Element, 18, 26, 29, 32, 354

Photoshop Elements 2024, 19, 24, 353

Photoshop Elements Mobile, 22

Photoshop Elements Mobile and Web Companion Apps, 22

PHOTOSHOP ELEMENTS TRICKS, 267

Photoshop Elements window, 35, 52, 55, 271

Pick a blur choice, 152

Pick **Photo Bin**, 140

picture data storage and creation., 36

pictures on Flickr, 26, 353

Pinned and Unpinned tabs, 308

pixel dimensions, 191, 195, 196, 198, 199

Pixel measurements, 196

Pixels, 24, 27, 28, 128, 129, 159, 160, 178, 259, 269

pixels per inch, 31, 195, 321

placing focus on soft edges, 50

Platinum, 71

pointer over the drawn path, 82

Polygonal Lasso tool, 184

Pop guided edit, 93

Pop Guided Edit, 93

Pop-up sliders within panels, 53

Portable Document Format, 30, 42

portion of an image, 236, 247

positioning elements, 47

Positive values for the Roundness adjuster, 88

Post images, 19

Posterize, 229, 259, 260

PPI, 28, 31, 196

PPI and DPI, 28

Precise editing, 29

Precisely convert to black and white, 219

Precisely sharpen a picture, 152

Preferences, 41, 47, 48, 52, 61, 63, 120, 175, 204, 245, 278, 279, 290, 291, 299, 300, 325, 343, 345, 346

preferred blur impact, 108

preferred text,, 80

pre-made settings, 73, 255

Preset dimensions, 86

preview box, 91, 213

Preview changes, 210

primary differences, 31

primary photo, 97, 139, 140, 267

Print, 36, 57, 85, 87, 196, 197, 290, 327, 328, 330, 331, 333, 335, 336

Print Bin Files, 36, 57

Printing choices, 331

Proceed with editing, 80, 86, 87, 88, 92, 94, 101, 105, 108, 111

Proceed with Editing, 103

Proceed with editing - In Fast, 92, 94, 101, 105, 108, 111

Proceed with editing in Quick, 80, 86, 87, 88

Process multiple files, 44

Process Multiple Files., 45

professional edition,, 18

professional-looking images, 69

proper evaluation of the visual quality, 29

proper evaluation of the visual quality of digital photographs, 29

Proportional, 167, 168

Proximity Match, 141

PSD files, 36, 37, 201, 305

PSD files are Adobe Photoshop's native file type, 36

Purple Wash, 72

Q

quality of the color of the picture, 60

Quick Actions, 19, 21, 22, 69, 75

Quick and Advanced modes, 49, 69, 74, 88, 118, 252, 253

quick fixes, 25

QUICK FIXES, 69

Quick Fixes and Effects, 24

QUICK FIXES AND EFFECTS, 69

Quick mode, 20, 21, 35, 47, 49, 54, 55, 69, 73, 74, 84, 86, 87, 92, 94, 101, 105, 108, 111, 181, 183, 205, 206, 207, 216, 252, 253, 255

Quick mode for editing, 35, 55

Quick Selection, 49, 50, 83, 103, 108, 118, 136, 222

Quickly create a slideshow, 316

quick-moving photo reels, 19

Quote Graphic, 21, 64, 68, 324, 326, 327

R

Radial Blur, 150

Radial gradient, 163

radial lines, 150

Radius, 139, 151, 152, 153, 186, 188

Radius Indicates, 153

RAM for viewing, 60

raster and vector graphics, 24, 38

Raster files, 29, 30, 31

Raster vs. vector graphics, 29

rasterization, 44

real-world terms, 29

Recent File List Contains, 41

Recompose a photo, 178

Recompose a picture, 179

Recompose options, 180

Rectangular Marquee tool, 31, 49, 134, 175

Rectangular Marquee tool creates, 135

rectangular selection borders, 135

red eye fix., 75

Red eye is a typical problem, 138

Red Tone, 72

redesigned user interface, 353

Redisplay disabled warning messages, 279

Reduce the image's size., 142
Reducing noise in camera raw images, 275
Refine Edge dialog, 187, 188
Refine Radius, 188
Refine Radius and Erase Refinements, 188
refine selection tool, 25
Refine the edge of your selection, 187
Refine your selection with the use of the edge
    selector., 183
refining edge adjustment, 25
Reflected gradient, 163
regular layer, 232, 236, 238
relaunch the application, 278
Remain organized, 19
Remove a layer style, 264
Remove Background, 21, 182
Remove big things from your photos, 268
Remove Blemishes, 110
Remove color in your photo., 231
Remove Object, 83
Remove red eye, 311
Remove region, 144
Remove the Hidden icon from the media files, 292
remove the selected contacts, 353
Remove things from your picture., 269
Remove warts and blemishes, 268
removing color, 25
removing warts, 26
Rename a preset, 282
Renaming files, 298
Render Filters, 256
Replace any transparent portions, 117
Replace Background, 21, 66, 267
replacement for Adobe Photoshop, 18
Reposition, 116
Required/Contents folder, 221
Resample an image, 198
Resample Image, 196, 197, 199
resampling, 153, 196, 197, 198, 223
Reset Auto Smart Tone Learning, 204
Reset option, 97
Reset Panels, 55
resize a canvas., 25
Resize Guided Edit, 84
Resize your canvas., 202

Resize your image., 202
Resize Your Images, 25
RESIZE YOUR IMAGES, 195
Resize your picture, if need be, 208
resized photo, 86
Resolution, 29, 40, 43, 45, 174, 176, 177, 198
resolution files, 62
resolution of the file, 44
Restart the program, 142
Restart the program and increase the RAM allotted.,
    142
Restore a catalog from one computer to another, 315
Restore default preferences, 278
Result from Processing Files, 46
retina of your photo subject, 138
revamped design, 19
RGB, 27, 33, 34, 35, 40, 43, 59, 118, 119, 120, 121,
    219, 220, 259, 274, 284
RGB color models, 120
Right edges, 132
Rotate button, 206
rotating an image, 35, 55
Roundness, 88, 157

S

saturating the colors in a landscape, 89
saturation, 19, 20, 32, 34, 72, 73, 88, 89, 90, 91, 120,
    154, 209, 210, 211, 212, 221, 231, 232, 255, 256,
    262, 272, 284
Saturation, 34, 89, 90, 91, 94, 114, 121, 206, 210,
    212, 213, 220, 221, 228, 256, 274
Save a file in GIF format, 58
Save a file in JPEG format, 60
Save a file in PNG format, 61
Save a file in TIFF format, 61
Save a subset of a library, 282
Save and make use of custom swatch libraries, 125
Save and Print, 327
Save As, 57, 58, 60, 61, 63, 73, 84, 92, 94, 101, 103,
    105, 108, 111, 253, 254, 256, 271, 317
Save As Original Folder, 63
Save Bin as an Album, 36, 57
Save changes, 57, 58, 276, 320
Save files, 57

save files without previews, 63
Save or delete metadata templates, 286
Save Over Current File, 61, 63
Save Transparency, 62
Save window, 125, 126
Save/Save As, 80, 86, 87, 88
Saving File Preferences, 61
saving files, 24, 62
Saving Files, 41, 61, 62, 63
saving files to the cloud, 24
Scan photos using a TWAIN driver, 271
Scan your photos, 270
scan your picture, 26
Scan your pictures., 282
scanning, 153, 223, 259, 270, 271
Scatter, 156
screen captures, 26
screen image sharpness, 28
screen of a television, 27
seamless manner, 117
Search on Adobe Stock, 21, 64
Seasons, 70
section of an image lighter, 89
Select a layer to edit, 233
Select **a library by selecting Replace Swatches**, 125
Select Adobe Stock., 67
Select **an impact from the list of possibilities**, 101
Select and Isolate Areas, 25
SELECT AND ISOLATE AREAS, 184
Select and Isolate Areas in Your Photos, 25
SELECT AND ISOLATE AREAS IN YOUR PHOTOS, 184
Select **atop the gradient bar**, 166
Select files in the Media view, 294
Select **Fit On Screen under View**, 130
Select **JPEG from the list of formats**, 60
Select multiple media files, 330
Select options from the Tool Options bar, 52
Select **Out of Bounds Effect**, 103
Select Puzzle Piece button, 106
Select Subject, 21, 66, 186, 267
Select the brush size, 92, 141
Select **the Eraser Tool**, 114
Select **the panel menu**, 53
select **Tool Options in the Taskbar**, 52
selecting an alternate choice, 123

selecting from pre-made presets, 19
selecting **Refine Effect**, 94
selecting the color, 109
selecting the Reset, 110
selection border, 31, 50, 132, 135, 136, 188, 190
Selection Brush tool, 50, 83, 185, 189, 190
Selection Edge, 189, 190
Selection guided edit, 94
Selection or Mask mode, 32
selection process, 187
Selection Tools, 22, 134, 135, 136, 166, 222
Selections, 31, 175, 184, 189
selection's boundary, 141
selection's edges, 31, 135, 145, 190
Selects can be pasted into a picture., 235
separate PSD file, 62
Sepia, 70, 72
Set color modes and units of measurement in the info panel, 284
Set up the profile for other service providers, 346
Setting up the profile for a preset service provider, 345
several eye replacements, 140
several images, 115
several Photoshop Elements books, 23
Shake Reduction, 226, 227
Shake Region, 227
Share files by email, 347
share the edited content back, 22
Share via Twitter, 93, 94, 101, 108, 111
share your images, 19
Share Your Photos and Videos, 26
SHARE YOUR PHOTOS AND VIDEOS, 342
Share your photos via email, 344
Share your picture via email., 353
share your pictures, 26
Share your pictures on Flickr., 353
sharing sites, 101
sharp the image, 69
Sharpen tool, 50, 151, 152
Sharpen your picture with the use of the sharpening tool., 183
Sharpening edges, 153, 223
sharpens details, 152
sharper edge, 88

sharpness of your picture, 231
Shift Edge, 188
Short Edge, 85
short reels, 353
Show Bounding Box, 132, 166
Show Grid, 36, 57
Show Highlight on Rollover, 132
Show or hide a layer, 233
Show Overlay, 147
Show Radius, 188
Show Regions, 115
Show Strokes, 115
Silver, 71
similar vein,, 338, 354
simple adjustments like correction of colors, 18
Simple B & W, 71
Simple Method, 106
simple modifications, 69
simple sharing, 20, 341
simpler editing, 22
Simplify, 164, 167, 168, 169, 237, 242
simplifying or flattening a layer, 25
size and proportions, 135
Skin Tone, 84, 215
SKIN TONE guided edit, 84
Slide the Clipped option, 147
slide the **Opacity control.**, 92
slideshows, 18, 23, 288, 316, 350
Small List or Large List, 281
Small Thumbnail or Large Thumbnail, 281
Smaller action cameras, 28
smaller brush size, 137
smaller file size, 60, 240
smaller mobile devices, 27
Smart Blending, 114
Smart Blur, 151
smart brush tool, 25
Smart Brush tool, 50, 143, 144, 145, 207
smart fix,, 75
Smart Radius, 188
Smartphone cameras, 28
Smooth Corners, 168
Smooth modes, 190
smooth skin, 21, 25, 224
Smooth Skin, 21, 110, 224

SMTP port, 347
smudge tool, 151, 152
Smudge tool, 50, 151
sneak peek, 24
Snow, 71
Social Media, 342, 343, 350, 351
social media or sharing options, 80, 86, 88, 93, 94, 108, 111
social media platforms, 26, 73, 254, 256
Soft Leak, 72
Soft Light, 127
Soft Lines, 71
software's native files type, 37
sophisticated tools for picture data storage, 36
Sort files in Media View, 291
Spacing, 156
special edits, 24, 110, 117
Special Edits, 65, 106, 108, 109, 178, 267
special effects, 89, 126, 128, 210, 232, 263
specific color components, 89
specific regions, 70, 106, 221
specific software features, 23
specified previews, 63
Specify a color management option, 208
Specify gradient transparency, 165
Spherical, 116
Split Tone, 72
Spot Healing Brush, 49, 50, 83, 118, 140, 142
Spot Healing Brush tool, 50, 140, 142
spot healing functions, 142
Spring, 70
Square, 167
standout features, 353
standout features of the 2024 edition, 353
start of every stroke, 152
Start using 2GB of free cloud storage, 23
STARTTLS, 347
Stippling, 71
stop Photoshop Elements, 200
storage of multiple lares, 37
Store Swatches, 125
storing and displaying high-quality pictures, 29
Straighten, 49, 118, 181, 182, 183, 277
straightened image, 181, 182, 183
Strength slider, 110

Strikethrough, 171

Stroke objects on a layer, 193

Stylish border text, 109

subsequent actions, 77, 134, 145, 165, 234, 240, 242, 250, 299, 304

Subtract, 94, 134, 137, 145, 189, 190, 208

Subtract areas, 94

Subtract from Selection, 137, 208

Subtract From Selection button, 137

Summer, 71

sunsets, 19

Supplementary choices, 276

Surface Blur, 151

surrounding, 31, 106, 117, 135, 136, 141, 143, 149, 153, 163, 173, 182, 185, 188, 190, 201, 224, 269, 275

Swap height and width are used, 180

Swap out a background, 267, 269

Swap out a face, 267, 269

Swatch panel, 123

Swatches panel, 121, 123, 124, 125, 126, 231

Switch between Album and Folder Views, 300

Switching to Light and Dark mode, 278

symbols, 19, 235, 244, 306

Sync selective media, 301

T

Tablet Choices, 155

Tablet Settings, 158

tapping **B on your keyboard**, 52

Text Alignment, 171

text around the quick selection's boundaries, 78

Text in an image, 243

Text in warp, 171

Text on Path Tool, 78

Text on Path tool., 81

Text on Selection Tool, 78, 80

Text on Shape tool, 81

Text on Shape Tool, 78, 80

Text Orientation Toggle, 171

Text window, 78

text-oriented, 171

Texture Fill, 257

texture for the canvas, 102

textures, 24, 74, 75, 76, 155, 190, 248

Textures, 69, 74, 75, 144, 254

Textures mimic different backdrops, 74, 75

Textures simulate various surfaces, 75

The "Out of Bounds" Guided Edit effect, 102

The 2024 version of Adobe Photoshop, 353

The 2024 version of Adobe Photoshop Elements, 353

the active window, 47

the **Adobe Stock website**, 68

the Advanced mode, 20, 49, 50, 54, 243, 252, 255, 281, 333

The align menu, 132

the **Alignment Tool**, 115

The amount of blur, 106, 108, 150

The angle of Brush, 102

the auto option, 75

the average value, 122

the backdrop layer, 106, 159

the background translucent, 99

the **Basics category**, 20

the blend color, 127, 128

the blur tool, 25

The Blur Tool, 149

The border of the selection emerges, 137

The brightness of the picture, 73

the Brush or Pencil tools, 126

the Brush Picker in the menu bar, 137

The Brush Size adjuster, 83, 84

The brush stroke's shape, 156

The brush tip, 149, 173

The Brush Tools, 155

the case of subdivisions, 48

The Clone Stamp, 146

the color field, 119

the color picker tool, 25, 90, 122, 212

the color swatch, 46, 48, 126, 130, 164, 194

The color that emerges, 126

The color that the painting, 126

The color that the painting or editing tool, 126

the color wheel, 34, 89, 120, 121, 210, 211

The color wheel, 34, 35

the context menu, 36, 56, 57, 187

The Cookie Cutter Tool, 177

the Create panel, 35, 55

The Crop Tool, 173

the **Default Colors** icon, 123
the default definition, 27
The default preferences for tools, 52
The Depth of Field Guided Edit, 106
the diamond beneath, 165
the Double Exposure guided edit, 100
The Double Exposure Guided Edit, 100
The Editor workspace, 39
the effect of applying a different color, 72
The Effect of The Puzzle, 105
The Effect panel, 252
the effects panel, 26, 263, 266
The Element Hub, 39
The Elliptical Marquee tool, 49, 134
The Eraser tool, 158
The Eyedropper tool's foreground color box, 122
The Eyedropper/Sampler Tool, 121
The Fibers filter, 257
The Filter, 247, 248, 251
The Filter / Adjustment menu, 247
the filters panel, 26
The flyout menu, 57
The flyout of the Photo Bin, 36
The fundamental color-programming unit, 27
The Gradient Tool, 163
The Guided Workspace's Tool Options bar, 97, 99, 110
the hand tool, 25, 130, 131
The Hand Tool, 130
The Healing Brush Tools, 142
The Healing Brush tool's selection, 143
The human eye sees color in terms of three characteristics, 34
The image's darker and lighter parts, 154
The impressionist Brush, 155
The Impressionist Brush tool, 155
the **Increase Contrast icon**, 92
The Info panel, 283
the info panel or status bar, 284
The Lasso tool, 50
The lens flare filter, 257
The Line Tool, 168
The Magic Eraser tool, 160
the **Magic Wand**, 31, 184, 222
the main photo, 140

The Marquee Selection, 134
The maximum size of an image, 200
The Media Browser area, 289
The Meme Maker Guided Edit, 96
the merging process to function, 115
The mode, 142, 147
the mouse button, 47, 53, 136, 137, 139, 143, 163, 174, 269, 321
The Move & Scale Object Guided Edit, 82
the move tool, 25, 74, 75, 131, 133, 183
The Move Tool, 131
The Multi-Photo Text Guided Edit, 97
The Navigator panel, 131
The new Artistic Effect options, 21
The newly added canvas, 201
The original color of the image, 126
The Paint Bucket, 161
The Paint Bucket (Fill) Tool, 161
The Painterly Guided Edit effect, 101
The palette menu, 171
the pan motion/layout options, 116
the panel out of the Panel Bin, 54
The Pattern Stamp Tool, 148
The Pencil Tool, 173
the perfect dimensions, 29
The Photo Bin, 35, 55, 114
The Photoshop Elements 2024 license, 353
The physical size of a pixel, 28
the pointer over the image, 81, 171
The Polygon Tool, 168
The Polygonal Lasso tool, 50
the primary subject, 66, 103
The Process Multiple Files command, 44
The quantity of pixels, 195
the Quick Fix pane, 46
The Quick Fix Toolbar, 69
the Quick mode result, 73, 255
The Recompose tool, 178, 180
The Recompose Tool, 178
The Rectangle Tool, 167
The Rectangle Tool, Ellipse Tool, and Rounded Rectangle Tool, 167
The Red Eye Removal Tool, 138
The Refine Edge dialog, 187
The Refine Selection Brush and Push Tool, 138

The resolution of a computer monitor, 27

The resolution of raster and vector files, 31

The revised version, 353

the RGB color components, 27

the Selection brush, 144

The selection brush tool, 32

The Shape Selection, 166

The Sharpen Tool, 152

the size of an image and the size of a canvas, 31

The size of the Font, 171

the size of the window while zooming, 130

The Smart Brush tool, 143

The Smart Brush Tools, 143

The Smudge Tool, 151

the social media, 80, 93, 94, 101, 105, 108, 111, 340

The source, 114, 143

The Sponge, 154

The Sponge, Dodge, and Burn Tools, 154

The Spot Healing, 140

the spot healing brush tool, 25

the standard of the industry for creative, 37

The stroke Thumbnail, 281

the style configurations, 79

the styles panel, 26, 266

The Styles panel, 262

the **Switch Colors icon**, 123

The Text and Border Overlay, 109

The Text and Border Overlay Guided Edit, 109

the text box, 41, 53, 119, 130, 146, 149, 154, 173, 207

the text options, 20

The threshold, 151, 153

the tool icon in the toolbox, 52

the Tool options bar, 135

the Tool Options bar,, 52, 129, 136, 141, 142, 148, 151, 157, 164, 166

the **Tool Options bar's** Fit Screen button., 129

The Toolbox, 49

the Try Sample Eyes list, 139

The Try Sample Eyes list displays, 111

The Unsharp Mask filter, 152

the use of guides and rulers modify your pictures, 68

the use of the action panel., 24

the use of the layers panel, 25

the use of the type tool, 25, 183

The visual impression of assembling puzzle pieces, 105

The whole of your photo catalog, 19

the window/screen, 131

the zoom tool, 25, 131

The Zoom Tool, 128

Things You Need to Know, 24

thousands of gorgeous stock photographs., 21

thousands of great stock photographs, 64

Threshold, 151, 153, 180, 229, 254

thumbnails of open photos, 35, 55

TIFF file, 62

Tinted Black, 71

Tips for creating visual effects with filters, 248

Tolerance, 156, 160, 161, 162

Toolbox in the advanced mode, 49

Toolbox in the Quick Mode, 49

Tools in the View group, 49

Tools panel, 187, 238

Toy Camera, 71

Tracking adjusts, 171

Transform a shape, 166

Transform an image into a normal layer and back again., 235

Transform and warp a layer, 241, 242

transform your photos, 69

transforming and warping a layer., 25

transparent sections, 127, 232

T-shirts and posters, 30

turn images into works of art., 21

two color models, 34

Type Tool, 78, 97, 98, 109

Type tool options, 171

Typing Tools, 169

U

Unconstrained, 167, 168

Underline, 171

uniform blur, 106, 107, 108

unique dark mode, 353

unique dimensions and pixel count, 29

Unique pattern, 193

unique text, 20

Units & Rulers, 47, 245, 325

Unselected portions of the image, 108
unsharp mask, 25
Unsharp Mask, 152, 153, 200, 223, 275
Unsharp Mask filter, 153, 223, 275
Unsharp Mask Filter, 153
Unsharp Mask finds pixels, 153, 224
unveiled Premium Elements 2024,, 353
Unwanted individuals or objects, 142
update the data, 209
Up-Down, 226
upload mobile images and videos to Elements, 22
upload mobile images and videos to Elements on the desktop and web, 22
uppercase characters, 63
upsample, 198
upsampling, 198
Use a tool, 51
use any of the action bar's Subject, 22
Use gradients and patterns, 20, 77
Use Lower Case, 63
use of a new blank file, 39
use of keywords, 64, 66, 67
use of mathematical methods, 30
use of Photoshop Elements, 18, 23, 24, 273, 335
use of tags for people, 19
use of the HSB, 34
use of the HSB and RGB color models, 34
use of the Lasso tool, 135
use peek-through overlays, 23
Use Photoshop Elements, 21, 96, 299
Use preset tool options, 279
Use Quick Highlight, 179
Use Shift key for Tool Switch, 52
Use System Font, 291
Use the built-in FUJIFILM Prints, 19
Use **the crop tool** to crop the image, 100
use the desktop application to edit, 23
Use the Preset Manager, 281
use the **Resize Border slider.**, 109
Use the right layouts, 23
Use the Text on Path tool, 81
user interface, 19, 291, 353
user interface and several additional capabilities, 353
User Profile icon, 68
users of Windows, 23

users of Windows and Mac computers, 23
Using Adobe Stock, 21
Using Text on Custom Path tool, 172
Using the automated cropping recommendations, 175
using the CORRECT SKIN TONE, 84
Using the Keyword Tags panel, 302
Using the Magic Eraser tool,, 160
Using the Text on Selection, 80, 172
Using the Text on the Shape tool, 171
utilizing Elements, 23

V

vacant character frames, 99
variety of patterns, 148
various amounts of red, 120
various conversion settings, 219
various effects, 70, 311
various selections, 31
vCard file on your computer, 353
Vector, 30, 167
Verify the Saving File Preferences dialog box, 61
version of your photo, 84, 251
Vertical Distortion, 78, 246
vertical films, 353
Vertical Type Tool, 78
Vibrance tabs, 206
video editing software, 33
video story, 26, 337, 338, 339, 340, 341
Videos are instantly tagged with Smart Tags, 19
View and find media files using the Timeline, 311
View and manage files by folders, 292
View Mode, 188
View the print size on the screen, 196
Viewing media files, 308
Viewing media files before adding location, 308
Viewing media files before adding location information, 308
Vignette Discarded, 116
Vignette Effect, 87
Vignette Effect Guided Edit, 87
Vimeo, 342, 343, 344, 350
Vintage, 72, 254
Vintage Leak, 72

visible spectrum, 35, 121

W

Warming Filter (81) and Cooling Filter, 261
Warming Filter (85) and Cooling Filter (80), 261
Warp a text in an image., 246
Web, 22, 23, 85, 86, 119, 284
Web Companion, 22
well-known pieces of art or common art genres, 21
What are pixels?, 38
What are presets?, 282
What is a native PSD file?, 36, 38
What is Anti-Aliasing?, 141
What is feathering?, 194
What is metadata?, 315
What is the use of the info panel?, 287
white background, 23, 44, 75, 182, 321
White Leak, 72
white paint produces pure black or white., 128
Whiten Teeth, 49, 110, 118, 207, 208
whole new experience, 19
Why select and isolate?, 184
Widely compatible, 29
Width and Height, 85, 167, 174, 199, 202
window resizes, 130
Windows byte order, 61

Windows only, 296, 351, 353
window's title bar, 128, 131
Winter, 71
With the use of auto curate, adjust your pictures., 315
wizard-like interface, 77, 91, 95, 106
Work with layer styles, 263
Work with panels, 54
Work with Photoshop Elements Layers, 25
WORK WITH PHOTOSHOP ELEMENTS LAYERS, 232
workflows to advanced color correction, 69
world of digital, 27
world of digital photography, 27
wow clients, 18
Write keyword Tag Information into your files, 305

Y

Yellow Streak, 72
Your email address's password, 347
YouTube, 26, 323, 340, 342, 343, 344, 350, 351

Z

Zoom In and Zoom Out, 49, 128
Zoom in or out, 128
Zoom tool, 49, 128, 129, 130, 183, 208, 274, 276

Made in the USA
Middletown, DE
26 August 2024